Interactive
Practice Book **ℯ𝒊**

Hampton-Brown
EDGE
Reading, Writing & Language

Sharon Daniela Cruz Perez

NATIONAL
GEOGRAPHIC
LEARNING | CENGAGE
Learning·

Acknowledgments

Grateful acknowledgment is given to the authors, artists, photographers, museums, publishers, and agents for permission to reprint copyrighted material. Every effort has been made to secure the appropriate permission. If any omissions have been made or if corrections are required, please contact the Publisher.

Photographic Credits

Cover: Standing in Awe of the Aurora, Northwest Territories, Canada, Robert Postma. Photograph © Robert Postma/First Light/Getty Images.

Acknowledgments continue on page Ack 1.

For product information and technology assistance, contact us at **Customer & Sales Support, 888-915-3276**

For permission to use material from this text or product, submit all requests online at **www.cengage.com/permissions**
Further permissions questions can be emailed to **permissionrequest@cengage.com**

National Geographic Learning | Cengage Learning
1 Lower Ragsdale Drive
Building 1, Suite 200
Monterey, CA 93940

Cengage Learning is a leading provider of customized learning solutions with office locations around the globe, including Singapore, the United Kingdom, Australia, Mexico, Brazil, and Japan. Locate your local office at **www.cengage.com/global**.

Visit National Geographic Learning online at **ngl.cengage.com**
Visit our corporate website at **www.cengage.com**

Printed in the USA.
RR Donnelley, Menasha, WI

ISBN: 978-1-285-44006-4 (Practice Book)
ISBN: 978-1-285-44347-8 (Practice Book Teacher's Annotated Edition)

Printed in the United States of America
17 18 19 20 21 22 23 24 25
10 9 8 7

▶ **The Experiment; Superstitions: The Truth Uncovered**

Prepare to Read: Key Vocabulary 6

Before Reading: *The Experiment* 8

    Literary Analysis: *Analyze Plot and Setting*
    Focus Strategy: *Preview and Predict*

   ▶ **Interact with the Text:** *Superstitions: The Truth Uncovered* 11

    Literary Analysis: *Analyze Text Features*
    Focus Strategy: *Preview and Set a Purpose*

Reflect and Assess 15

    Writing: *Write About Literature*

Integrate the Language Arts 16

    Literary Analysis: *Analyze Plot: Climax*
    Vocabulary Study: *Prefixes*

▶ **Building Bridges; The Right Words at the Right Time**

Prepare to Read: Key Vocabulary 18

Before Reading: *Building Bridges* 20

    Literary Analysis: *Analyze Character*
    Focus Strategy: *Clarify Ideas*

   ▶ **Interact with the Text:** *The Right Words at the Right Time* 23

    Literary Analysis: *Analyze Text: Memoir*
    Focus Strategy: *Clarify Ideas*

Reflect and Assess 27

    Writing: *Write About Literature*

Integrate the Language Arts 28

    Literary Analysis: *Dialect*
    Vocabulary Study: *Prefixes*

▶ **The Open Window; One in a Million**

Prepare to Read: Key Vocabulary 30

Before Reading: *The Open Window* 32

    Literary Analysis: *Analyze Character and Plot*
    Focus Strategy: *Clarify Vocabulary*

   ▶ **Interact with the Text:** *One in a Million* 35

    Literary Analysis: *Analyze Cultural Perspectives: Folk Tale*
    Focus Strategy: *Clarify Vocabulary*

Reflect and Assess 37

    Writing: *Write About Literature*

Integrate the Language Arts 38

    Literary Analysis: *Compare Settings*
    Vocabulary Study: *Suffixes*

▶ **Ambush**

Close Reading 40

    Literary Analysis: *Analyze Character and Plot*
    Writing: *Write About Viewpoint*

▶ **Unit Review**

Key Vocabulary 46

Unit 2

▶ **Genes: All in the Family; How to See DNA**

    Prepare to Read: Key Vocabulary **48**

    Before Reading: *Genes: All in the Family* **50**

       Literary Analysis: *Analyze Author's Purpose*
       Focus Strategy: *Self-Question*

    ▶ **Interact with the Text:** *How to See DNA* **53**

       Literary Analysis: *Analyze Author's Purpose*
       Focus Strategy: *Self-Question*

    Reflect and Assess **57**

       Writing: *Write About Literature*

    Integrate the Language Arts **58**

       Literary Analysis: *Summarize*
       Vocabulary Study: *Context Clues*

▶ **Do Family Meals Matter?; Fish Cheeks**

    Prepare to Read: Key Vocabulary **60**

    Before Reading: *Do Family Meals Matter?* **62**

       Literary Analysis: *Analyze Author's Purpose*
       Focus Strategy: *Find Question-Answer Relationships*

    ▶ **Interact with the Text:** *Fish Cheeks* **65**

       Literary Analysis: *Analyze Author's Purpose*
       Focus Strategy: *Find Question-Answer Relationships*

    Reflect and Assess **69**

       Writing: *Write About Literature*

    Integrate the Language Arts **70**

       Literary Analysis: *Analyze Descriptive Language*
       Vocabulary Study: *Context Clues*

▶ **Only Daughter; Calling a Foul**

    Prepare to Read: Key Vocabulary **72**

    Before Reading: *Only Daughter* **74**

       Literary Analysis: *Analyze Author's Purpose*
       Focus Strategy: *Question the Author*

    ▶ **Interact with the Text:** *Calling a Foul* **77**

       Literary Analysis: *Analyze Author's Viewpoint*
       Focus Strategy: *Question the Author*

    Reflect and Assess **81**

       Writing: *Write About Literature*

    Integrate the Language Arts **82**

       Literary Analysis: *Analyze Style*
       Vocabulary Study: *Context Clues*

▶ **The Color of Water**

    Close Reading **84**

       Literary Analysis: *Analyze Author's Purpose; Analyze Author's Viewpoint*
       Writing: *Write About Viewpoint*

▶ **Unit Review**

    Key Vocabulary **90**

▶ **Heartbeat; Behind the Bulk**

    Prepare to Read: Key Vocabulary **92**

    Before Reading: *Heartbeat* **94**

       Literary Analysis: *Analyze Point of View*
       Focus Strategy: *Make Inferences*

    ▶ **Interact with the Text:** *Behind the Bulk* **97**

       Literary Analysis: *Analyze Point of View*
       Focus Strategy: *Make Inferences*

    Reflect and Assess **101**

       Writing: *Write About Literature*

    Integrate the Language Arts **102**

       Literary Analysis: *Analyze Point of View*
       Vocabulary Study: *Word Families*

▶ **I Go Along; Theme for English B**

    Prepare to Read: Key Vocabulary **104**

    Before Reading: *I Go Along* **106**

       Literary Analysis: *Analyze Point of View*
       Focus Strategy: *Make Inferences*

    ▶ **Interact with the Text:** *Theme for English B* **109**

       Literary Analysis: *Analyze Structure: Poetry*
       Focus Strategy: *Make Inferences*

    Reflect and Assess **113**

       Writing: *Write About Literature*

    Integrate the Language Arts **114**

       Literary Analysis: *Analyze Style*
       Vocabulary Study: *Latin and Greek Roots*

▶ **The Pale Mare; The Caged Bird**

    Prepare to Read: Key Vocabulary **116**

    Before Reading: *The Pale Mare* **118**

       Literary Analysis: *Analyze Point of View*
       Focus Strategy: *Make Inferences*

    ▶ **Interact with the Text:** *Caged Bird* **121**

       Literary Analysis: *Analyze Structure: Poetry*
       Focus Strategy: *Make Inferences*

    Reflect and Assess **125**

       Writing: *Write About Literature*

    Integrate the Language Arts **126**

       Literary Analysis: *Analyze Point of View*
       Vocabulary Study: *Word Families*

▶ **Outliers**

    Close Reading **128**

       Literary Analysis: *Analyze Author's Purpose; Analyze Author's Viewpoint*
       Writing: *Write About Viewpoint*

▶ **Unit Review**

    Key Vocabulary **134**

Unit 4

► **Enabling Or Disabling?; This I Believe**

    Prepare to Read: Key Vocabulary **136**

    Before Reading: *Enabling Or Disabling?* **138**

        Literary Analysis: *Analyze Development of Ideas*
        Focus Strategy: *Identify Main Ideas*

    ► **Interact with the Text:** *This I Believe* **141**

        Literary Analysis: *Analyze Development of Ideas*
        Focus Strategy: *Relate Main Ideas and Supporting Details*

    Reflect and Assess **145**

        Writing: *Write About Literature*

    Integrate the Language Arts **146**

        Literary Analysis: *Analyze Style*
        Vocabulary Study: *Multiple-Meaning Words*

► **Brother Ray; Power of the Powerless: A Brother's Lesson**

    Prepare to Read: Key Vocabulary **148**

    Before Reading: *Brother Ray* **150**

        Literary Analysis: *Analyze Text Structure: Chronology*
        Focus Strategy: *Summarize Nonfiction*

    ► **Interact with the Text:** *Power of the Powerless* **153**

        Literary Analysis: *Analyze Text Structure: Chronology*
        Focus Strategy: *Summarize Nonfiction*

    Reflect and Assess **159**

        Writing: *Write About Literature*

    Integrate the Language Arts **160**

        Literary Analysis: *Compare Literature and Film*
        Vocabulary Study: *Context Clues*

► **He Was No Bum; miss rosie**

    Prepare to Read: Key Vocabulary **162**

    Before Reading: *He Was No Bum* **164**

        Literary Analysis: *Analyze Text Structure: Chronology*
        Focus Strategy: *Determine What's Important*

    ► **Interact with the Text:** *miss rosie* **167**

        Literary Analysis: *Analyze Language: Simile and Metaphor*
        Focus Strategy: *Determine What's Important*

    Reflect and Assess **169**

        Writing: *Write About Literature*

    Integrate the Language Arts **170**

        Literary Analysis: *Analyze Repetition and Alliteration*
        Vocabulary Study: *Multiple-Meaning Words*

► **Household Words**

    Close Reading **172**

        Literary Analysis: *Analyze Development of Ideas; Analyze Text Structure: Chronology*
        Writing: *Write About Development of Ideas*

► **Unit Review**

    Key Vocabulary **178**

► **Jump Away; Showdown with Big Eva**

Prepare to Read: Key Vocabulary **180**

Before Reading: *Jump Away* **182**

    Literary Analysis: *Analyze Theme*
    Focus Strategy: *Make Connections*

    ► **Interact with the Text:** *Showdown with Big Eva* **185**

    Literary Analysis: *Analyze Theme*
    Focus Strategy: *Make Connections*

Reflect and Assess **191**

    Writing: *Write About Literature*

Integrate the Language Arts **192**

    Literary Analysis: *Analyze Mood and Tone*
    Vocabulary Study: *Relate Words*

► **Fear; Violence Hits Home**

Prepare to Read: Key Vocabulary **194**

Before Reading: *Fear* **196**

    Literary Analysis: *Analyze Theme*
    Focus Strategy: *Make Connections*

    ► **Interact with the Text:** *Violence Hits Home* **199**

    Literary Analysis: *Analyze Development of Ideas*
    Focus Strategy: *Make Connections*

Reflect and Assess **205**

    Writing: *Write About Literature*

Integrate the Language Arts **206**

    Literary Analysis: *Analyze Suspense*
    Vocabulary Study: *Relate Words*

► **Abuela Invents the Zero; Karate**

Prepare to Read: Key Vocabulary **208**

Before Reading: *Abuela Invents the Zero* **210**

    Literary Analysis: *Analyze Theme*
    Focus Strategy: *Make Connections*

    ► **Interact with the Text:** *Karate* **213**

    Literary Analysis: *Analyze Language: Irony*
    Focus Strategy: *Make Connections*

Reflect and Assess **217**

    Writing: *Write About Literature*

Integrate the Language Arts **218**

    Literary Analysis: *Analyze Flashback*
    Vocabulary Study: *Antonyms*

► **Why We Must Never Forget**

Close Reading **220**

    Literary Analysis: *Analyze Theme; Analyze Irony*
    Writing: *Write About Theme*

► **Unit Review**

Key Vocabulary **226**

Unit 6

▶ **16: The Right Voting Age; Teen Brains Are Different**

    Prepare to Read: Key Vocabulary **228**

    Before Reading: *16: The Right Voting Age* **230**

        Literary Analysis: *Analyze Argument and Evidence*
        Focus Strategy: *Draw Conclusions*

    ▶ **Interact with the Text:** *Teen Brains Are Different* **233**

        Literary Analysis: *Analyze Text Structure: Main Idea and Details*
        Focus Strategy: *Draw Conclusions*

    Reflect and Assess **237**

        Writing: *Write About Literature*

    Integrate the Language Arts **238**

        Literary Analysis: *Evaluate the Author's Purpose and Viewpoint*
        Vocabulary Study: *Specialized Vocabulary*

▶ **Should Communities Set Teen Curfews?; Curfews: A National Debate**

    Prepare to Read: Key Vocabulary **240**

    Before Reading: *Should Communities Set Teen Curfews?* **242**

        Literary Analysis: *Analyze Evidence*
        Focus Strategy: *Compare Arguments*

    ▶ **Interact with the Text:** *Curfews: A National Debate* **245**

        Literary Analysis: *Analyze Argument: Word Choice*
        Focus Strategy: *Compare Arguments*

    Reflect and Assess **249**

        Writing: *Write About Literature*

    Integrate the Language Arts **250**

        Literary Analysis: *Analyze Persuasive Techniques*
        Vocabulary Study: *Analogies*

▶ **What Does Responsibility Look Like?; Getting a Job**

    Prepare to Read: Key Vocabulary **252**

    Before Reading: *What Does Responsibility Look Like?* **254**

        Literary Analysis: *Analyze Argument and Reasons*
        Focus Strategy: *Form Generalizations*

    ▶ **Interact with the Text:** *Getting a Job* **257**

        Literary Analysis: *Analyze Author's Tone and Purpose*
        Focus Strategy: *Form Generalizations*

    Reflect and Assess **263**

        Writing: *Write About Literature*

    Integrate the Language Arts **264**

        Literary Analysis: *Evaluate Functional Documents*
        Vocabulary Study: *Multiple-Meaning Words*

▶ **Trashing Teens**

    Close Reading **266**

        Literary Analysis: *Analyze Argument and Evidence; Analyze Argument: Word Choice*
        Writing: *Write About Viewpoint*

▶ **Unit Review**

    Key Vocabulary **272**

▶ **Novio Boy: Scene 7, Part 1; Oranges**

Prepare to Read: Key Vocabulary 274

Before Reading: *Novio Boy: Scene 7, Part 1* 276

    Literary Analysis: *Compare Representations: Script and Performance*
    Focus Strategy: *Form Mental Images*

   ▶ **Interact with the Text:** *Oranges* 280

    Literary Analysis: *Analyze Elements of Poetry*
    Focus Strategy: *Form Mental Images*

Reflect and Assess 283

    Writing: *Write About Literature*

Integrate the Language Arts 284

    Literary Analysis: *Compare Themes*
    Vocabulary Study: *Idioms*

▶ **Novio Boy: Scene 7, Part 2; Your World**

Prepare to Read: Key Vocabulary 286

Before Reading: *Novio Boy: Scene 7, Part 2* 288

    Literary Analysis: *Analyze Structure: Script*
    Focus Strategy: *Identify Sensory Images*

   ▶ **Interact with the Text:** *Your World* 291

    Literary Analysis: *Analyze Structure: Rhyme and Rhythm*
    Focus Strategy: *Use Sensory Images*

Reflect and Assess 293

    Writing: *Write About Literature*

Integrate the Language Arts 294

    Literary Analysis: *Rhythm and Meter*
    Vocabulary Study: *Idioms*

▶ **To Helen Keller; Marked/Dusting**

Prepare to Read: Key Vocabulary 296

Before Reading: *To Helen Keller* 298

    Literary Analysis: *Analyze Style*
    Focus Strategy: *Identify Emotional Responses*

   ▶ **Interact with the Text:** *Marked/Dusting* 301

    Literary Analysis: *Analyze Word Choice: Figurative Language*
    Focus Strategy: *Assess Emotional Responses*

Reflect and Assess 305

    Writing: *Write About Literature*

Integrate the Language Arts 306

    Literary Analysis: *Analyze Alliteration and Consonance*
    Vocabulary Study: *Connotation and Denotation*

▶ **I Believe in All That Has Never Yet Been Spoken/Make Music with Your Life**

Close Reading 308

    Literary Analysis: *Compare Representations*
    Writing: *Write About Images*

▶ **Unit Review**

Key Vocabulary 312

Prepare to Read

▷ **The Experiment**
▷ **Superstitions: The Truth Uncovered**

Key Vocabulary

A. How well do you know these words? Circle a rating for each word. Check your understanding of each word by circling *yes* or *no*. Then, complete the sentences. If you are unsure of a word's meaning, refer to the Vocabulary Glossary, page 792, in your student text.

Rating Scale	
1	I have never seen this word before.
2	I am not sure of the word's meaning.
3	I know this word and can teach the word's meaning to someone else.

Key Word	Check Your Understanding	Deepen Your Understanding
❶ belief (bu-**lēf**) *noun* **Rating:** 1 2 3	A person's **belief** is always a well-known fact. **Yes** **No**	It is my strongest belief_____ _____ _____ _____ _____ .
❷ escape (is-**kāp**) *verb* **Rating:** 1 2 3	You would want to **escape** an ocean filled with hungry sharks. **Yes** **No**	If I were trapped on a desert island, I would try to escape by _____ _____ _____ _____ .
❸ evidence (**e**-vu-duns) *noun* **Rating:** 1 2 3	A written note left at the scene of a crime can be a good piece of **evidence.** **Yes** **No**	Detectives study pieces of evidence, such as _____ _____ _____ _____ _____ .
❹ experiment (ik-**spair**-u-munt) *noun* **Rating:** 1 2 3	An **experiment** never solves a problem. **Yes** **No**	An example of an experiment I have performed is _____ _____ _____ _____ .

Key Word	Check Your Understanding	Deepen Your Understanding
5 failure (**fāl**-yur) *noun* **Rating:** 1 2 3	Everyone likes **failure**. Yes No	The worst failure of communication I ever had was _____ _____ _____ _____ _____.
6 misfortune (mis-**for**-chun) *noun* **Rating:** 1 2 3	A family that loses their home in a storm is experiencing **misfortune**. Yes No	I experienced misfortune when _____ _____ _____ _____ _____.
7 mistaken (mi-**stā**-kun) *verb* **Rating:** 1 2 3	It is possible for a woman to be **mistaken** for her identical twin sister. Yes No	I am often mistaken for _____ _____ _____ _____ _____.
8 superstition (sü-pur-**sti**-shun) *noun* **Rating:** 1 2 3	The idea that Friday the 13th is an unlucky day is a common **superstition**. Yes No	One superstition I have heard of is _____ _____ _____ _____ _____.

B. Use one of the Key Vocabulary words to write about a superstition or powerful belief you have. How does it influence you?

_____

_____

LITERARY ANALYSIS: Analyze Plot and Setting

The events, or what the characters do, in a story are the **plot.** The **setting** is where and when the story takes place. The events of the story are affected by the setting.

A. Read the passage below. Look for details that describe the setting and plot. Write them in the chart.

Look Into the Text

> There was no way out.
>
> The walls of his cell were built of thick cement blocks. The huge door was made of steel. The floor and ceiling were made of concrete, and there were no windows. The only light came from a light bulb that was covered by a metal shield.
>
> There was no way out, or so it seemed to him.
>
> He had volunteered to be part of a scientific experiment and had been put in the cell to test the cleverness of the human mind. The cell was empty, and he was not allowed to take anything into it. But he had been told that there was one way to escape from the cell, and he had three hours to find it.

Setting	Plot

B. Use the information in the chart to complete the sentence about the plot and setting.

The volunteer might have difficulty _____

_____

_____.

FOCUS STRATEGY: Preview and Predict

HOW TO PREVIEW AND PREDICT

1. **Preview** Look at the title, pictures, and key words for clues.

2. **Predict** As you read, ask yourself: *What will happen next?*

A. Read the passage. Use the strategies above to preview and predict what will happen next. Then answer the questions below.

Look Into the Text

The shield! The shield around the light bulb! His mind raced. The metal shield could be used as a tool—the tool he needed! He had found the way to escape! He moved under the shield and looked closely at it. One good strong pull would free it, he decided. He reached up, grabbed hold of it, and pulled. But the shield stayed attached to the ceiling. He grabbed the shield again, twisting it as he pulled. He felt it rip free, and he fell to the floor clutching his treasure.

The shield was shaped like a cone and had been fastened to the ceiling by three long metal prongs. These prongs were sharp. But they were not strong enough to cut through steel or concrete or cement.

1. Do you think the volunteer will be able to escape? Why or why not?

_____

_____

2. What do you think will happen next?

_____

_____

B. Reread the passage above. Circle the words and ideas that you used to answer the question.

Selection Review The Experiment

 What Influences How You Act?
Find out how beliefs affect people.

A. In "The Experiment," you found out how a person's beliefs can affect his actions. Complete the chart below.

Cause-and-Effect Chart

Beliefs	Actions
There is no way out of the cell.	The man begins to look for a way out.

B. Use the information you wrote in the chart to answer the questions.

1. Why does the man believe there was no way out of the cell?

_____

_____

2. What belief does the man have about himself that may have affected the experiment? Use **belief** in your response.

_____

_____

3. How might the story be different if there was not a metal shield or light bulb in the cell?

_____

_____

SUPERSTITIONS:
The Truth Uncovered • by Jamie Kiffel

Connect Across Texts

In "The Experiment," a man's **belief** determines his actions. In this magazine article, find out the truth about some beliefs called **superstitions**.

Some people believe in superstitions to explain **the unexplainable**. Often that means explaining bad luck. Old Mr. Smith's house burned down? He must have forgotten to knock on wood after he said his home **was fireproof**. But where did strange beliefs like this come from, and why did people believe them? Here are the straight facts behind some superstitions.

SUPERSTITION 1
Ravens predict death.

Where It Came From Ravens are **scavengers**, so they were often **spotted** at cemeteries and battlefields—places associated with dying. People started thinking the birds could predict death.

What's the Truth? People who spot ravens could be in for some good luck—not death. According to legend, Vikings sailing the ocean would release **captive ravens** and follow them toward land. If the birds returned, the sailors knew land was still far away. And **tame ravens** are very friendly. "They act like puppies," says Patricia Cole of New York City's Prospect Park Zoo. "They'll sit on your lap, let you scratch their heads, and play tug-of-war!"

The raven became a symbol of death, but some people admire the bird for its intelligence and fearless behavior.

Key Vocabulary
belief *n.*, something you think is true
superstition *n.*, an idea based on fear, not science or logic

In Other Words
the unexplainable things they can't figure out
was fireproof could not burn down
scavengers animals that eat dead things
spotted seen
captive ravens ravens kept on the ship
tame ravens ravens that are not wild

Interact with the Text

1. Text Features
Text features such as subtitles provide more information about the content of an article. Underline the main title of the article and the subtitle. How does the subtitle clarify the title?

_____

_____

_____

_____

_____

2. Preview/Set a Purpose
Look at the photos, the caption, and the subheadings. What do you think you will learn about in this section?

_____

_____

_____

3. Text Features
Photos and diagrams support the text. Explain how the diagram, "Triangles in a Doorway," clarifies and supports the text in Superstition 2.

_____

_____

_____

_____

_____

_____

_____

_____

4. Interpret
Underline the words that explain why people threw salt over their left shoulder. Why was salt so valuable?

_____

_____

_____

_____

_____

_____

_____

_____

_____

_____

_____

_____

_____

SUPERSTITION 2
Walking under a ladder is bad luck.

Where It Came From In ancient times, people believed that triangles were **sacred**. Walking through a triangle could break the triangle's good powers and let evil things **escape**. In this case, the triangle is formed by the ladder and the ground.

What's the Truth? Triangles aren't sacred. They are just three connected points that, unlike the points of a line, aren't in a row. Math experts such as Professor Albert L. Vitter think of rectangular forms—such as doorways—as two triangles. (Picture a line from one corner of a doorway to its diagonal corner.) According to this notion, when you walk through a doorway you are walking through two triangles. Of course, you know by your own experience that it's perfectly safe to do this!

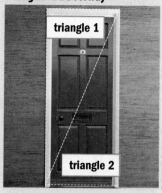
Triangles in a Doorway

triangle 1

triangle 2

▲ Interpret the Diagram
Explain how a doorway is like two triangles.

SUPERSTITION 3
Throwing salt over your left shoulder wards off evil.

Where It Came From In the days before refrigeration, salt was very valuable because people used it to preserve meat, fish, and other foods. People worried that evil spirits might try to steal their salt, especially if it spilled. So they tossed salt over their left shoulders into the eyes of any salt-stealing **demons** to stop them.

Key Vocabulary
escape _v._, to get free

In Other Words
sacred special, holy
wards off evil keeps away evil
demons bad spirits, devils

What's the Truth? Even if there were really demons, throwing salt in their eyes might slow them down for a little while, but it wouldn't stop them. In fact, salt occurs naturally in tears. It and the proteins in tears keep germs away and help prevent eye infections.

Ninety-eight percent of a tear is water. Tears also contain small amounts of sodium chloride, the chemical name for salt.

SUPERSTITION 4
Breaking a mirror means trouble.

Where It Came From People used to believe that your reflection was actually your **soul**. So if you broke a mirror, you'd break—and therefore lose—your soul.

What's the Truth? The image in a mirror is **a phenomenon of** light. "When you look at any object in a mirror, what you're actually seeing is reflected light," says Lou Bloomfield, author of *How Things Work: The Physics of Everyday Life*. When you stand in front of a mirror, reflected light from your body bounces off the mirror's surface. That's why you see your reflection.

Reflection in a Mirror

Light bounces off you and bounces back.

mirror

you

your reflection

△ Interpret the Diagram When light from your body hits the surface of the mirror, what happens next? What does this action cause you to see in the mirror?

In Other Words

soul spirit, inner self
a phenomenon of something that happens with

7. Interpret
In your own words, describe why this superstition is false.

_____

_____

_____

_____

_____

_____

_____

_____

SUPERSTITION 5
Knocking on wood keeps misfortune away.

Where It Came From People used to believe that gods lived inside trees. If you knocked on wood when you wanted a favor, the tree gods would help you.

What's the Truth? In the past, people may have **mistaken** tree-dwelling insects for gods, says Linda Butler, **an entomologist** at West Virginia University. "Lots of noisy insects live inside trees," she says. "For instance, the larva of the pine sawyer beetle makes a loud gnawing sound when it chews on wood." ❖

The pine sawyer beetle got its name from the sawing noise the larva makes as it chews the wood.

Key Vocabulary
    misfortune n., bad luck
    mistaken v., mixed up, confused

In Other Words
an entomologist a person who studies insects

Selection Review Superstitions: The Truth Uncovered

A. Complete the chart below. Explain why people believed each superstition, and the truth about each.

Superstition	Why People Believed It	The Truth
Ravens predict death.		
Walking under a ladder is bad luck.		
Throwing salt wards off evil.		

B. Answer the questions.

1. How do the text features help you understand what the magazine article is about?

    _____

2. What do superstitions cause people to do? Give one example from the text and what it caused people to believe.

    _____

    _____

WRITING: Write About Literature

A. Plan your writing. Read the opinion below. Decide if you agree or disagree with it. List examples from each text to support it.

> **Opinion:** People make up superstitions when they want to feel in control of something they don't understand.

The Experiment	Superstitions: The Truth Uncovered

B. What is your opinion? Write an opinion statement. Remember to use examples from both texts and your own experience to support your opinion.

_____

_____

_____

_____

_____

_____

_____

_____

_____

LITERARY ANALYSIS: Analyze Plot: Climax

A good story has a plot that keeps you guessing. Stories often start when a character has a **problem**. The **rising action** is the events that lead up to the **climax**, which is the most exciting part. The **falling action** is the events that follow the climax, and any leftover problems are solved during the **resolution**.

A. The plot diagram below contains elements of the plot of "The Experiment." Complete the diagram by filling in the missing events, the climax, and the resolution.

Plot Diagram

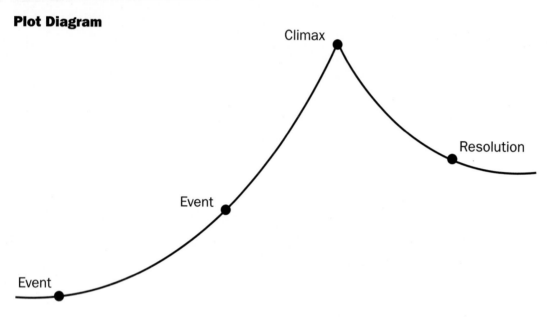

B. Brainstorm two alternate climaxes and two alternate resolutions.

Climax:

1. _____

2. _____

Resolution:

1. _____

2. _____

C. Choose one climax and resolution. Write a paragraph that tells the new ending to the story.

Just then, the man saw _____

_____

_____.

VOCABULARY STUDY: Prefixes

A **prefix** is a word part added at the beginning of a word in order to change the word's meaning.

A. *Dis-* is a common prefix that means "not" or "the opposite of." Write what you think each word means. Use a resource to check if you are not sure. Then write a sentence using the word.

Word	What It Means	Sentence
disability	to not be able to do something	
disagree		
disband		
discourage		
disengage		

B. What are other words you know that contain the prefix *dis-*? List them in the chart below. Write the definition of each word. Use a dictionary to confirm the meanings.

Word	Definition
discolor	to change the color

C. Use the chart above to write a sentence for each word you listed.

1. _____

2. _____

3. _____

4. _____

Prepare to Read

▶ **Building Bridges**
▶ **The Right Words at the Right Time**

Key Vocabulary

A. How well do you know these words? Circle a rating for each word. Check your understanding of each word by circling *yes* or *no*. Then, write a definition in your own words. If you are unsure of a word's meaning, refer to the Vocabulary Glossary, page 792, in your student text.

Rating Scale	
1	I have never seen this word before.
2	I am not sure of the word's meaning.
3	I know this word and can teach the word's meaning to someone else.

Key Word	Check Your Understanding	Deepen Your Understanding
❶ career (ku-**rear**) *noun* **Rating:** 1　2　3	Usually, a **career** in medicine requires a college degree and many years of job training. **Yes**　　　**No**	My definition: _____ _____ _____ _____ _____.
❷ comedian (ku-**mē**-dē-un) *noun* **Rating:** 1　2　3	A **comedian** has the ability to make people laugh. **Yes**　　　**No**	My definition: _____ _____ _____ _____ _____.
❸ consent (kun-**sent**) *noun* **Rating:** 1　2　3	It is best to have a friend's **consent** before borrowing his bicycle. **Yes**　　　**No**	My definition: _____ _____ _____ _____ _____.
❹ engineer (en-ju-**near**) *noun* **Rating:** 1　2　3	An **engineer** needs an education to plan difficult projects. **Yes**　　　**No**	My definition: _____ _____ _____ _____ _____.

Key Word	Check Your Understanding	Deepen Your Understanding
5 obstacle (**ahb**-sti-kul) *noun* **Rating:** 1 2 3	A strong person gives up when there is an **obstacle** in the way. Yes No	My definition: _____ _____ _____ _____ _____.
6 project (**prah**-jekt) *noun* **Rating:** 1 2 3	Starting a **project** can be hard, but completing it is rewarding. Yes No	My definition: _____ _____ _____ _____ _____.
7 react (rē-**akt**) *verb* **Rating:** 1 2 3	Most people **react** calmly in a car accident. Yes No	My definition: _____ _____ _____ _____ _____.
8 stubborn (**stu**-burn) *adjective* **Rating:** 1 2 3	A person is **stubborn** by not admitting he or she is wrong. Yes No	My definition: _____ _____ _____ _____ _____.

B. Use one of the Key Vocabulary words to describe a goal in your life. What might keep you from reaching it?

_____

_____

LITERARY ANALYSIS: Analyze Character

Authors show what a character is like with **description** and **dialogue.**

A. Read the passage. In the chart below, write how description and dialogue show what Mama Lil is like.

Look Into the Text

Mama Lil and I had been butting heads ever since I could remember. And the older I got, the more at odds we were.

She thought I weighed too much and dressed badly. I thought she smoked too much and overdid it with her fake gold chains. Time after time, she'd asked me, "How you ever gonna land a decent man with them chunky arms and those T-shirts that put your navel on parade? No self-respecting seventeen-year-old should be letting it all hang out like *that*."

Mama Lil	
Description:	Dialogue:

B. Answer the question about Mama Lil.

What do description and dialogue tell you about Mama Lil? _____

_____

_____

FOCUS STRATEGY: Clarify Ideas

HOW TO CLARIFY IDEAS

1. **Reread** When you don't understand what the words mean, ask a question. Then reread to answer it.

2. **Read On** Keep reading to clarify what you don't understand.

A. Read the passage. Use the strategies above to clarify the ideas as you read. Answer the questions below.

Look Into the Text

> Truth be told, Mama Lil was scared of something she didn't know. She hardly ever left our neighborhood in Brooklyn. To her, the Brooklyn Bridge was a mystery.
>
> And I think that deep down Mama Lil was afraid something bad would happen to me, the same way it happened to my mama and daddy. Also, Mama Lil couldn't read or write very well. I read most of her mail to her and helped her sign her checks.

1. What does Bebe mean when she says Mama Lil was "scared of something she didn't know"?

   _____

   _____

2. How is Mama Lil and Bebe's relationship different from a typical adult and child's relationship?

   _____

   _____

B. Write the strategy you used to answer each question.

   _____

   _____

Selection Review Building Bridges

 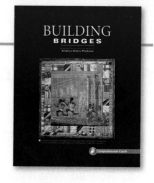

What Influences How You Act?
Find out how people get to where they want to go.

A. In "Building Bridges," Bebe has a goal. The way she acts toward Mama Lil determines the story's outcome. Complete the map below.

Goal-and-Outcome Map

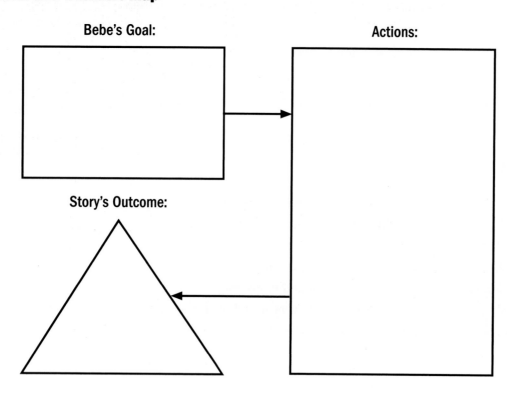

Bebe's Goal:

Actions:

Story's Outcome:

B. Use what you know about the characters to answer the questions.

1. Why does Mama Lil not want Bebe to work on the bridge renovation?

_____

_____

2. How does Bebe react to Mama Lil? Use **react** in your answer.

_____

_____

3. How might Bebe's relationship with Mama Lil change after this incident?

_____

_____

Connect Across Text
In "Building Bridges," Bebe knows what she wants in life. Read this memoir about what causes a teen to change his life.

THE RIGHT WORDS
AT THE RIGHT TIME

by John Leguizamo

I was a nerd in junior high. A really bad nerd. I was seriously out of touch, especially the way I dressed…

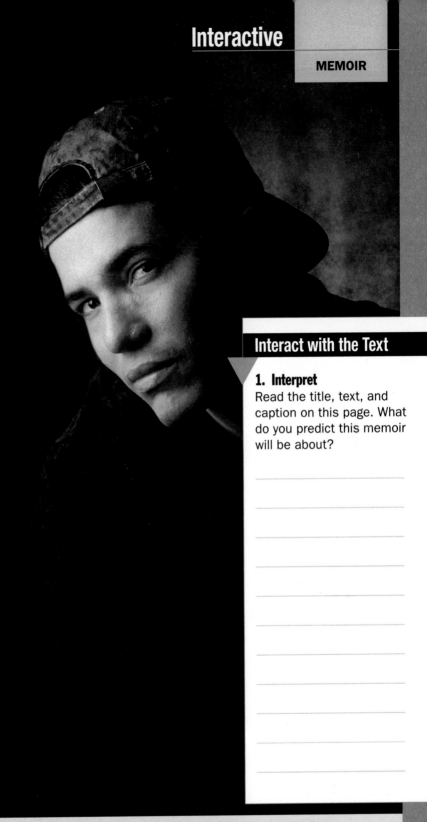

Interact with the Text

1. Interpret
Read the title, text, and caption on this page. What do you predict this memoir will be about?

_____

_____

_____

_____

_____

_____

_____

_____

_____

_____

_____

Key Vocabulary
comedian *n.*, a person who makes people laugh

▲ John Leguizamo's family moved from Colombia to the United States when he was four. He grew up to become an award-winning actor, **comedian**, producer, and writer.

2. Clarify Ideas
Remember that breaking up a sentence when you read will help you find the main idea. Underline the sentence that illustrates the author's realization about his looks. In your own words, explain the main idea of the sentence.

_____

_____

_____

_____

_____

_____

3. Analyze a Memoir
Highlight words and phrases that show what the author was like when he was growing up. How do you know he is not like that anymore? Explain.

_____

_____

_____

_____

_____

_____

_____

_____

_____

_____

_____

_____

_____

When you're a poor kid at a poor school, you worry a lot about how you look all the time, how much money you're spending on clothes and all that. I had problems, man. I wore **high waters**. And my shoes? Forget about it. I had fake sneakers—you know, the kind your mother finds in those big wire bins.

"Hey, John, here's one I like! Go find the one that matches!"

"I found it, Ma, but it's only a three and a half."

"Don't worry. We'll cut out the toes."

So there I am, pants too high, sneakers too tight, underwear without leg holes. I was the **Quasimodo of Jackson Heights**. Then it hits me: this is no way to get girls. So I had my mission then: become cool.

I totally changed. I hung out with the gangsters. Cut class. By the time I got to high school, I was getting in trouble all the time.

What I loved most was **cracking** jokes in school. I liked keeping the kids laughing. Even the teachers laughed sometimes, which was the best part. See, I was still so **out of it** in a way—too cool to hang with

Leguizamo has become a successful comedian and actor. He has been nominated for two Tony Awards for work in theater. He won an Emmy Award in 1999 for work in television.

In Other Words
high waters pants that were too short
Quasimodo of Jackson Heights strange-looking one in my neighborhood. Quasimodo is a deformed man in *The Hunchback of Notre Dame*, a book by Victor Hugo.

cracking telling
out of it odd, different from everyone else

the nerds, not cool enough to be with the *real* cool guys—I figured my only value was to be funny. I enjoyed people enjoying me.

Anyway, one day during my junior year, I was walking down the hallway, making jokes as usual, when Mr. Zufa, my math teacher, pulled me aside. I got collared by the teachers all the time, so I didn't think much about it. Mr. Zufa looked at me and started talking.

"Listen," he says, "instead of being so **obnoxious** all the time—instead of wasting all that energy in class—why don't you rechannel your hostility and humor into something productive? Have you ever thought about being a comedian?"

I didn't talk back to Mr. Zufa like I usually would have. I was quiet. I probably said something like, "Yeah, cool, man," but for the rest of the day, I couldn't get what he said out of my head.

It started to hit me, like, "Wow, I'm going to be a loser all my life." And I really didn't want to be a loser. I wanted to be somebody.

But that one moment Mr. Zufa collared me was the turning point in my life. Everything kind of **converged**, you know? The planets aligned.

But the big change didn't happen overnight.

Eventually, I got into New York University, where I did student films. One of the movies won **a Spielberg Focus Award**, and suddenly my life changed.

In Other Words
obnoxious annoying
converged came together, worked out
a Spielberg Focus Award an award given by Steven Spielberg, a famous movie director

4. Interpret
What happened as a result of Mr. Zufa's lecture?

_____

_____

_____

_____

_____

_____

_____

_____

5. Analyze a Memoir
Leguizamo explains that he did not immediately change from "a loser" into "somebody." What do you think were some of the steps he took in order to change?

_____

_____

_____

_____

_____

_____

_____

_____

_____

6. Interpret
Leguizamo is now an adult, recalling his days in school. In your own words, explain why he is still so grateful to Mr. Zufa.

_____

_____

_____

_____

_____

_____

I got an agent and wound up as a guest villain on **Miami Vice**. That started my **career**.

I've run into Mr. Zufa a bunch of times since high school and told him how his advice turned my life around. And I'm not just saying that. Here's a guy who was able to look beneath all the stuff I pulled in class and find some kind of merit in it, something worth pursuing. How cool is that? ❖

Key Vocabulary
  career *n.*, life's work, profession
• **react** *v.*, to respond
  obstacle *n.*, something that prevents you from doing something

In Other Words
Miami Vice a popular TV show

Selection Review   The Right Words at the Right Time

A. Underline the main part of the sentence below. Then circle the parts of the sentence that support it. Use the punctuation to help you see the parts.

> Anyway, one day during my junior year, I was walking down the hallway, making jokes as usual, when Mr. Zufa, my math teacher, pulled me aside.

B. Answer the questions.

1. How is this memoir similar to a story? How is it different?

_____

_____

2. Is there an adult who has had a positive impact on your life? How has this person influenced your decisions? Write your ideas in a brief paragraph.

_____

_____

_____

_____

_____

Reflect and Assess

WRITING: Write About Literature

A. Plan your writing. List examples of how Bebe and Leguizamo make choices.

Bebe	John Leguizamo

B. What have you learned about making choices by reading about Bebe and Leguizamo? Write a journal entry describing what you've learned. Give examples from both texts.

_____

_____

_____

_____

_____

_____

_____

_____

_____

_____

Integrate the Language Arts

LITERARY ANALYSIS: Dialect

Dialect is a version of language used by a specific group or used in a specific region. Dialect can include special expressions and pronunciations.

A. List three examples of dialect from "Building Bridges." Use context clues to explain what each example means.

Example of Dialect	Meaning
"That grit-work ain't no place for you."	"Hard work like that is not for you."

B. Describe how the use of dialect helped you better understand each character in "Building Bridges."

_____

_____

_____

C. List examples of dialect from "The Right Words at the Right Time.""

_____

_____

_____

VOCABULARY STUDY: Prefixes

A **prefix** is a word part that is added to the beginning of a word. It changes the word's meaning.

A. *Pre-* is a common prefix that means before. Write what you think each word means. Confirm the definition for each word in the dictionary.

Word	Meaning
precaution	something you do in advance to avoid danger
predict	
prepay	
prevent	
preview	

B. The chart below shows some common prefixes and their meanings. Complete the chart by listing words that contain each prefix.

Prefix	Meaning	Words
dis-	not, opposite of	disappear
non-	not	
re-	back or again	
sub-	below, less than, under	
un-	not	

C. Write a definition for each of these words.

reconsider _____

unsatisfactory _____

dishonest _____

nonstop _____

subconscious _____

Prepare to Read

▶ **The Open Window**
▶ **One in a Million**

Key Vocabulary

A. How well do you know these words? Circle a rating for each word. Check your understanding of each word by choosing the correct synonym. Then complete the sentences. If you are unsure of a word's meaning, refer to the Vocabulary Glossary, page 792, in your student text.

Rating Scale

1	I have never seen this word before.
2	I am not sure of the word's meaning.
3	I know this word and can teach the word's meaning to someone else.

Key Word	Check Your Understanding	Deepen Your Understanding
① confident (**kon**-fu-dunt) *adjective* **Rating:** 1 2 3	To be **confident** is to be _____. careful certain	A time I was confident was when _____ _____ _____ _____ _____ .
② convince (kun-**vins**) *verb* **Rating:** 1 2 3	To **convince** is to _____. persuade lie	Advertisements convince people that _____ _____ _____ _____ _____ .
③ doubt (**dowt**) *verb* **Rating:** 1 2 3	If you **doubt** something, you _____ it. believe question	When I doubt what a friend tells me, I respond by _____ _____ _____ _____ _____ .
④ foolish (**fü**-lish) *adjective* **Rating:** 1 2 3	To be **foolish** is to be _____. serious unwise	People are foolish when _____ _____ _____ _____ _____ .

Key Word	Check Your Understanding	Deepen Your Understanding
5 nerves (**nurvz**) *noun* **Rating:** 1 2 3	To suffer from **nerves** is to experience _____. **anxiety** **pride**	To get rid of an attack of nerves, I can _____ _____ _____ _____ _____ .
6 shock (**shok**) *noun* **Rating:** 1 2 3	To experience **shock** is to be filled with extreme _____. **enthusiasm** **surprise**	I would be in shock if _____ _____ _____ _____ _____ .
7 tragedy (**tra**-ju-dē) *noun* **Rating:** 1 2 3	A **tragedy** is a type of _____. **celebration** **misfortune**	Someone I know experienced a tragedy when _____ _____ _____ _____ _____ .
8 worthless (**wurth**-lus) *adjective* **Rating:** 1 2 3	Something that is **worthless** is _____. **useless** **interesting**	An example of an object that I have that is worthless is _____ _____ _____ _____ .

B. Use one of the Key Vocabulary words to write about a time someone influenced your behavior.

_____

_____

Before Reading The Open Window

LITERARY ANALYSIS: Analyze Character and Plot

You can learn what a character is like from **dialogue** and a character's **actions.** Their actions create the plot.

A. Read the passage below. Pay attention to dialogue and to Framton's actions, or the plot. In the chart, write what the dialogue tells you about Framton.

Look Into the Text

> Framton Nuttel tried to think of something to talk about with the girl. He also wondered what he would say to the aunt. At his sister's recommendation, he had come to their home in the country to rest and cure his nerves. But he doubted whether this visit with total strangers was going to help him.
>
> "I know how it will be," his sister had said before he left for the country. "You won't speak to anyone down there. Your nerves will be worse than ever from moping."

Framton's Actions	What the Dialogue Says	What Is Framton Like?
Framton goes to the country to rest his nerves.		

B. Answer the question about the plot.

Will Framton's visit to the country be restful? Why or why not? _____

_____

_____

FOCUS STRATEGY: Clarify Vocabulary

HOW TO CLARIFY VOCABULARY

1. **Find Context Clues** Look for clue words near the unfamiliar word.

2. **Analyze the Clues** Combine the clues with what you know to figure out the meaning of the unfamiliar word.

3. **Replace** Use the meaning in the sentence. Check that it makes sense.

A. Read the passage. Use the strategies above to clarify vocabulary. Answer the questions below.

Look Into the Text

"On this day three years ago, her husband, her two young brothers, and their little brown dog left through that window to go hunting. They never came back. On the way to their favorite hunting spot, they all drowned. It had been a very wet summer. Places that used to be safe to walk across were not safe. The marsh gave way suddenly without warning. Their bodies were never recovered. That was the dreadful part of it."

1. What word don't you know? _____

2. What words and phrases give you clues to the word's meaning?_____

_____

3. What do you already know about these words and phrases? _____

_____

4. What is the meaning of the word?_____

B. Rewrite the sentence by replacing the original word with the meaning.

_____

_____

Does it make sense? Circle *yes* or *no*.   **Yes**   **No**

What Influences How You Act?
Find out how easily people can be fooled.

A. In "The Open Window," you found out how easy it was for Vera to influence Framton to run away. Complete the chart with Framton's and Vera's words and actions.

Characters	Words	Actions
Framton		
Vera		

B. Use the information in the chart to answer the questions about the characters and the plot.

1. Why is Framton an easy person to shock and influence?

_____

_____

2. How might the story have been different if Vera had been less confident? Use **confident** in your answer.

_____

_____

3. Why do you think Vera chooses to treat Framton this way?

_____

_____

One in a Million
a traditional Middle Eastern tale

Connect Across Texts

In "The Open Window," the girl **convinces** Framton of something. What is Hodja convinced of in this folk tale?

Nasruddin Hodja looked at his donkey and frowned. The beast was **a bag of bones** and had a dirty, shaggy coat. It stood under a tree, **dully chewing a clump of grass**. "Look at you," Hodja sneered. "You are completely **worthless** to me. All you do is stand under that tree. You refuse every order I give you!"

The lazy donkey didn't even look at Hodja. It kept **chomping away**.

"That's it!" Hodja cried in frustration. "I'm going to sell you!"

So the next day Hodja led the scrawny creature to the crowded marketplace in the center of the village. He was grateful for the thirty **dinars** a **foolish** man offered him for the beast. Hodja went on with his business as the buyer led the hopeless creature away.

Later, as Hodja wound his way out of the marketplace, he noticed a crowd of eager shoppers. Curious to see what treasure they were after, Hodja pushed through to the center of the group. He was startled to see his donkey! The beast's new owner was shouting, "Look at this fine animal! Have you ever seen a better donkey? See how clean and strong it is! You will never find a better worker. Who will bid for this exceptional creature?"

The buyers pressed forward eagerly. "What a prize! What a find!" they murmured excitedly. One shopper offered forty dinars for the donkey.

Interact with the Text

1. Analyze Cultural Perspectives: Folk Tale
The setting of a folk tale reflects the culture it comes from. Underline words that tell you about the setting. Write a sentence describing where Hodja lives.

_____

_____

_____

2. Clarify Vocabulary
Circle the clues that help you figure out what *sneered* means. Rewrite the sentence, replacing *sneered* with the meaning.

_____

_____

_____

_____

_____

_____

Key Vocabulary
- **convince** *v.*, to make someone believe something
- **worthless** *adj.*, useless
- **foolish** *adj.*, not wise, silly

In Other Words
- **a bag of bones** very thin
- **dully chewing a clump of grass** chewing some grass in a slow, bored way
- **chomping away** eating, chewing
- **dinars** gold coins

3. Interpret

How might he have acted differently if the new owner did not praise the donkey? Why?

_____

_____

_____

_____

_____

_____

_____

Another man offered fifty. A third offered fifty-five!

Puzzlement furrowed Hodja's brow. "I thought that donkey was just an ordinary animal," he said to himself, scratching his scraggly beard. "Was I a fool? It is obviously very special. It's one in a million . . ."

The new owner swept his arm toward the donkey and cried, "How can you **pass up** the chance to own such a magnificent beast? See how the muscles ripple under the smooth, silky coat. Look at those bright, intelligent eyes . . ."

Hodja squeezed his way to the front of the crowd. The man's **flowery words** floated through the warm air, filling Hodja's ears. "Seventy-five dinars once," the man yelled. "Seventy-five dinars twice . . ."

Hodja's skin tingled. He raised his hand excitedly and shouted, "I bid eighty dinars!" ❖

In Other Words

Puzzlement furrowed Hodja's brow. Hodja looked confused.

pass up miss, not take

flowery words nice words, nice description

Cultural Background

Nasruddin Hodja is a popular archetype, or certain type of character, in Middle Eastern tales. Sometimes he is a fool, but sometimes he is wise. He is known by different names throughout the Middle East.

Selection Review One in a Million

A. Below is one word from "One in a Million." Write two clues from the selection that help you understand the word's meaning. Then write what the word means.

Word	First Clue	Second Clue	Word Meaning
scrawny	bag of bones		

B. Answer the questions.

1. How did knowing you were reading a folk tale help you to clarify the vocabulary?

   _____

   _____

2. Imagine you are the seller of Hodja's donkey. Describe it to a buyer. Reread the text to find ideas.

   _____

   _____

Reflect and Assess

WRITING: Write About Literature

A. Plan your writing. Read the opposing opinions. Put an *X* next to the opinion you agree with. Then list three examples from each text to support it.

☐ **Opinion 1:** The characters in these stories were tricked because they were foolish.

☐ **Opinion 2:** The characters in these stories were tricked because they met confident, talented liars.

The Open Window	One in a Million

B. What is your opinion? Write an opinion statement. Then write a paragraph that includes your opinion statement and supports it with evidence from both texts. Remember to use the text evidence you listed in the chart to support your statement.

_____

_____

_____

_____

_____

_____

_____

Integrate the Language Arts

LITERARY ANALYSIS: Compare Settings

The **setting** is where and when a story takes place. Authors can tell the setting directly or they can suggest the setting and let you imagine it.

A. List details about the settings of both selections.

The Open Window	One in a Million
Framton is at a house in the country.	

B. Answer the questions.

1. Compare the way each author describes the setting.

_____

_____

2. What picture did you form in your mind of the setting of "One in a Million"?

_____

_____

3. How does the setting of "The Open Window" affect the characters?

_____

_____

C. Imagine that "The Open Window" takes place in a big city. Describe how the characters and plot of the story might be different.

_____

_____

_____

_____

VOCABULARY STUDY: Suffixes

A **suffix** is a word part added to the end of a word. A suffix changes a word's meaning.

A. –*Ful* is a common suffix that means "full of." Write what you think each word means. Confirm the definition of each word in the dictionary.

Word	Meaning
careful	with care
harmful	
mindful	
thoughtful	
useful	

B. The chart below shows some common suffixes and their meanings. Complete the chart by listing words you've heard that contain each suffix.

Suffix	Meaning	Words
-logy	the study of	biology
-ly	like	
-ment	result	
-ness	the state of	
-ous	possessing the quality of	

C. Write a definition for each of these words.

clearly _____

judgment _____

weakness _____

zoology _____

tremulous _____

Read for Understanding

1. Genre What kind of text is this passage? How do you know?

_____

_____

_____

_____

2. Topic Write a topic sentence to tell what the text is mostly about.

_____

_____

_____

_____

_____

_____

Reread and Summarize

3. Key Ideas In each section, circle three words or phrases that express the key ideas in that section. Note next to each word or phrase why you chose it.

· Section 1: paragraphs 1–4
· Section 2: paragraphs 5–8

4. Summary Use your topic sentence and notes from item 3 to write a summary of the selection.

_____

_____

_____

_____

_____

_____

_____

_____

_____

Ambush

BY TIM O'BRIEN

1 When she was nine, my daughter Kathleen asked if I had ever killed anyone. She knew about the war; she knew I'd been a soldier. "You keep writing these war stories," she said, "so I guess you must've killed somebody." It was a difficult moment, but I did what seemed right, which was to say, "Of course not," and then to take her onto my lap and hold her for a while. Someday, I hope, she'll ask again. But here I want to pretend she's a grown-up. I want to tell her exactly what happened, or what I remember happening, and then I want to say to her that as a little girl she was absolutely right. This is why I keep writing war stories:

2 He was a short, slender young man of about twenty. I was afraid of him—afraid of something—and as he passed me on the trail I threw a grenade that exploded at his feet and killed him.

3 Or to go back:

4 Shortly after midnight we moved into the ambush site outside My Khe. The whole **platoon** was there, spread out in the dense brush along the trail, and for five hours nothing at all happened. We were working in two-man teams—one man on guard while the other slept, switching off every two hours—and I remember it was still dark when Kiowa shook me awake for the final watch. The night was foggy and hot. For the first

In Other Words
Ambush Surprise Attack
platoon group of soldiers

Historical Background
The **Vietnam War** took place from 1954-75 throughout Southeast Asia. The government of North Vietnam, supported by China and the Soviet Union, fought to take over the government of South Vietnam, supported by the United States.

few moments I felt lost, not sure about directions, **groping** for my helmet and weapon. I reached out and found three **grenades** and lined them up in front of me; the pins had already been straightened for quick throwing. And then for maybe half an hour I kneeled there and waited. Very gradually, in tiny slivers, dawn began to break through the fog, and from my position in the brush I could see ten or fifteen meters up the trail. The mosquitoes were fierce. I remember slapping at them, wondering if I should wake up Kiowa and ask for some repellent, then thinking it was a bad idea, then looking up and seeing the young man come out of the fog. He wore black clothing and rubber sandals and a gray **ammunition** belt. His shoulders were slightly stooped, his head cocked to the side as if listening for something. He seemed at ease. He carried his weapon in one hand, muzzle down, moving without any hurry up the center of the trail. There was no sound at all—none that I can remember. In a way, it seemed, he was part of the morning fog, or my own imagination, but there was also the reality of what was happening in my stomach.

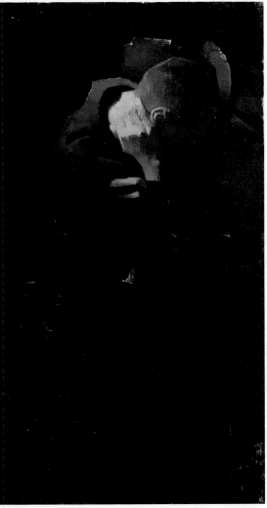

Over four million of these made and sold every week, Diarmuid Kelley (b.1972). Oil on canvas, private collection, The Bridgeman Art Library.

▲ Critical Viewing: Effect What is the mood, or feeling, of this painting? How does it relate to the mood of the story?

In Other Words
groping searching awkwardly
grenades small bombs
ammunition bullet

Reread and Analyze

5. Author's Craft
Reread paragraph 1. Double underline the text that expresses why the narrator is telling his story.

6. Analyze Technique
Reread paragraph 1. Highlight text that tells what the narrator is thinking. Decide what this tells you about him. Then, write down his traits below.

_____

_____

_____

_____

_____

7. Analyze Character
Reread paragraph 2. Circle a word and underline an action that tells you more about the narrator.

8. Analyze Character
Reread paragraph 4. Underline actions that the narrator takes. Highlight his thoughts. What have you learned about him?

_____

_____

_____

_____

_____

_____

_____

_____

9. Relate Characters and Plot Underline the narrator's actions in the second half of paragraph 4. Highlight his thoughts and explanations.

10. Relate Characters and Plot What do you think? Did the narrator act deliberately? Use evidence from the text to support your answer.

I had already pulled the pin on a grenade. I had come up to a **crouch**. It was entirely automatic. I did not hate the young man; I did not see him as the enemy; I did not ponder issues of morality or politics or military duty. I crouched and kept my head low. I tried to swallow whatever was rising from my stomach, which tasted like lemonade, something fruity and sour. I was terrified. There were no thoughts about killing. The grenade was to make him go away—just evaporate—and I leaned back and felt my mind go empty and then felt it fill up again. I had already thrown the grenade before telling myself to throw it. The brush was thick and I had to lob it high, not aiming, and I remember the grenade seeming to freeze above me for an instant, as if a camera had clicked, and I remember ducking down and holding my breath and seeing little wisps of fog rise from the earth. The grenade bounced once and rolled across the trail. I did not hear it, but there must've been a sound, because the young man dropped his weapon and began to run, just two or three quick steps, then he hesitated, **swiveling** to his right, and he glanced down at the grenade and tried to cover his head but never did. It occurred to me then that he was about to die. I wanted to warn him. The grenade made a popping noise—not soft but not loud either—not what I'd expected—and there was a puff of dust and smoke—a small white puff—and the young man seemed to jerk upward as if pulled by invisible wires. He fell on his back. His rubber sandals had been blown off. There was no wind. He lay at the center of the trail, his right leg bent beneath him, his one eye shut, his other eye a huge star-shaped hole.

I did not hate the young man…

In Other Words
crouch low, bent-leg position
swiveling turning

Fallen Timbers/Fallen Time, 1989, David A. Given with Arturo Alonzo Sandoval. Mixed media, National Vetereans Art Museum, Chicago Illinois.

▲ **Critical Viewing: Effect** How is the United States flag used in this piece of art? What effect does this have?

5   It was not a matter of live or die. There was no real **peril**. Almost certainly the young man would have passed by. And it will always be that way.

6   Later, I remember, Kiowa tried to tell me that the man would've died anyway. He told me that it was a good kill, that I was a soldier and this was a war, that I should shape up and stop staring and ask myself what the dead man would've done if things were reversed.

7   None of it mattered. The words seemed far too complicated. All I could do was **gape** at the fact of the young man's body.

8   Even now I haven't finished sorting it out. Sometimes I forgive myself, other times I don't. In the ordinary hours of life I try not to **dwell on** it, but now and then, when I'm reading a newspaper or just sitting alone in a room, I'll look up and see the young man coming out of the morning fog. I'll watch him walk toward me, his shoulders slightly stooped, his head cocked to the side, and he'll pass within a few yards of me and suddenly smile at some secret thought and then continue up the trail to where it bends back into the fog. ❖

In Other Words
peril danger
gape stare
dwell on think a lot about

Reread and Analyze

11. Analyze Character
Highlight what Kiowa says in paragraph 6. What do his words tell you about his relationship with the narrator?

_____

_____

_____

_____

_____

12. Analyze Character
Reread paragraphs 7–8. Looking back on his actions, how does the narrator feel about them now? Support your answer with evidence from the story.

_____

_____

_____

_____

_____

_____

_____

_____

_____

_____

_____

Discuss

13. **Synthesize** With the class, list things in column 1 that you learned about the narrator. In column 2, list devices and techniques the author used to portray the character.

_____   _____
_____   _____
_____   _____

Next, with the class, discuss how the author uses these details to explain the narrator's actions. Make notes.

_____
_____
_____

14. **Write** Use your notes from question 13 to write about the ways that the author uses the setting, the plot, and the character's thoughts and actions to portray the character. Use the questions below to organize your thoughts. If you need more space, continue your writing on another piece of paper.

- What is the narrator like?

- What do you learn about the narrator in the first paragraph?

- Analyze the author's descriptive details about the narrator: How do these details add up to portray the narrator?

- Analyze the author's choice of setting: How does the setting add to the picture of the narrator?

- Analyze the author's use of plot. How does the action change the narrator?

_____
_____
_____
_____
_____
_____
_____
_____

Connect with the **EQ** What Influences How You Act?

Think about how fear influences people's actions.

15. **Viewpoint** Can we know ahead of time how we will act in a new situation? How might the author answer this question?

_____

_____

_____

_____

_____

16. **Theme** What is the author's message about what influences our actions?

_____

_____

_____

_____

_____

Key Vocabulary Review

A. Read each sentence. Circle the word that best fits into each sentence.

1. A person might change his or her (**career** / **superstition**) several times.

2. It is important to get someone's (**evidence** / **consent**) if you want to borrow something.

3. People usually (**react** / **escape**) to a joke by laughing.

4. You might feel (**stubborn** / **confident**) if someone compliments you.

5. A (**worthless** / **foolish**) person might think school is unimportant.

6. A deadly house fire is a (**tragedy** / **failure**).

7. Most people have to overcome an (**experiment** / **obstacle**) to reach their goals.

8. A (**project** / **belief**) requires hard work and preparation.

B. Use your own words to write what each Key Vocabulary word means. Then write a synonym for each word.

Key Word	My Definition	Synonym
1. belief		
2. comedian		
3. convince		
4. doubt		
5. experiment		
6. misfortune		
7. mistaken		
8. shock		

Unit 1 Key Vocabulary

belief	• consent	escape	foolish	obstacle	stubborn
career	• convince	• evidence	misfortune	• project	superstition
comedian	doubt	experiment	mistaken	• react	tragedy
confident	engineer	failure	nerves	shock	worthless

• **Academic Vocabulary**

C. Complete the sentences.

1. An **engineer** is someone who _____
_____.

2. I suffer from **nerves** when _____
_____.

3. A person might try to **escape** if _____
_____.

4. A detective might study **evidence** to determine _____
_____.

5. I know a person who is **stubborn** about _____
_____.

6. One **superstition** people might believe in is _____
_____.

7. A pair of glasses with no lenses is **worthless** because _____
_____.

8. I experienced a **failure** when _____
_____.

Prepare to Read

▶ **Genes: All in the Family**
▶ **How to See DNA**

Key Vocabulary

A. How well do you know these words? Circle a rating for each word. Check your understanding of each word by circling *yes* or *no*. Then, complete the sentences. If you are unsure of a word's meaning, refer to the Vocabulary Glossary, page 792, in your student text.

Rating Scale
1 I have never seen this word before.
2 I am not sure of the word's meaning.
3 I know this word and can teach the word's meaning to someone else.

Key Word	Check Your Understanding	Deepen Your Understanding
❶ control (kun-**trōl**) *verb* **Rating:** 1 2 3	People can **control** how tall they will be. **Yes** **No**	One thing I control in my life is _____ _____ _____ _____ _____ .
❷ extraction (ik-**strak**-shun) *noun* **Rating:** 1 2 3	A doctor can perform an **extraction** of a rusty nail from a patient's foot. **Yes** **No**	After a tooth extraction, people usually _____ _____ _____ _____ .
❸ inherit (in-**hair**-ut) *verb* **Rating:** 1 2 3	If you **inherit** a ring, you buy it with your own money. **Yes** **No**	Something I would like to inherit is _____ _____ _____ _____ .
❹ molecule (**mo**-li-kyūl) *noun* **Rating:** 1 2 3	A **molecule** of water is much larger than a school bus. **Yes** **No**	When scientists look at molecules, they need special equipment, such as _____ _____ _____ .

Key Word	Check Your Understanding	Deepen Your Understanding
5 sequence (**sē**-kwuns) *noun* **Rating:** 1 2 3	The **sequence** of the alphabet is *d, t, u, c, r, l.* **Yes** **No**	The sequence of events in my morning routine is _____ _____ _____ _____ _____.
6 trait (**trāt**) *noun* **Rating:** 1 2 3	A physical **trait**, such as hair or eye color, comes from a person's biological parents. **Yes** **No**	The trait I have that I like best is _____ _____ _____ _____ _____.
7 transmit (trans-**mit**) *verb* **Rating:** 1 2 3	When you cough on someone, you usually **transmit** germs. **Yes** **No**	One way to transmit a message without speaking is _____ _____ _____ _____ _____.
8 unique (yū-**nēk**) *adjective* **Rating:** 1 2 3	My sister's hair color is **unique** because it looks just like mine. **Yes** **No**	A unique thing about my friend is _____ _____ _____ _____ _____.

B. Use one of the Key Vocabulary words to write about a physical characteristic you have. How do you feel about it?

_____

_____

Before Reading Genes: All in the Family

Analyze Author's Purpose

Writers decide which form of writing to use based on what information they want to tell their readers. Knowing an author's purpose, or reason for writing, helps you evaluate the information. Writers can write to narrate, to inform or explain, to persuade or argue, to express feelings, or to tell how to do something. In science writing, writers use key terms and facts to communicate important ideas.

A. Read the passage below. Identify the facts and key terms about genes. Write the facts and key terms in the Main-Idea Tree.

> ### Look Into the Text
>
> ### What Is a Gene?
> The word *gene* has several meanings, but in essence, a gene is an instruction that tells your body how to work. The instruction is stored as a code in the molecule DNA.

Main-Idea Tree

What Is a Gene?

Fact:
Fact:
Key Term: code
Key Term:

B. Answer the questions.

1. What is the author's purpose for writing? _____

_____

_____

2. How does the author achieve his purpose? _____

_____

_____

FOCUS STRATEGY: Self-Question

How to SELF-QUESTION

1. **Ask Questions** Pay attention to important ideas, text features, and diagrams.

2. **Write Your Questions** Write *Who, What, Where, When, Why,* and *How* questions.

3. **Answer the Questions** Use the text and visuals to help answer your questions.

A. Read the passage. Use the strategies above to self-question as you read. Complete the chart below.

Look Into the Text

Where Do My Genes Come From?

Your genes come from your parents, theirs come from their parents, and so on—all the way back to the first living thing that ever existed. Genes are passed down through families, and that's why you probably look a bit like your parents. Physical characteristics, like long eyelashes, red hair, freckles, or blue eyes, run in families because they are controlled by genes.

Type of Question	Ask Your Questions	Answer Your Questions
Where?	Where do your genes come from?	
Why?		
What?		
How?		

B. How did self-questioning help you understand the passage better?

_____

_____

Selection Review Genes: All in the Family

 EQ **How Do Families Affect Us?**
Explore the science behind family resemblances.

A. In "Genes: All in the Family," you learned how scientific facts explain family resemblances. Complete the web below with facts from the article.

Idea Web

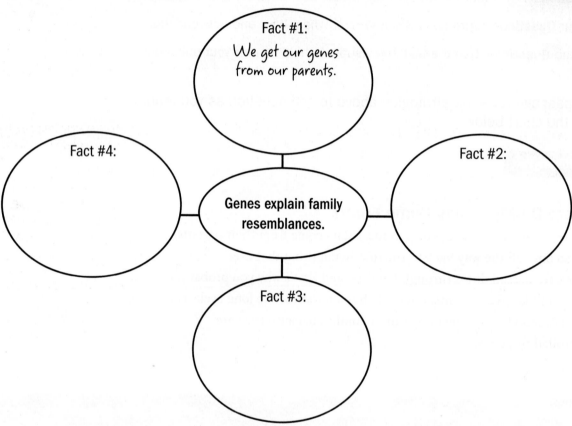

Fact #1:
We get our genes from our parents.

Fact #4:

Fact #2:

Genes explain family resemblances.

Fact #3:

B. Use the information in the web to answer the questions.

1. Why do people often look similar to their parents?

_____

_____

2. How is each child in a family unique? Use the word **unique** in your answer.

_____

_____

3. Why is it important for scientists to study the relationship between genes and families?

_____

_____

How to See DNA

SCIENCE PROCEDURE

by the
Genetic Science
Learning Center

Connect Across Texts

You read about DNA in "Genes: All in the Family." In this science procedure, you will discover what DNA looks like.

The **traits** that you **inherit** from your parents are **determined** by DNA. This is true for all living things: The cells of every plant and animal contain DNA **molecules**. DNA carries the genetic information that determines what the plants and animals will look like, among other traits. You may wonder, though: What does DNA look like? Try this activity to find out.

How to See DNA

Purpose: In this activity, you will free DNA from the cells of green split peas. Then you will be able to see what DNA looks like.

You Will Need:
- 1/2 cup green split peas
- 1/8 teaspoon salt
- 1 cup cold water
- blender
- strainer
- measuring cups and spoons
- liquid detergent
- small glass tubes or containers
- meat tenderizer
- rubbing alcohol
- small wooden stir sticks

Interact with the Text

1. Ask Questions
What questions do you have after reading the introduction to the science procedure? Write one of your questions.

_____

_____

_____

_____

_____

2. Author's Purpose
Circle the sentence in which the author explains the goal of this science procedure. Write the goal in your own words.

_____

_____

_____

_____

_____

_____

_____

Key Vocabulary

trait *n.*, a certain way something is, a feature of something

inherit *v.*, to get things from family members who lived before us

molecule *n.*, a very small particle or piece of a substance

In Other Words

determined controlled

3. Interpret

Circle three words or phrases from Steps 1 and 2 that you might see in a recipe. How are recipes and science procedures similar?

_____

_____

_____

_____

_____

_____

_____

4. Ask Questions

What question might the diagram *Pea Cell Structure* answer? Write a question and the answer.

_____

_____

_____

_____

_____

_____

_____

_____

_____

_____

_____

_____

_____

_____

_____

Step 1

Blender Insanity!

Put the split peas, salt, and cold water in a blender. Put the blender lid in place. Blend on high for 15 seconds. The blender separates the pea cells from each other, so you now have a really thin pea-cell soup.

Step 2

Soapy Peas

Pour the pea mixture through a strainer into a measuring cup. Add 2 tablespoons of liquid detergent to the strained peas. Swirl to mix.

Let the mixture sit for 5–10 minutes.

Why Do This?

Each pea cell is surrounded by a membrane, or outer covering. Inside the membrane is a nucleus. The nucleus is protected by another membrane. And inside the nucleus is the DNA.

To see the DNA, you have to break through both membranes. Detergent can handle this task.

A cell's membrane has lipid (fat) molecules with proteins connecting them. When detergent comes near the cell, it captures the lipids and proteins, breaking down the cell membrane and freeing the DNA from the nucleus.

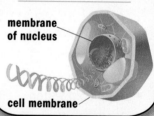

Pea Cell Structure

membrane of nucleus

cell membrane

Step 3

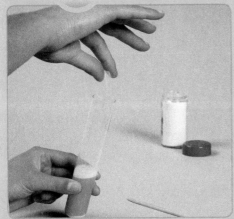

Enzyme Power

Pour the mixture into the glass containers. Fill each container one-third full. Then, add a **pinch** of meat tenderizer (enzymes) to each container and stir gently. Be careful! If you stir too hard, you'll break up the DNA, making it harder to see.

Why Do This?

You may wonder why you are adding meat tenderizer to the soapy pea mixture.

Meat tenderizer contains enzymes, proteins that help chemical reactions happen more quickly. Without enzymes, your body would **grind to a halt**.

The DNA in the nucleus of a cell is protected by other kinds of proteins. Enzymes cut through those proteins.

Step 4

Alcohol Separation

Tilt your glass container. Slowly pour rubbing alcohol into the container and down the side. It should form a layer on top of the pea mixture. Continue pouring until you have about the same amount of alcohol as pea mixture in the container.

DNA will rise from the layer of pea mixture into the alcohol layer. Use a wooden stick to draw the DNA from the alcohol. After you finish, you will have completed a DNA **extraction**!

Why Does This Happen?

Turn the page and find out...

5. Author's Purpose
Remember that writers of science procedures include step-by-step directions. Underline the most important direction words in Step 3. How are the direction words helpful?

_____

_____

_____

_____

_____

_____

_____

6. Author's Purpose
It is important to use the correct materials when following a science procedure. Mark an X next to the material described in the *Why Do This?* box. What would happen if the author forgot to name this ingredient?

_____

_____

_____

_____

_____

_____

_____

_____

_____

7. Ask Questions

Circle an interesting fact in the *Why Does This Happen?* box. Write a question you have about it.

_____

_____

_____

_____

_____

_____

Why Does This Happen?

Alcohol is **less dense than** water, so it floats on top. Because two separate layers are formed, all of the fats (lipids) and protein that you broke up in Steps 2 and 3, along with the DNA, have to decide: "Hmmm, which layer should I go to?"

Most particles and molecules will stay below the alcohol or dissolve in it. The DNA will float in the alcohol and will not be dissolved. This makes it easy to extract. ❖

In Other Words

less dense than not as thick as

Selection Review How to See DNA

A. Look at the question you wrote on page 53. Complete the sentences below.

1. The answer to my question is _____

_____.

2. I found the answer by _____

_____.

3. After learning this, I _____

_____.

B. Answer the questions.

1. What text features did the author include to help you understand this science procedure?

_____

_____

2. Which features helped you most in understanding the procedure?

_____

_____

Reflect and Assess

WRITING: Write About Literature

A. Plan your writing. Read the opposing opinions. Put an *X* next to the opinion you agree with. List examples from each selection to support your opinion.

☐ **Opinion 1:** Genes are mainly responsible for determining who we are.

☐ **Opinion 2:** Genes are not the only thing responsible for determining who we are.

Genes: All in the Family	How to See DNA

B. What is your opinion? Write an opinion paragraph. Use the evidence you listed in the chart to support your opinion.

_____

_____

_____

_____

_____

_____

_____

_____

_____

Integrate the Language Arts

LITERARY ANALYSIS: Summarize

When you want to understand something, it can be a good idea to **summarize** it. When you summarize an article, you retell the most important ideas from it. Follow these steps to write a summary of "How to See DNA."

A. Identify the topic. _____

_____

B. Make a list of the major points in the article.

_____

_____

_____

_____

_____

_____

C. Write the important information in a paragraph. _____

_____

_____

_____

_____

_____

_____

_____

_____

D. Did you include information from the "Why Do This?" sections of the article? Why or why not?

_____

_____

VOCABULARY STUDY: Context Clues

Context clues, or clues in a text, can help you figure out the meaning of an unfamiliar word. Two types of context clues include definitions and appositive definitions.

A. Read the text below. Circle the context clues that can help you figure out the meanings of the underlined words.

> Every person has a <u>unique</u>, or one of a kind, set of genes (except for identical twins). <u>Genomes</u> are sets of genes. There is a complete set of genes inside every cell in your body. To fit into this tiny space, the genes are packed up in an <u>ingenious</u>, or clever, way. Since you have two sets of genes, you have two options for everything. The option that takes priority is called the <u>dominant</u> gene.

B. Use the context clues that you circled, and write the meaning of each underlined word from the text above. Use a dictionary to check the definition.

Word	What It Means
dominant	
genomes	
ingenious	
unique	

C. Use the information in the chart to complete the sentences.

1. If your mother's genes are **dominant**, you look like _____

   _____

2. Each set of **genomes** gives a person _____

   _____

3. The **ingenious** plan worked because _____

   _____

4. Every person is **unique** because _____

   _____

Prepare to Read

▶ Do Family Meals Matter?
▶ Fish Cheeks

Key Vocabulary

A. How well do you know these words? Circle a rating for each word. Check your understanding of each word by circling *yes* or *no.* Then, in your own words, write a definition for the word. If you are unsure of a word's meaning, refer to the Vocabulary Glossary, page 792, in your student text.

Rating Scale

1 I have never seen this word before.

2 I am not sure of the word's meaning.

3 I know this word and can teach the word's meaning to someone else.

Key Word	Check Your Understanding	Deepen Your Understanding
❶ appreciate (u-**prē**-shē-āt) *verb* **Rating:** 1 2 3	When you **appreciate** people, they usually become angry. Yes No	My definition: _____ _____ _____ _____ _____ .
❷ beneficial (be-nu-**fi**-shul) *adjective* **Rating:** 1 2 3	If something is **beneficial** you should throw it away immediately. Yes No	My definition: _____ _____ _____ _____ _____ .
❸ bond (**bond**) *noun* **Rating:** 1 2 3	Brothers can have a strong **bond**, even when they live in different cities. Yes No	My definition: _____ _____ _____ _____ _____ .
❹ consume (kun-**süm**) *verb* **Rating:** 1 2 3	Most cars **consume** gasoline. Yes No	My definition: _____ _____ _____ _____ _____ .

Key Word	Check Your Understanding	Deepen Your Understanding
5 data (**dā**-tu) *noun* **Rating:** 1 2 3	People who ask you to answer a set of questions could be collecting **data**. Yes No	My definition: _____ _____ _____ _____ _____ .
6 research (ri-**surch**) *noun* **Rating:** 1 2 3	Scientists use their **research** results to find new ways to cure illnesses. Yes No	My definition: _____ _____ _____ _____ _____ .
7 survey (**sur**-vā) *noun* **Rating:** 1 2 3	When you take a **survey**, you use a book to find the answers. Yes No	My definition: _____ _____ _____ _____ _____ .
8 united (yū-**nī**-tud) *adjective* **Rating:** 1 2 3	People who are **united** split into groups with opposite goals. Yes No	My definition: _____ _____ _____ _____ _____ .

B. Is spending time with your family important? Write a sentence using two of the Key Vocabulary words to tell what you think.

_____

_____

Before Reading Do Family Meals Matter?

LITERARY ANALYSIS: Analyze Author's Purpose

The purpose of a **research report** is to present and explain factual information that a researcher has gathered about a topic.

A. Read the passage below. Find the facts about family meals. Restate the facts in the chart. Then, write how the authors use the data to explain the information in the report.

> ### Look Into the Text
>
> ### Views on Family Meals
>
> Is eating together really becoming less important to the American family? In a study called Project EAT (Eating Among Teens), 98% of the parents said that it was important to eat at least one meal together each day. Sixty-four percent of the adolescents in the study agreed with their parents.

Views	Facts or Data	What the Data Means
Parents		
Teens		

B. Compare the data. Complete the sentence about the research report.

The research report on family meals shows that _____

_____

_____

_____

FOCUS STRATEGY: Find Question-Answer Relationships

HOW TO FIND QUESTION-ANSWER RELATIONSHIPS

Focus Strategy

1. **"Right There" Answers** You can often find answers right in the text.

2. **"Think and Search" Answers** Sometimes you need to put information together from different parts of the report to find an answer.

A. Read the passage. Use the strategies above to find question-answer relationships as you read. Answer the questions below.

Look Into the Text

> A survey for the National Center on Addiction and Substance Abuse found that:
> • 86% of teens who had dinner with their families five or more nights a week said they had never tried smoking, compared with 65% who had dinner with their families two nights a week or less
> • 68% of teens who had dinner with their families five nights a week or more reported never trying alcohol, compared to 47% of teens who ate dinner with their families two nights a week or less.
> • teens eating a family dinner five or more times a week were almost twice as likely to receive *A*s in school compared to teens who had a family dinner two or fewer times a week (20% vs. 12%)

1. What effect did eating dinner with their families five nights or more have on teens?

_____

_____

2. Which of the two strategies did you use to answer question 1?

_____

_____

B. Return to the passage above, and circle the words or sentences that gave you the answer to the first question.

Selection Review Do Family Meals Matter?

How Do Families Affect Us?
Learn about the impact of family meals.

A. In "Do Family Meals Matter?" you found out how family meals affect teens. Use the information in the research report to complete the web.

Details Web

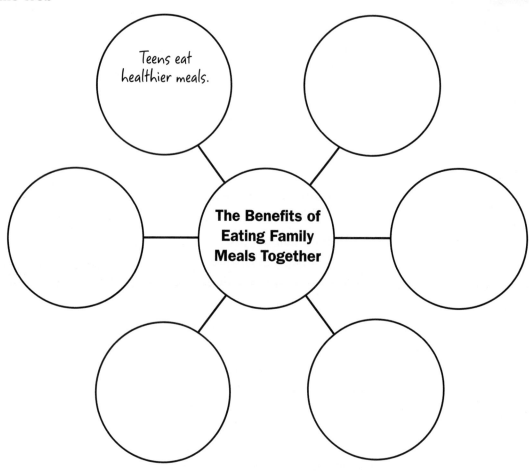

Teens eat healthier meals.

The Benefits of Eating Family Meals Together

B. Use the information in the web to answer the questions.

1. Why do the researchers believe families should eat together?

_____

_____

2. How do the authors use data in their report? Use **data** in your answer.

_____

_____

3. What are some more ways parents and teenagers could develop strong family bonds?

_____

_____

Connect Across Texts

"Do Family Meals Matter?" discusses families eating together. In this anecdote, Amy Tan describes a memorable family meal.

FISH CHEEKS

BY AMY TAN

I fell in love with the minister's son the winter I turned fourteen. He was not Chinese, . . .

Interact with the Text

1. Interpret
Look at the photo. Read the title, text, and "Connect Across Texts." What do you predict this anecdote will be about?

_____

_____

_____

_____

_____

_____

_____

▲ The author, Amy Tan, has written numerous books including *The Joy Luck Club*, which was retold in a movie of the same name, and *The Chinese Siamese Cat*, which inspired the children's TV show "Sagwa."

_____

_____

_____

_____

_____

_____

_____

_____

_____

_____

_____

_____

_____

_____

_____

but as white as Mary in the manger. For Christmas I prayed for this blond-haired boy, Robert, and a slim new American nose.

When I found out that my parents had invited the minister's family over for Christmas Eve dinner, I cried. What would Robert think of our **shabby** Chinese Christmas? What would he think of our noisy Chinese relatives who lacked proper American manners? What terrible disappointment would he feel upon seeing not a roasted turkey and sweet potatoes but Chinese food?

On Christmas Eve, I saw that my mother had outdone herself in creating a strange menu. She was pulling black veins out of the backs of fleshy prawns. The kitchen was littered with **appalling** mounds of raw food: A slimy rock cod with bulging fish eyes that **pleaded** not to be thrown into a pan of hot oil. Tofu, which looked like stacked wedges of rubbery white sponges. A bowl soaking dried **fungus** back to life. A plate of squid, crisscrossed with knife markings so they resembled bicycle tires.

prawns or shrimp

tofu

And then they arrived—the minister's family and all my relatives in a clamor of doorbells and rumpled Christmas packages. Robert grunted hello, and I pretended he was not **worthy of existence**.

Dinner threw me deeper into **despair**. My relatives licked the ends of their chopsticks and reached across the table, dipping into the

In Other Words
shabby low-quality
appalling terrible
pleaded begged
fungus mushrooms
worthy of existence important to me
despair hopelessness

dozen or so plates of food. Robert and his family waited patiently for platters to be passed to them. My relatives murmured with pleasure when my mother brought out the whole steamed fish. Robert **grimaced**. Then my father poked his chopsticks just below the fish eye and plucked out the soft meat. "Amy, your favorite," he said, offering me the tender fish cheek. I wanted to disappear.

At the end of the meal my father leaned back and belched loudly, thanking my mother for her fine cooking. "It's a polite Chinese custom, to show you are satisfied," he explained to our astonished guests. Robert was looking down at his plate with a reddened face. The minister managed to muster a quiet burp. I was stunned into silence for the rest of the night.

After all the guests had gone, my mother said to me, "You want be same like American girls on the outside." She handed me an early gift. It was a miniskirt in beige tweed. "But inside, you must always be Chinese. You must be proud you different. **You only shame is be ashame.**"

The minister managed to muster a quiet burp.

And even though I didn't agree with her then, I knew that she understood how much I had suffered during the evening's dinner.

In Other Words

grimaced made an unhappy expression
You only shame is be ashame. The only thing you should be embarrassed about is that you are embarrassed.

4. Ask Questions
On pages 66 and 67, underline the phrases that explain why Tan was so ashamed of her family customs. Write a question you would like to ask the author. How do you think Tan would answer?

_____
_____
_____
_____
_____
_____
_____
_____

5. Interpret
What is Tan's mother trying to make her understand?

_____
_____
_____
_____
_____
_____
_____
_____
_____
_____
_____
_____
_____
_____

6. Ask Questions

Underline the sentence that explains why Tan's mother made this specific meal. How do you feel about Tan's family now?

_____

_____

_____

_____

_____

_____

It wasn't until many years later—long after I had gotten over my crush on Robert—that I was able to **appreciate** fully her lesson and the true purpose behind our particular menu. For Christmas Eve that year, she had chosen all my favorite foods. ❖

Key Vocabulary

• **appreciate** *v.*, to understand that something is good, to act grateful for it, to value it

Selection Review Fish Cheeks

A. Look through "Fish Cheeks" again. Write a question and answer in the chart for both types of Question-Answer relationships.

Relationship	Question	Answer
Author and Me		
On My Own		

B. Answer the questions.

1. How does Tan's use of descriptive language help you understand her anecdote about Christmas Eve dinner?

_____

_____

2. Which details from the meal would you remember most vividly ten years from now?

_____

_____

Reflect and Assess

WRITING: Write About Literature

A. Plan your writing. Write what you liked and disliked about the two selections in the chart below.

	Do Family Meals Matter?	Fish Cheeks
Likes		
Dislikes		

B. Which selection held your interest more? Why? Write a critical review. Support your review with information from the chart.

_____

_____

_____

_____

_____

_____

_____

_____

_____

_____

_____

LITERARY ANALYSIS: Analyze Descriptive Language

Writers use **descriptive language** to help their readers picture characters, objects, and places. When writers use descriptive language, they appeal to the five senses.

A. Read the examples of descriptive language from "Fish Cheeks." Then describe how each helped you to picture the scene.

Description	The Picture I See
"The kitchen was littered with appalling mounds of raw food."	
"At the end of the meal my father leaned back and belched loudly . . ."	
"My relatives licked the ends of their chopsticks . . ."	
"Tofu, which looked like stacked wedges of rubbery white sponges."	

B. Read the sentences from "Fish Cheeks" below. Write which of the five senses they appeal to.

1. Then my father poked his chopsticks just below the fish eye and plucked out the soft meat. _____

2. I was stunned into silence for the rest of the night. _____

3. She handed me an early gift. It was a miniskirt in beige tweed. _____

4. What terrible disappointment would he feel upon seeing not a roasted turkey and sweet potatoes but Chinese food? _____

C. Write about a memorable meal you have had. Use descriptive language that appeals to the five senses.

_____

_____

_____

VOCABULARY STUDY: Context Clues

Context clues are the words and phrases that surround an unfamiliar word and help you figure out the meaning of the unfamiliar word. One type of context clue is an example. Words that signal an example include *such as, including, like,* and *for example.*

A. Circle the context clues that helped you find the meanings of the words and phrases below. Then write what you think the underlined word or phrases mean.

Sentence(s) from the Text	What the Words/ Phrases Mean
"Young people are more likely to avoid <u>problem behavior</u>, such as drug or alcohol use, the more their parents are involved in their lives."	
"Eating together more often was linked to <u>better eating habits</u>. This included eating more fruits and vegetables, less fried food, and fewer soft drinks."	
"They gave a <u>variety</u> of reasons, including indifference, lack of time, and arguing and fighting at the dinner table."	

B. Complete the sentences.

1. A person might try to avoid problem behavior because _____

_____

2. By choosing better eating habits _____

_____

3. There are a variety of ways to be healthy including _____

_____

C. Use the words and phrases you learned to write a paragraph about the importance of eating healthy meals.

_____

_____

_____

Prepare to Read

▶ Only Daughter
▶ Calling a Foul

Key Vocabulary

A. How well do you know these words? Circle a rating for each word. Check your understanding of each word by circling *yes* or *no*. Then, complete the sentences. If you are unsure of a word's meaning, refer to the Vocabulary Glossary, page 792, in your student text.

Rating Scale	
1	I have never seen this word before.
2	I am not sure of the word's meaning.
3	I know this word and can teach the word's meaning to someone else.

Key Word	Check Your Understanding	Deepen Your Understanding
1 **abusive** (u-**byū**-siv) *adjective* **Rating:** 1 2 3	An **abusive** action is helpful. Yes No	Companies that are abusive to the environment _____ _____ _____ _____ _____ .
2 **approval** (u-**prü**-vul) *noun* **Rating:** 1 2 3	In American society, nodding your head in agreement is a sign of **approval**. Yes No	I would give my approval if a classmate wanted to _____ _____ _____ _____ _____ .
3 **behavior** (bi-**hā**-vyur) *noun* **Rating:** 1 2 3	People's **behavior** is what they say and do. Yes No	I was proud of my friend's behavior when _____ _____ _____ _____ _____ .
4 **circumstance** (**sur**-kum-stans) *noun* **Rating:** 1 2 3	It would be a lucky **circumstance** if someone returned your lost backpack. Yes No	One circumstance that can affect my schoolwork is _____ _____ _____ _____ _____ .

Key Word	Check Your Understanding	Deepen Your Understanding
5 destiny (**des**-tu-nē) *noun* **Rating:** 1 2 3	Everyone has exactly the same **destiny** in life. **Yes** **No**	I think it is my destiny to _____ _____ _____ _____ .
6 embarrass (im-**bair**-us) *verb* **Rating:** 1 2 3	If you **embarrass** a friend, you make him feel happy and proud. **Yes** **No**	Sometimes I embarrass my family when I _____ _____ _____ _____ .
7 role (**rōl**) *noun* **Rating:** 1 2 3	Most actors want a leading **role** in a play. **Yes** **No**	The most important role I play in my family is _____ _____ _____ _____ _____ .
8 valuable (**val**-yū-bul) *adjective* **Rating:** 1 2 3	Something that is **valuable** has no worth. **Yes** **No**	Something that is not valuable to me anymore is _____ _____ _____ _____ _____ .

B. In what ways can parents affect their children? Use one of the Key Vocabulary words in your answer.

_____

_____

Before Reading Only Daughter

Analyze Author's Purpose

A **memoir** tells about a specific time in the writer's life and is told in the writer's own words. It includes:

- details about people and events
- why the people and events are important to the writer

A. Read the passage below. Find the clues that tell you this is a memoir. Complete the chart.

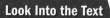

> Once, several years ago, when I was just starting out my writing career, I was asked to write my own contributor's note for an anthology I was part of. I wrote: "I am the only daughter in a family of six sons. *That* explains everything."
>
> Well, I've thought about that ever since, and yes, it explains a lot to me, but for the reader's sake I should have written: "I am the only daughter in a *Mexican* family of six sons." Or even: "I am the only daughter of a Mexican father and a Mexican-American mother." Or: "I am the only daughter of a working-class family of nine." All of these had everything to do with who I am today.

Elements of a Memoir	Clues from Passage
Event	The writer remembers writing a note about herself as an only daughter.
People	
Importance of event and people	

B. What will you will learn about the writer after reading her memoir?

_____

_____

FOCUS STRATEGY: Question the Author

HOW TO QUESTION THE AUTHOR

1. **Use a Double-Entry Journal** Write questions for the author in one column of a two-column chart.

2. **Answer Your Question** Answer the questions as you read on. The answer may be right there.

3. **Think Beyond the Text** Use what you already know from your life and the author's life to answer questions.

A. Read the passage. Use the strategies above to question the author as you read. Answer the questions below.

Look Into the Text

> Being only a daughter for my father meant my destiny would lead me to become someone's wife. That's what he believed. But when I was in fifth grade and shared my plans for college with him, I was sure he understood. I remember my father saying, "*Que bueno, mi'ja,* that's good." That meant a lot to me, especially since my brothers thought the idea hilarious. What I didn't realize was that my father thought college was good for girls—for finding a husband.

1. Write a question for the author.

_____

_____

2. Think beyond the text, and answer your question.

_____

_____

B. How did the reading strategy help you answer your question?

_____

_____

_____

Selection Review Only Daughter

How Do Families Affect Us?
Read about how the behavior of parents can make a difference.

A. In "Only Daughter," you found out how the behavior of a parent can affect other family members. Complete the chart below about Cisneros's father and how his actions and beliefs affected her.

Cause-and-Effect Chart

Father's Actions and Beliefs	How It Affects Cisneros
He thinks college is for finding a husband.	She studies English instead of looking for a wealthy man to marry.

B. Use the information in the chart to answer the questions.

1. Why is most of Cisneros's memoir about her father?

_____

_____

2. When does Cisneros finally feel like she had gained her father's approval? Use **approval** in your answer.

_____

_____

3. How might Cisneros's life have been different if her father had encouraged her to become a writer?

_____

_____

Connect Across Texts

In "Only Daughter," Sandra Cisneros describes how her father affected her life. In this news commentary, Stan Simpson tells how other parents have an impact on their children.

STAN
SIMPSON

Calling a Foul

Bill Cardarelli was impressed by a high school basketball player. He thought she would be a fine addition to the St. Joseph College women's team he coached.

Then he saw her dad in action as **a spectator**.

"He was absolutely bad-mouthing the coach," Cardarelli recalled. "I mean yelling: 'You don't know how to coach! What are you doing?'"

The kid was no longer that **valuable** to Cardarelli.

"I stopped **recruiting her**," he said. "Because you knew what was **in line for** the next coach to get that guy."

Bad-behaving parents at sports events have become a painful reality.

The stuff that happens after the game is just as shocking. A Connecticut parent spit at a high school basketball coach because he didn't like how the coach was coaching. Referees and coaches have been physically attacked after school games. And it's not unusual for parents to be banned from a game until they can control their emotions.

State high school athletic directors say it is more difficult than ever to attract coaches and game officials. They're not willing to put up with **abusive** parents.

Now there's a bill that would make it a crime to attack a sports official at a game.

Time-out.

Has it really come to this? Do we need a law to remind adults that they should act like grownups at sports events?

"That's a sad **commentary**," said John Shukie, president of the Connecticut Association of Athletic Directors. "It's kind of **an indictment of** where sports have been going in our society. The importance people place

Interact with the Text

1. Author's Viewpoint
Underline the author's opinions in the first column. What is he trying to tell the reader?

_____

_____

_____

_____

_____

_____

2. Author's Viewpoint
Circle three facts in the second column. Why does the author include these facts?

_____

_____

_____

_____

_____

_____

_____

Key Vocabulary
valuable *adj.*, having worth, important
abusive *adj.*, hurtful, cruel, harsh

In Other Words
a spectator someone watching the game
recruiting her trying to get her to join my team
in line for going to happen to
commentary statement about the issue
an indictment of a negative comment about

3. Interpret
Underline the reason the author thinks parents behave rudely at sporting events. What effect does this ultimately have on their children?

_____

_____

_____

_____

_____

_____

_____

4. Ask Questions
Circle what the writer thinks should be done to repeat offenders. How does he view these parents' behavior? How does he support his opinion?

_____

_____

_____

_____

_____

_____

_____

_____

_____

_____

_____

on winning and losing is greater than ever now."

The small percentage of **overzealous** parents out there has become an unwelcome part of youth athletics. You can't stop these parents. You can only hope to keep them under control. Many want their children to be successful athletes so badly that they don't notice their kids are NOT good enough to get athletic scholarships. It doesn't matter how many trophies their kids won in sports when they were really little. The parents **embarrass** themselves and their kids with their angry performances.

"We have lost our sense of **decorum**," says athletic director June Bernabucci of Hartford. "Parents and all adults have to stop **living vicariously through** their children and their sports activities."

No law in the world will stop a fuming parent from fighting with a coach or an official. But every parent of a student athlete should sign an agreement that outlines consequences for his or her bad **behavior**:

- I will not confront a coach or sports official after a game ends.

- I will not shout insults at other athletes on either team.

- I will not use **profanity**.

- I will sit in the stands, support the team, and pretend that I'm the adult.

Yeah, maybe it's a little childish. But wait until you hear the consequences.

Repeat offenders would be **banned** from games, unless they wear a huge sign: *As a parent, I stink.* ❖

Key Vocabulary
embarrass *v.*, to make someone feel confused, uneasy, or ashamed
behavior *n.*, the way a person acts, conduct

In Other Words
overzealous extreme, intense
decorum good behavior
living vicariously through pushing their own dreams on
profanity bad words
banned kept away from

About the Writer

Stan Simpson (1962–) writes a weekly column for the *Hartford Courant*, a newspaper in Hartford, Connecticut. He also hosts a weekly news radio program. His work addresses a wide range of issues, including education, criminal justice, and local politics.

Key Vocabulary
- **role** *n.*, a part you play on stage or in real life

Interact with the Text

5. Interpret
Underline the issues the author writes about. Why do you think the author writes about this issue?

_____

_____

_____

_____

_____

_____

_____

Selection Review Calling a Foul

A. Choose one opinion and one fact from the article. Use the strategies to question the author.

Fact: _____

_____

Question: _____

_____

Opinion: _____

_____

Question: _____

_____

1. How did questioning the author help you understand the text better?

_____

_____

_____

_____

Selection Review continued

B. The author writes his opinion about parents' behavior at sports events, but he also includes facts. Complete the T chart, separating the article's facts and opinions. Then answer the questions below.

T Chart

Facts	Opinions

1. How did identifying the facts and opinions in this news commentary help you understand the text?

   _____

   _____

2. This news commentary focused on the bad behavior of some parents. What do you think those parents would say about this news commentary? Write a paragraph.

   _____

   _____

   _____

   _____

   _____

   _____

   _____

   _____

   _____

   _____

   _____

Reflect and Assess

WRITING: Write About Literature

A. Write three things parents do to support their children in a positive way. Provide examples from one or both texts to support each item.

Positive Things Parents Can Do
1.
2.
3.

B. Use the examples you listed from both texts to write a short guide for parents.

Integrate the Language Arts

▶ Only Daughter
▶ Calling a Foul

LITERARY ANALYSIS: Analyze Style

The words that authors choose and the way these words are arranged create the author's **style** of writing. Style may change depending on the form, or genre, and the effect the author wants to have on the readers.

A. Read the excerpt from "Calling a Foul." Circle any words or phrases that indicate the author's direct, informal style.

> "You can't stop these parents. You can only hope to keep them under control. Many want their children to be successful athletes so badly that they don't notice their kids are NOT good enough to get athletic scholarships. It doesn't matter how many trophies their kids won in sports when they were really little."

B. Write the examples that you circled and which element of style the author is using.

Examples from the Text	Author's Style

C. Imagine that you are the child of one of the parents the author describes. Write a letter to your parent. Use the same style of writing as this author.

_____

_____

_____

_____

_____

_____

_____

_____

_____

VOCABULARY STUDY: Context Clues

Synonyms are words that have about the same meaning. **Antonyms** are words that have the opposite meaning. **Context clues** with synonyms and antonyms can help you figure out the meanings of unfamiliar words.

A. Read each example from "Calling a Foul" and circle a synonym or antonym for the underlined word or phrase.

1. "'He was absolutely bad-mouthing the coach,' Cardarelli recalled. 'I mean yelling. . . .'"

2. "'That's a sad commentary'. . . It's kind of an indictment of where sports have been going in our society.'"

3. "The small percentage of overzealous parents out there has become an unwelcome part of youth athletics. . . . You can only hope to keep them under control."

4. "No law in the world will stop a fuming parent from fighting with a coach or an official."

B. Write what you think each word or phrase means based on the context clues you circled above.

Word or Phrase	What It Means
bad-mouthing	
fuming	
indictment	
overzealous	

C. Now that you know each word's meaning, write sentences using the words below.

bad mouthing _____

_____

fuming _____

_____

indictment _____

_____

overzealous _____

_____

text is this passage? How
do you know?

_____

_____

_____

2. Topic Write a topic
sentence to tell what the
text is mostly about.

_____

_____

_____

Reread and Summarize

3. Key Ideas In each
section, circle three words
or phrases that express the
key ideas in that section.
Note next to each word or
phrase why you chose it.

· Section 1: paragraphs 1–4
· Section 2: paragraphs 5–12
· Section 3: paragraph 13

4. Summary Use your
topic sentence and notes
from item 3 to write a
summary of the selection.

_____

_____

_____

_____

_____

_____

_____

_____

_____

_____

from

The Color of Water

by James McBride

1   It was kill or be killed in my house, and Mommy understood that, in
fact created the system. You were **left to your own devices** or so you
thought until you **were at your very wits' end**, at which time she would
step in and rescue you. I was terrified when it came my turn to go to
school. Although P.S. 118 was only eight blocks away, I wasn't allowed
to walk there with my **siblings** because kindergarten students were
required to ride the bus. On the **ill-fated morning**, Mommy chased me
all around the kitchen trying to dress me as my siblings laughed at my
terror. "The bus isn't bad," one quipped, "except for the snakes." Another
added, "Sometimes the bus never brings you home." **Guffaws** all around.

2   "Be quiet," Mommy said,
inspecting my first-day-of school
attire. My clothes were clean, but
not new. The pants had been Billy's,
the shirt was David's, the coat had
been passed down from Dennis to
Billy to David to Richie to me. It
was a gray coat with a fur collar
that had literally been chewed up

Comforters, Ron Waddams © 1983, Acrylic on board, courtesy
Larren Art Trust, Beaconsfield, England.

In Other Words

left to your own devices on your own
were at your very wits' end couldn't think
   of anything else to do
siblings brothers and sisters
ill-fated morning morning of my first day
Guffaws Laughter

by somebody. Mommy dusted it off with a whisk broom, set out eight or nine bowls, poured oatmeal in each one, left instructions for the eldest to feed the rest, then ran a comb through my hair. The sensation was like a tractor pulling my curls off. "C'mon," she said, "I'll walk you to the bus stop." Surprise reward. Me and Mommy alone. It was the first time I remember ever being alone with my mother.

3   It became the **high point** of my day, a memory so sweet it is burned into my mind like a tattoo, Mommy walking me to the bus stop and every afternoon picking me up, standing on the corner of New Mexico and 114th Road, clad in a brown coat, her black hair tied in a colorful scarf, watching with the rest of the parents as the yellow school bus swung around the corner and came to a stop with a hiss of air brakes.

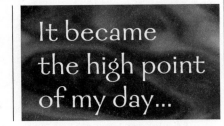

It became the high point of my day...

4   Gradually, as the weeks passed and the terror of going to school **subsided**, I began to notice something about my mother, that she looked nothing like the other kids' mothers. In fact, she looked more like my kindergarten teacher, Mrs. Alexander, who was white. Peering out the window as the bus rounded the corner and the front doors flew open, I noticed that Mommy stood apart from the other mothers, rarely speaking to them. She stood behind them, waiting calmly, hands in her coat pockets, watching intently through the bus windows to see where I was, then smiling and waving as I yelled my greeting to her through the window. She'd quickly grasp my hand as I stepped off the bus, ignoring the stares of the black women as she **whisked** me away.

In Other Words
high point best part
subsided was less powerful, decreased
whisked quickly took

Why did the author write this selection?

_____

_____

_____

_____

6. Author's Viewpoint
Reread paragraph 1. Underline the text where the author describes his mother. What does this show about the author's view of his mother?

_____

_____

_____

_____

7. Details Reread paragraphs 1 through 4. Highlight the details that the author uses to show how he feels about his mother. Why does the author choose these details to tell about his mother?

_____

_____

_____

_____

_____

_____

_____

8. Details Reread paragraphs 5 through 10. Double underline the details that show how Mommy responds to the author's questions about why she is different. What do these details show about the author's view of her?

_____

_____

_____

_____

_____

_____

9. Word Choice Underline the word _Forget_ in paragraph 10. Why does the author repeat this word?

_____

_____

_____

Find and underline other repeated words in paragraph 10. Then circle words that tell what Mommy feels is important and should be remembered. How does recalling her words support the author's viewpoint?

_____

_____

_____

_____

_____

_____

School's Out, 1936, Allan Rohan Crite. Oil on canvas, Smithsonian American Art Museum.

▲ **Critical Viewing: Character** How do the adults and children in this painting get along? How does the artist illustrate the relationships?

5   One afternoon as we walked home from the bus stop, I asked Mommy why she didn't look like the other mothers.

6   "Because I'm not them," she said.

7   "Who are you?" I asked.

8   "I'm your mother."

9   "Then why don't you look like Rodney's mother, or Pete's mother? How come you don't look like me?"

10   She sighed and shrugged. She'd obviously **been down this road** many times. "I do look like you. I'm your mother. You ask too many questions. Educate your mind. School is important. Forget Rodney and Pete. Forget their mothers. You remember school. Forget everything else. Who cares about Rodney and Pete! When they go one way, you go the other way. Understand? When they go one way, you go the other way. You hear me?"

In Other Words
been down this road answered this question

11   "Yes."

12   "I know what I'm talking about. Don't follow none of them around.
You **stick to** your brothers and sisters, that's it. Don't tell nobody your
business neither!" End of discussion.

13   A couple of weeks later
the bus dropped me off
and Mommy was not there.
I **panicked**. Somewhere in
the back of my mind was
the memory of her warning
me, "You're going to have to
learn to walk home by yourself," but that memory blinked like a distant
fog light in a stormy sea and it drowned in my panic. I was lost. My house
was two blocks away, but it might as well have been ten miles because I
had no idea where it was. I stood on the corner and **bit back** my tears.
The other parents regarded me sympathetically and asked me my address,
but I was afraid to tell them. In my mind was Mommy's warning, drilled
into all twelve of us children from the time we could walk: "Never, ever,
ever tell your business to nobody," and I shook my head no, I don't know
my address. They **departed** one by one, until a sole figure remained, a
black father, who stood in front of me with his son, saying, "Don't worry,
your mother is coming soon." I ignored him. He was blocking my view, the
tears clouding my vision as I tried to peer behind him, looking down the
block to see if that familiar brown coat and white face would appear in
the distance. It didn't. In fact there wasn't anyone coming at all, except
a bunch of kids and they certainly didn't look like Mommy. They were a
motley crew of girls and boys, ragged, with wild hairdos and unkempt
jackets, hooting and making noise, and only when they were almost upon
me did I recognize the faces of my elder siblings and my little sister Kathy
who trailed behind them. I ran into their arms and collapsed in tears as
they gathered around me, laughing. ❖

> "You stick to your brothers and sisters, that's it."

In Other Words
stick to stay with
business personal information
panicked got very worried and scared
bit back tried to stop
departed left
motley crew mixed group

Reread and Analyze

10. Author's Viewpoint
Underline the main events in paragraph 13. How does the author show that his mother's lesson worked?

_____

_____

_____

_____

How did his mother rescue him when he was at his wit's end?

_____

_____

_____

_____

Discuss

11. **Synthesize** With the class, list some of the details that the author uses to support his viewpoint. Discuss why the author chooses those details.

_____

_____

_____

Then, with the class, discuss how authors use details and word choice to express and support their viewpoints. Make notes.

_____

_____

_____

_____

12. **Write** Use your notes from question 11 to write about the ways that authors use details and word choice to support their viewpoints. Use the questions below to organize your thoughts.

   A. What is the author's viewpoint?

      1. What details does the author use to support his viewpoint?

      2. Evaluate the author's use of details: Why does the author choose these details to support his viewpoint?

      3. Evaluate the author's word choice: How does the author's choice of words help reinforce his viewpoint?

      4. Do the author's use of details and choice of words help you understand his viewpoint? Explain.

_____

_____

_____

_____

_____

_____

_____

Connect with the **EQ** How Do Families Affect Us?

Consider what is most important in a family.

13. **Viewpoint** How would the author answer the Essential Question? How do you know?

_____

_____

_____

_____

_____

_____

14. **Theme** What is the writer's message about why a family matters?

_____

_____

_____

_____

_____

_____

Key Vocabulary Review

A. Read each sentence. Circle the word that best fits into each sentence.

1. Locking up your bike is an example of protecting (**valuable / beneficial**) property.

2. Each person has (**united / unique**) characteristics.

3. A recipe follows a specific (**sequence / trait**) of steps.

4. People are (**united / abusive**) when they all work together.

5. Scientists collect (**circumstances / data**) when they do experiments.

6. You need a microscope to study a (**molecule / survey**).

7. People use e-mail to (**inherit / transmit**) information.

8. An archaeologist may have to perform an (**extraction / approval**) to remove artifacts from the ground.

B. Use your own words to write what each Key Vocabulary word means. Then write a synonym for each word.

Key Word	My Definition	Synonym
1. approval		
2. beneficial		
3. control		
4. destiny		
5. embarrass		
6. research		
7. role		
8. trait		

abusive	• beneficial	control	• extraction	• role	• transmit
• appreciate	• bond	• data	inherit	• sequence	• unique
approval	• circumstance	destiny	molecule	• survey	united
behavior	• consume	embarrass	• research	trait	valuable

• **Academic Vocabulary**

C. Answer the questions using complete sentences.

1. Why might someone conduct a **survey**?

_____

_____

2. Describe a **circumstance** that might make you late for something.

_____

_____

3. Describe a time when your **behavior** changed what people thought of you.

_____

_____

4. What person do you **appreciate** the most?

_____

_____

5. Who do you have a special **bond** with?

_____

_____

6. What is your favorite food to **consume**?

_____

_____

7. What qualities did you **inherit** from a family member?

_____

_____

8. Why do animal shelters rescue pets from **abusive** owners?

_____

_____

Prepare to Read

▶ Heartbeat
▶ Behind the Bulk

Key Vocabulary

A. How well do you know these words? Circle a rating for each word. Check your understanding of each word by marking an *X* next to the correct definition. Then complete the sentences. If you are unsure of a word's meaning, refer to the Vocabulary Glossary, page 792, in your student text.

Rating Scale

1 | I have never seen this word before.
2 | I am not sure of the word's meaning.
3 | I know this word and can teach the word's meaning to someone else.

Key Word	Check Your Understanding	Deepen Your Understanding
1 appearance (u-**pear**-uns) *noun* **Rating:** 1 2 3	☐ a person's actions ☐ the way a person looks	One way to change your appearance is _____ _____ _____ _____ .
2 depressed (di-**prest**) *adjective* **Rating:** 1 2 3	☐ happy and charming ☐ sad and gloomy	To cheer up a friend who is depressed, you can _____ _____ _____ _____ .
3 distorted (di-**stor**-ted) *adjective* **Rating:** 1 2 3	☐ true and accurate ☐ not true and not real	An object can look distorted if you _____ _____ _____ _____ .
4 illusion (i-**lü**-zhun) *noun* **Rating:** 1 2 3	☐ something that is not real ☐ something that is hard to find	One example of an illusion I have seen is _____ _____ _____ _____ .

Key Word	Check Your Understanding	Deepen Your Understanding
❺ normal (**nor**-mul) *adjective* **Rating:** 1 2 3	☐ usual or regular ☐ unnatural or irregular	On a normal weekend, I like to _____ _____ _____ _____ .
❻ solution (su-**lü**-shun) *noun* **Rating:** 1 2 3	☐ the act of solving a problem ☐ the act of cleaning	When I have trouble finding a solution to a problem, I ___ _____ _____ _____ .
❼ transform (trans-**form**) *verb* **Rating:** 1 2 3	☐ to copy ☐ to change	One way to transform an empty room is to _____ _____ _____ _____ .
❽ weight (wāt) *noun* **Rating:** 1 2 3	☐ a measurement of diameter ☐ a measurement of heaviness	One way to lose weight is to _____ _____ _____ _____ .

B. Use one of the Key Vocabulary words to write about a time you learned something new about yourself.

_____

_____

Before Reading Heartbeat

LITERARY ANALYSIS: Analyze Point of View

A first-person narrator tells the story using *I*, *me*, and *my*. A first-person narrator describes characters and events from his or her **point of view.** When a first-person narrator records the thoughts and feelings of others, his or her perspective may not be reliable.

A. Read the passage below. Complete the chart with the thoughts and feelings that tell you each character's point of view.

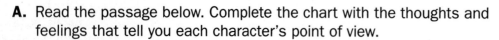

> **Look Into the Text**
>
> My nickname's "Heartbeat," because my friends swear that you can actually see the pulse on my bare chest. I've always been skinny. Everyone assumes I'm a weakling because I'm so thin (I prefer "lean and mean" or "wiry"), despite being a three-sport athlete. I decided to do something about it this fall when Sarah, the girl I have a crush on, said "Oh my God . . . you are so skinny." She was visibly repulsed by my sunken chest as I stepped off the soccer bus after practice. I silently vowed to do everything within my power to become the "after" picture. I was sixteen years old, but looked like I was eleven.

Character	Character's Thoughts and Feelings	Are They Reliable?
"Heartbeat"	knows he's not a weakling	
Sarah		

B. Answer the questions about the characters' points of view.

Does appearance matter to Heartbeat, the narrator? To Sarah? Why or why not?

_____

_____

FOCUS STRATEGY: Make Inferences

HOW TO MAKE INFERENCES

1. You Read Look for clues in the text.

2. You Know Think about what your experience tells you.

3. And So Combine what you already know with what you read to make an inference.

A. Use the strategies to make inferences as you read. Complete the chart.

Look Into the Text

> For the rest of the fall, I did countless push-ups and curled free weights until I couldn't bend my arms. I got ridiculously strong and defined, but I wasn't gaining weight. I wanted to be *thicker.* I didn't care about getting stronger if nobody could tell. I did research, and started lifting heavier weights at lower reps and supplemented my meals with weight-gainer shakes, egg whites, boiled yams, and tubs of cottage cheese.

You Read	You Know	And So
"I did countless push-ups and curled free weights"	Lifting weights usually makes you bigger.	

1. What inference can you make about the narrator?

_____

_____

2. How did using the strategy help you understand the text better?

_____

_____

B. Underline the clues that helped you make your inference.

Unit 3: True Self **95**

Selection Review Heartbeat

EQ | **Do We Find or Create Our True Selves?**
Explore whether appearance matters.

A. In "Heartbeat," the narrator, Dave, decides to change his appearance to make someone else like him. Write what Dave does in the chart.

Why Dave Wants to Change	What Dave Does to Change
Sarah tells him he is skinny.	Dave works out but does not gain weight.

B. Use the information in the chart to answer the questions.

1. Why does Dave begin to wear T-shirts under his sweaters and shirts?

_____

_____

2. Why doesn't his solution work? Use **solution** in your answer.

_____

_____

3. Do you think he will feel differently about his appearance in the future? Why or why not?

_____

_____

_____

Behind the Bulk

BY CATE BAILY

Connect Across Texts

In "Heartbeat," Dave learns to accept the way he looks. Read this informative article about a young man who tries to build up his body.

Every time he passed a mirror, Craig flexed his muscles. He wanted to look "insanely big—like an action figure."

"When I walked into a room, I wanted **heads to turn**," he says. People did notice Craig's 225-pound, 5-foot 9-inch **frame**. But what they didn't see was the physical damage and **psychological turmoil** going on inside.

The story behind the bulk was five years of **steroid abuse** and a struggle with muscle dysmorphia. Muscle dysmorphia is a condition in which a person has a **distorted** image of his or her body. Men with this condition think that they look small and weak, even if they are large and muscular.

Illegal and Grim

It all started when Craig was 18. Before a summer trip to Orlando, Florida, he was feeling overweight. He wanted to look good, so he resolved to get fit. Running on the treadmill, he slimmed down fast, losing 20 pounds in a month.

But lean wasn't Craig's ideal. "I wanted people to say, 'That guy's huge.'" He lifted **weights** and experimented with steroidal **supplements**, also called dietary supplements. These drugs promise to build muscles. Despite potential risks and unclear effectiveness, they can be bought legally over the counter at many stores.

But what Craig was looking for couldn't be bought in a store. So he turned to anabolic steroids.

Anabolic steroids have some **legitimate** medical uses when taken under a doctor's supervision. But to use steroids for muscle-building in a healthy body is illegal. This didn't

Interact with the Text

1. Point of View
Circle a pronoun that tells you this informative article is written in third-person point of view. How has the writer incorporated Craig's thoughts and ideas?

_____

_____

_____

2. Inferences
Underline a phrase that tells you why steroidal supplements are dangerous. What can you infer about why people take supplements?

_____

_____

_____

_____

_____

_____

Key Vocabulary
- **distorted** *adj.*, twisted out of shape, not representing the truth
  weight *n.*, heavy gym equipment used for exercising

In Other Words
heads to turn people to notice me
frame body
psychological turmoil mental confusion
steroid abuse incorrect use of a medical drug
supplements pills
legitimate real, valuable

3. Inferences
Underline words and phrases that describe Craig's relationships with other people. What can you infer about how Craig's struggle affected those relationships?

_____

_____

_____

_____

_____

_____

_____

4. Point of View
Highlight facts that tell you the effects steroids had on Craig. Why did the author include the information?

_____

_____

_____

_____

_____

_____

_____

_____

_____

_____

stop Craig. Neither did the many **grim potential side effects**.

Craig thought he knew exactly what he was getting into. Like 4% of high school seniors and an

How Weight Training Builds Muscle

Muscle fibers contain long myofibrils, which are made up of strands of protein. When you lift weights, the protein strands get larger. This causes the muscle fibers to expand.

Muscle Before Training

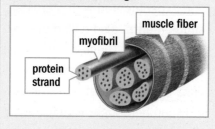

Muscle After Training

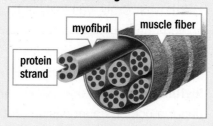

▲ Interpret the Diagrams Which part of a muscle fiber gets larger and causes the muscle fiber to expand?

estimated hundreds of thousands of adults, he took steroids anyway.

Heart Problems

Craig's **appearance** was that important to him. "The scale was my enemy. Every pound meant so much to me," he says.

Craig constantly compared himself to others. He drove his friends and family crazy asking, "Is that guy bigger than me? What about that guy?"

He never had complete satisfaction. "Some days, I'd be **arrogant**, wearing shorts to show off my quads. Other days, I'd be a disaster. On those days, I'd have to wear big, baggy clothes."

Craig's steroid use **escalated** over time. He had begun by taking oral steroids (pills) exclusively. But when he heard that injectable steroids were more effective, he overcame a fear of needles. At his worst, he was injecting three to four times and taking ten pills a day.

The drugs **took their toll**. Craig's hair fell out. Acne popped up all over his back. His face swelled. Then, something even more serious happened: he started having chest pains.

Key Vocabulary
appearance _n._, the way someone or something looks

In Other Words
grim potential side effects other bad things the steroids could do to his body
arrogant really proud
escalated increased
took their toll hurt Craig's body

Steroids Can Cause...

- Baldness
- Mood Swings
- Acne
- Heart Attack, Stroke
- Stunted Growth
- Liver Cancer, Tumors, Cysts
- Kidney Damage

▲ **Interpret the Diagram** Name three problems that steroids can cause.

New Priorities

Craig was having other problems, too. Craig, then 25, was screaming and yelling at his wife a lot. Ultimately, his marriage ended. He lost a **custody battle** over his 1-year-old son, Jake. Craig's wife said that Craig couldn't see their child until he passed a drug test.

That was the moment when everything changed for Craig. He knew he had to quit.

On Father's Day, Craig **went cold turkey**. He knew he needed help, so his parents found him a psychiatrist, who treated him through **the better part of a** year.

Today, Craig's **priorities** have changed. He still wants to be a head-turner, but for a different reason. "Now I'd rather be walking into a room with my son and have people thinking, 'Wow, he's the greatest dad in the world.'" ❖

In Other Words

custody battle legal fight with his wife
went cold turkey completely quit taking steroids
the better part of a most of the
priorities values

5. Inferences
Underline phrases that tell why Craig decided to quit taking steroids. What can you infer about his decision?

6. Point of View
Circle the sentence that tells what Craig wants people to notice about him now. Explain why the author ends the article with Craig's quote.

Selection Review Behind the Bulk

A. Read the two details from the article about Craig's experiences with steroids.

> **Detail 1:** Craig developed acne and lost his hair.
> **Detail 2:** Craig's marriage fell apart.

  1. What can you infer about the effects of steroid use?

_____

_____

_____

_____

  2. Based on Craig's story, why do you think people take steroids?

_____

_____

_____

_____

B. Answer the questions.

  1. How would the article be different if the information had been presented in the first-person rather than the third-person point of view?

_____

_____

_____

_____

  2. What is your opinion about steroid use? Write a statement. Use at least two pieces of text evidence from the article.

_____

_____

_____

_____

_____

_____

_____

_____

_____

Reflect and Assess

WRITING: Write About Literature

A. Plan your writing. List the reasons why Dave in "Heartbeat" and Craig in "Behind the Bulk" worry about how they look to others.

Dave	Craig
Dave thinks his nickname, "Heartbeat," makes him sound weak.	Craig wanted people to notice him.

B. Why do people worry about how they look to others? Write a short explanation. Support your explanation with reasons Dave and Craig have from the chart.

People worry about how they look because _____

_____

_____

_____

_____

_____

_____

_____

_____

Integrate the Language Arts

LITERARY ANALYSIS: Analyze Point of View

In **third-person limited point of view**, the narrator describes the actions, thoughts, and feelings of a person or character.

A. In "Behind the Bulk," the information was told from a third-person limited point of view. Write Craig's actions, thoughts, and feelings in the chart below.

Actions	Thoughts	Feelings
compared himself to others		

B. Choose one example from each column in the chart above. Rewrite each example from the point of view of the people listed below.

1. Craig's friends:

_____

_____

2. Craig's wife:

_____

_____

3. Craig's son:

_____

_____

C. Explain how the article would have been different, for you as a reader, if the author had not used third-person limited point of view. How would you feel about Craig?

If the author had not used third-person limited point of view, _____

_____

_____

_____

VOCABULARY STUDY: Word Families

Knowing the meaning of word in a **word family** can help you understand the meaning of another word in the same family. For example, if you know that *appearance* means "the way you look," you might guess that *appear* means "to be seen."

A. Read each Key Vocabulary word in the chart. Write a word you know that is from the same word family. Then write what the related word means. Use a dictionary to check the meaning.

Key Vocabulary	Related Word	Definition
distorted		
normal		
transform		

B. Think of related words you know from each word family and list as many as you can in the chart.

Word	Related Words I Know
athletic	
escalated	
opted	
ridiculous	

C. Use one of the words you know from the chart above in a sentence. Check your sentences by confirming the meaning of each word in a dictionary.

1. _____

2. _____

3. _____

4. _____

Unit 3
Pages 210–231

Prepare to Read
▶ I Go Along
▶ Theme for English B

Key Vocabulary

A. How well do you know these words? Circle a rating for each word. Check your understanding of each word by circling the synonym. Then complete the sentences. If you are unsure of a word's meaning, refer to the Vocabulary Glossary, page 792, in your student text.

Rating Scale

1	I have never seen this word before.
2	I am not sure of the word's meaning.
3	I know this word and can teach the word's meaning to someone else.

Key Word	Check Your Understanding	Deepen Your Understanding
❶ advanced (ud-**vanst**) *adjective* **Rating:** 1 2 3	An **advanced** class is a _____ class. **high-level** **beginning**	Someday I would like to take advanced classes in _____ _____ _____ _____ .
❷ category (**ca**-tu-gor-ē) *noun* **Rating:** 1 2 3	A **category** is a _____. **individual** **group**	My favorite category of music is _____ _____ _____ _____ .
❸ poet (**pō**-ut) *noun* **Rating:** 1 2 3	A **poet** is an _____. **author** **historian**	One poet that I really like is _____ _____ _____ _____ .
❹ potential (pu-**ten**-shul) *noun* **Rating:** 1 2 3	If you show **potential**, you show _____. **inability** **ability**	I think I have the potential to _____ _____ _____ _____ .

Key Word	Check Your Understanding	Deepen Your Understanding
5 **program** (**prō**-gram) *noun* Rating: 1 2 3	A **program** is a _____. song show	I recently saw a TV program that was about _____ _____ _____ _____ _____ .
6 **realize** (**rē**-u-līz) *verb* Rating: 1 2 3	To **realize** something is to _____ it. know guess at	I would like my teachers to realize that _____ _____ _____ _____ _____ .
7 **serious** (**sear**-ē-us) *adjective* Rating: 1 2 3	A **serious** person is _____. thoughtful amusing	The times I am most serious are when _____ _____ _____ _____ _____ .
8 **understand** (un-dur-**stand**) *verb* Rating: 1 2 3	To **understand** something is to _____ it. misinterpret comprehend	If I had to talk about something I understand, it would be _____ _____ _____ _____ .

B. Use two of the Key Vocabulary words to tell something about yourself.

_____

_____

Before Reading I Go Along

LITERARY ANALYSIS: Analyze Point of View

A story that has a **first-person narrator** gives the reader a personal perspective of story events. This character's perspective is called a **point of view**. The writer uses a first-person pronoun, like *we* or *us*.

A. Read the passage. Circle the phrases or sentences that show that the narrator is using the first-person point of view. Write the text clues in the chart.

> **Look Into the Text**
>
> Anyway, Mrs. Tibbetts comes into the room for second period, so we all see she's still in school. This is the spring she's pregnant, and there are some people making bets about when she's due. The smart money says she'll make it to Easter, and after that we'll have a sub teaching us. Not that we're too particular about who's up there at the front of the room, not in this class.
>
> Being juniors, we also figure we know all there is to know about sex. We know things about sex no adult ever heard of. Still, the sight of a pregnant English teacher slows us down some. But she's married to Roy Tibbetts, a plumber who was in the service and went to jump school, so that's okay. We see him around town in his truck.

Elements of First-Person Narrator Point of View	Text Clues
First-person pronouns	
Reader is placed in the setting, with the other characters	
Narrator seems to speak for all but may not be reliable	

B. Why does the narrator use the pronoun *we* to describe his thoughts and feeling about Mrs. Tibbetts?

The narrator uses *we* because _____

_____.

FOCUS STRATEGY: Make Inferences

Focus Strategy

HOW TO MAKE INFERENCES

1. **Notice the details** as you read.

2. **Make an inference** to fill in information that is missing from the text.

3. **Think again** about the inference you made.

4. **Keep reading** to find more evidence to support your inference.

A. Read the passage. Use the strategies above to make an inference about the narrator as you read. Answer the questions below.

Look Into the Text

> They're still milling around in the aisle, but there are plenty of seats. I find an empty double and settle by the window, pulling my ball cap down in front. It doesn't take us long to get out of town, not this town. When we go past 7-Eleven, I'm way down in the seat with my hand shielding my face on the window side. Right about then, somebody sits down next to me. I flinch.

1. What can you infer about the narrator?

   _____

   _____

2. Circle the details that support the inference you made for question 1. What information was missing that you had to infer?

   _____

   _____

B. How does the last sentence in the passage provide evidence for your inference?

   _____

   _____

   _____

Selection Review I Go Along

I Go Along
by Richard Peck

EQ **Do We Find or Create Our True Selves?**
Find out about people who put themselves in categories.

A. In "I Go Along," you read how Gene's field trip makes him question his real potential. Write what happens on the field trip and what it shows about each character in the Character Description Map.

Character Description Map

Character	What the Character Says and Thinks	What This Shows About the Character
Gene	Gene thinks his teacher knows no one in his class will go to the reading.	Gene thinks he understands the feelings of his classmates.
Sharon		

B. Use the information in the map to answer the questions.

1. Why do you think Gene decides to go on the field trip to the poetry reading?

_____

_____

2. Does Gene have more potential than he believes he does? Why or why not? Use the word **potential** in your response.

_____

_____

_____

3. How will Gene's experience at the poetry reading and with Sharon change him?

_____

_____

Connect Across Texts
In "I Go Along," Gene thinks about how people fit in at school. In
this poem, the speaker also thinks about **categories** of people.

Theme for
English B
by Langston Hughes

The instructor said,

> *Go home and write*
>
> *a page tonight.*
>
> *And let that page come out of you —*
>
> 5 *Then, it will be true.*

I wonder if it's that simple?

I am twenty-two, colored, born in Winston-Salem.

I went to school there, then Durham, then here

to this college on the hill above Harlem.

10 I am the only colored student in my class.

The steps from the hill lead down into Harlem,

through a park, then I cross St. Nicholas,

Eighth Avenue, Seventh, and I come to the Y,

the Harlem Branch Y, where I take the elevator

15 up to my room, sit down, and write this page:

It's not easy to know what is true for you or me

at twenty-two, my age. But I guess I'm what

Key Vocabulary
- **category** *n.*, a group of items that are similar in some way

Interact with the Text

1. Analyze Structure: Poetry
Reread lines 1–5. How do you know you are reading a poem and not a short story?

_____

_____

_____

_____

2. Analyze Structure: Poetry
Reread lines 6–15. Circle clues that tell you about the speaker. What is the speaker like?

_____

_____

_____

_____

_____

_____

_____

3. Inferences
Reread lines 18–19. What is an important part of the speaker's identity? Explain the speaker's message in your own words.

_____

_____

_____

_____

_____

4. Analyze Structure: Poetry
Reread lines 20–35. Underline words that tell you who the audience is. Is there more than one audience? Explain.

_____

_____

_____

_____

_____

5. Inferences
Reread lines 30–35. Circle sentences that give you clues to the speaker's message. Write his message in your own words.

_____

_____

_____

_____

_____

The Savoy Ballroom was an exciting dance spot in Harlem, New York, from the 1920s to the 1950s.

I feel and see and hear, Harlem, I hear you:

hear you, hear me — we two — you, me, talk on this page.

20   (I hear New York, too.) Me — who?

Well, I like to eat, sleep, drink, and be in love.

I like to work, read, learn, and understand life.

I like a pipe for a Christmas present,

or records — Bessie, bop, or Bach.

25   I guess being colored doesn't make me _not_ like

the same things other folks like who are other races.

So will my page be colored that I write?

Being me, it will not be white.

But it will be

30   a part of you, instructor.

You are white —

yet a part of me, as I am a part of you.

That's American.

Sometimes perhaps you don't want to be a part of me.

35   Nor do I often want to be a part of you.

Key Vocabulary
understand _v._, to know the meaning of something well

Musical Background
Bessie is Bessie Smith, an American jazz singer of the 1920s and '30s. _Bop_, also called bebop, is a form of jazz that started in the 1940s. Johann Sebastian _Bach_ was a composer of classical music.

But we are, that's true!
As I learn from you,
I guess you learn from me —
although you're older — and white —
40 and somewhat more free.

This is my page for English B. ❖

6. Analyze Structure: Poetry
Reread lines 36–40. How does the poet use everyday language and grammar in his poem?

_____

_____

_____

_____

_____

_____

_____

_____

_____

7. Interpret
Why do you think Hughes wrote this poem? What does he want readers to realize? Use the word **realize** in your answer.

_____

_____

_____

_____

_____

_____

_____

_____

_____

_____

Selection Review Theme for English B

A. Answer the questions.

    1. Why is it important to make inferences when reading poetry?

    _____

    _____

    2. What inferences did you make while reading "Theme for English B"?

    _____

    _____

B. Answer the questions.

    1. Why is the musical quality of poetry important? How did the rhythm and the sounds of the words help you understand this poem?

    _____

    _____

    _____

    _____

    _____

    _____

    2. Why do you think the writer chose a poem to express what he had to say?

    _____

    _____

    _____

    _____

    _____

    3. Do you think the speaker found or created himself? Use details from the poem to support your opinion.

    _____

    _____

    _____

    _____

    _____

Reflect and Assess

WRITING: Write About Literature

A. Plan your writing. Read the opinion statement below. Decide if you agree or disagree. List examples from both selections to support your choice.

Opinion: The people and things around us have a big impact on who we are.

I Go Along	Theme for English B

B. What is your opinion? Write an opinion statement. Remember to use the text evidence you listed in the chart to support your opinion.

_____

_____

_____

_____

_____

_____

_____

_____

LITERARY ANALYSIS: Analyze Style

An author uses language in a way that creates a particular **style** and has a certain effect on readers. The techniques authors use to create style include repeating words or phrases, using a combination of long and short sentences, or using incomplete sentences.

A. Read the passage from "I Go Along" below. Look for techniques the author uses to create a style. Then complete the chart.

> First of all, he's only in his twenties. Not even a beard, and he's not dressed like a poet. In fact, he's dressed like me: Levi's and Levi's jacket. Big heavy-duty belt buckle. Boots, even. A tall guy, about a hundred and eighty pounds. It's weird, like there could be poets around and you wouldn't realize they were there.

Style Technique	Example
Repeated words	
Short sentences	
Incomplete sentences	
Word choice	

C. Write a short paragraph explaining how this author's style affects you as a reader.

_____

_____

_____

_____

_____

_____

_____

VOCABULARY STUDY: Latin and Greek Roots

Knowing **Latin and Greek roots** and what they mean can help you learn more words in English. For example, you learned that *audience* comes from the Latin root *aud* and means "to hear." The word *program* comes from the Greek root *gram* and means "letter" or "written."

A. Find the root in each word, guess its meaning, and then confirm its definition using a dictionary.

Word	What I Think It Means	Definition
audiotape		
auditorium		
cardiogram		
telegram		

B. The charts below show some common roots and their meanings. Complete the chart by listing words you've heard that contain each root.

Greek Root	Meaning	Words I've Used
cyclo	circular, wheel	cyclone, bicycle
micro	small	

Latin Root	Meaning	Words I've Used
dict	hear	
port	carry	

C. Use the charts above to write a definition of each of these words.

cycle _____

microscope _____

dictate _____

portable _____

Prepare to Read

▶ **The Pale Mare**
▶ **Caged Bird**

Key Vocabulary

A. How well do you know these words? Circle a rating for each word. Check your understanding of each word's meaning by circling *yes* or *no*. Then write a definition in your own words. If you are unsure of a word's meaning, refer to the Vocabulary Glossary, page 792, in your student text.

Rating Scale
1 I have never seen this word before.
2 I am not sure of the word's meaning.
3 I know this word and can teach the word's meaning to someone else.

Key Word	Check Your Understanding	Deepen Your Understanding
1 claim (**klām**) *verb* **Rating:** 1 2 3	When you win the lottery, you should **claim** the prize money. **Yes** **No**	My definition: _____ _____ _____ _____ _____
2 freedom (**frē**-dum) *noun* **Rating:** 1 2 3	In the United States, people do not have any **freedom**. **Yes** **No**	My definition: _____ _____ _____ _____ _____
3 goal (**gōl**) *noun* **Rating:** 1 2 3	Every new year, many people set a **goal** for what they want to accomplish. **Yes** **No**	My definition: _____ _____ _____ _____ _____
4 ideals (ī-**dē**-ulz) *noun* **Rating:** 1 2 3	Most people agree that lying and cheating are good **ideals** to live by. **Yes** **No**	My definition: _____ _____ _____ _____ _____

Key Word	Check Your Understanding	Deepen Your Understanding
5 **implore** (im-**plor**) *verb* **Rating:** 1 2 3	When you **implore** someone, you beg him or her. **Yes**　　　**No**	My definition: _____ _____ _____ _____
6 **roots** (**rüts**) *noun* **Rating:** 1 2 3	People who have **roots** have ties to places and people. **Yes**　　　**No**	My definition: _____ _____ _____ _____
7 **struggle** (**stru**-gul) *verb, noun* **Rating:** 1 2 3	People who **struggle** when dancing find it very easy to move to the music. **Yes**　　　**No**	My definition: _____ _____ _____ _____
8 **tradition** (tru-**di**-shun) *noun* **Rating:** 1 2 3	In some families it is a **tradition** to watch football after Thanksgiving dinner. **Yes**　　　**No**	My definition: _____ _____ _____ _____

B. Use one of the Key Vocabulary words to write about something that is important to you as a person.

_____

_____

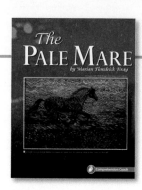

LITERARY ANALYSIS: Analyze Point of View

A **first-person narrator** is the character in the story who tells it in his or her own words. The narrator includes his or her own thoughts or opinions. Because the narrator is writing from his or her own viewpoint, readers need to question what he or she says about other characters and events.

A. Read the passage below. Underline the words and phrases that tell about the narrator's thoughts and feelings. Use these clues to complete the chart.

Look Into the Text

> I sigh. My expertise isn't what he needs. Any fool can take orders. It's not complicated to yell "Four chicken burritos, one green sauce, three red, two large Cokes, two medium 7Ups." No, it's not my expertise in serving food that my precious parents want to preserve. It's that damn tradition again, our *familia* thing, the one that leads to *la raza*, the bigger picture of our people, who we are as Latin Americans. At least that's how Papa and Mama see it. But I don't see things just that way. Not anymore.

Narrator's Thoughts and Feelings About Herself	Narrator's Thoughts and Feelings About Her Parents

B. Answer the question about the narrator's viewpoint.

How does the narrator feel about her situation? _____

_____

_____

FOCUS STRATEGY: Make Inferences

HOW TO MAKE INFERENCES

1. Read the Text Look for the way the narrator says things.

2. Think About Your Own Experience Use it to make an inference.

3. Write Your Ideas On a Self-Stick Note Place it on the text.

4. Read On Notice how your ideas about the narrator change.

A. Read the passage. Use the strategies above to make inferences as you read. Answer the questions below.

Look Into the Text

Each of my strides jars a different, recent memory. Earlier this week at school, my teacher exclaiming over my work in physics, "Excellent work, Consuela. I'll write a letter of recommendation for you. You should really apply to Cal Tech and MIT. You're coming to the weekend astronomy camp, right?" My heart sang. The stars. For the last two years, they are all I've wanted to do: Study them, chart their fierce light, listen to them, learn what they are saying. Stars do talk—really—with radio waves for words. But when I got home from school, an eclipse was on.

1. What changes when Consuela gets home? How do you think her parents feel about her going to camp?

_____

_____

2. Which of the four strategies did you use to answer question 1? Explain how you used one or more strategies.

_____

_____

_____

B. Return to the passage above, and circle the words or phrases that helped you answer the first question.

Selection Review The Pale Mare

EQ **Do We Find or Create Our True Selves?**
Discover some struggles that people must face about their identity.

A. In "Pale Mare," you found out how people can struggle while trying to discover who they are. Complete the Story Map with events from the story.

Story Map:

Beginning:

↓

Middle:

↓

End:

1. What is Consuela struggling with?

_____

_____

2. Why does Consuela give the horses their freedom? Use **freedom** in your answer.

_____

_____

3. Which event from the story helps Consuela discover who she truly is?

_____

_____

_____

Connect Across Texts

In "The Pale Mare," Consuela's **goal** is to have the **freedom** to be who she really is. What does this poem say about freedom?

CAGED BIRD

by *Maya Angelou*

A free bird leaps
on the back of the wind
and floats downstream
till the current ends
5 and dips his wing
in the orange sun rays
and dares to claim the sky.

Interact with the Text

1. Inferences

Circle the words in this stanza that tell about the free bird's actions. What can you infer about it?

_____

_____

_____

_____

2. Analyze Structure: Poetry

Poems have beats that give each line a certain rhythm. Count the beats in each line of the stanza and write the number of beats at the end of each line. How do the beats give the last line special emphasis?

_____

_____

_____

_____

_____

_____

Key Vocabulary

- **goal** *n.*, a purpose
  freedom *n.*, the power to do, say, or be whatever you want
  claim *v.*, to say you have the right to something

In Other Words

current wind

3. Inferences

Highlight the words that the poet uses to describe the bird's cage. What can you infer about the cage?

_____

_____

_____

_____

_____

_____

_____

_____

_____

_____

4. Interpret

Underline the words in the fourth stanza that describe the feelings of the caged bird. What causes the bird to feel this way? Why do you think the bird sings?

_____

_____

_____

_____

_____

_____

_____

_____

_____

_____

_____

_____

_____

_____

But a bird that stalks
down his narrow cage
10   can seldom see through
his bars of rage
his wings are clipped and
his feet are tied
so he opens his throat to sing.

15   The caged bird sings
with a fearful trill
of things unknown
but longed for still
and his tune is heard
20   on the distant hill
for the caged bird
sings of freedom.

The free bird thinks of another breeze
and the trade winds soft through the sighing trees
25   and the fat worms waiting on a dawn-bright lawn
and he names the sky his own.

But a caged bird stands on the grave of dreams
his shadow shouts on a nightmare scream
his wings are clipped and his feet are tied
30   so he opens his throat to sing.

In Other Words
rage anger
trill sound, song
longed for wanted

The caged bird sings
with a fearful trill
of things unknown
but longed for still
35 and his tune is heard
on the distant hill
for the caged bird
sings of freedom.

5. Analyze Structure: Poetry
Underline the lines that describe the caged bird's song. What does this symbolize?

_____

_____

_____

_____

_____

_____

_____

_____

_____

_____

6. Inferences
What do you think the poet means by "his tune is heard on the distant hill"?

_____

_____

_____

_____

_____

_____

_____

_____

_____

_____

_____

_____

Selection Review Caged Bird

A. The poet uses symbols to represent ideas. Make an inference about each symbol's meaning.

> **Symbol 1:** the cage
> **Symbol 2:** the free bird

1. Inference for Symbol 1: _____

_____

_____

2. Inference for Symbol 2: _____

_____

_____

B. Answer the questions.

1. How do the rhyme and rhythm of the poem make it enjoyable to read?

_____

_____

2. List the two birds' similarities and differences in the Venn Diagram. Then answer the question.

Venn Diagram

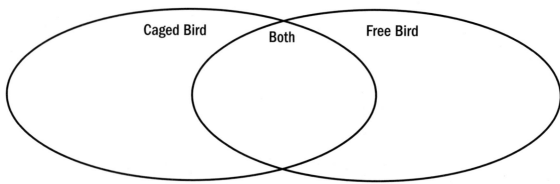

How are the two birds in the poem alike and different?

_____

_____

_____

_____

_____

_____

Reflect and Assess

WRITING: Write About Literature

A. Plan your writing. Write details from each selection that describe the effects of having freedom.

Cause-and-Effect Chart

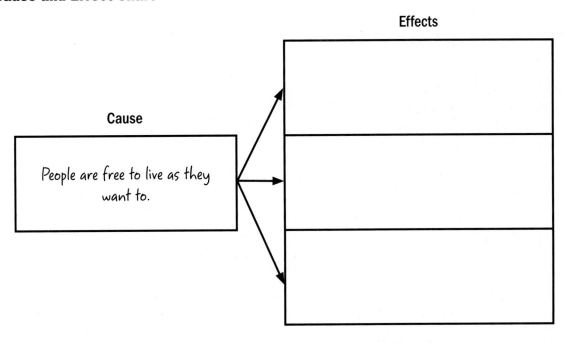

B. Write a cause-and-effect paragraph explaining what happens when someone has freedom. Support your writing with examples from the selections that you wrote in the chart.

_____

_____

_____

_____

_____

_____

_____

_____

_____

_____

_____

_____

_____

_____

_____

LITERARY ANALYSIS: Analyze Point of View

Stories can be written from first-person or third-person point of view. Some stories are told from a **third-person omniscient point of view**, by a narrator who is "all knowing." The narrator explains everything that is going on in the story, including each character's thoughts and feelings.

A. Listed below are details you could find out from an omniscient narrator. Write examples of what you might have learned in "Pale Mare" if it were written from an omniscient point of view.

Details	Examples from "Pale Mare"
Character's secret thoughts	
Events the main character doesn't know about	
Things that have happened in the past	
Things that might happen in the future	
What every character in the story is thinking	

B. Rewrite the following sentences from "The Pale Mare" from an omniscient point of view.

1. I didn't know why I was crying, but tears slid down my chin onto my shirt collar.

_____

_____

2. "That's right," I say admiringly. "Don't even look back." I turn and fade away into the night as shouts from security erupt from a nearby barn.

_____

_____

C. Write a brief, fictional conversation between you and a friend using omniscient point of view. How does this help you understand another person's feelings?

_____

_____

VOCABULARY STUDY: Word Families

Word families are groups of words that are related by meaning. Sometimes, knowing the meaning of one word in a family can help you understand what a related word means. For example, the word *connect* and *connection* are in the same word family. If you know the meaning of *connect*, you can figure out *connection*.

A. Read each word in the chart. Write a word you know that is from the same family. Then write what the related word means. Use a dictionary to check the meaning.

Word	Related Word	Related Word Definition
astronomer		
direct		
ideals		
light		
tradition		

B. Think of related words you know from each family and list as many as you can in the chart.

Word	Words I Know
celebrate	
precipitate	
president	
science	

C. Use each word you listed in the chart above in a sentence. Check your sentences by confirming the meaning of each word in the dictionary.

1. _____

2. _____

3. _____

4. _____

Read for Understanding

1. Genre What kind of text is this passage? How do you know?

_____

_____

_____

_____

2. Topic Write a topic sentence to tell what the text is mostly about.

_____

_____

_____

_____

Reread and Summarize

3. Key Ideas In each section, circle three words or phrases that express the key ideas in that section. Note next to each word or phrase why you chose it.

· Section 1: paragraphs 1–5
· Section 2: paragraphs 6–13

4. Summary Use your topic sentence and notes from item 3 to write a summary of the selection.

_____

_____

_____

_____

_____

_____

_____

From Outliers

by Malcolm Gladwell

1   For almost a generation, **psychologists** around the world have been **engaged** in a spirited debate over a question that most of us would consider to have been settled years ago. The question is this: is there such a thing as **innate** talent? The obvious answer is yes. Achievement is talent plus preparation. The problem with this view is that the closer psychologists look at the careers of the gifted, the smaller the role innate talent seems to play and the bigger the role preparation seems to play.

2   **Exhibit A in** the talent argument is a study done in the early 1990s by the psychologist K. Anders Ericsson and two colleagues at Berlin's elite Academy of Music. With the help of the Academy's professors, they divided the school's violinists into three groups. In the first group were the stars, the students with the **potential** to become world-class soloists. In the second were those judged to be merely "good." In the third were students who were unlikely to ever play professionally and who intended to be music teachers in the public school system. All of the violinists were then asked the same question: over the course of your entire career, ever since you first picked up the violin, how many hours have you practiced?

3   Everyone from all three groups started playing at roughly the same age, around five years old. In those first few years, everyone practiced roughly the same amount, about two or three hours a week. But when the students were around the age of eight, real differences started to

Key Vocabulary
● **potential** _n._, possibility; the ability to do something, given the chance

In Other Words
Outliers People Who Do Extraordinary Things
psychologists behavior experts
engaged involved
innate natural or inborn
Exhibit A in The first piece of evidence related to

emerge. The students who would end up the best in their class began to practice more than everyone else: six hours a week by age nine, eight hours a week by age twelve, sixteen hours a week by age fourteen, and up and up, until by the age of twenty they were practicing—that is, purposefully and single-mindedly playing their instruments with the intent to get better—well over thirty hours a week. In fact, by the age of twenty, the **elite** performers had each totaled ten thousand hours of practice. By contrast, the merely good students had totaled eight thousand hours, and the future music teachers had totaled just over four thousand hours.

4   Ericsson and his colleagues then compared amateur pianists with professional pianists. The same pattern emerged. The amateurs never practiced more than about three hours a week over the course of their childhood, and by the age of twenty they had totaled two thousand hours of practice. The professionals, on the other hand, steadily increased their practice time every year, until by the age of twenty they, like the violinists, had reached ten thousand hours.

5   **The striking thing** about Ericsson's study is that he and his colleagues couldn't find any "naturals," musicians who **floated effortlessly to** the top while practicing a fraction of the time their peers did.

In Other Words

elite top, best
The striking thing What was amazing
floated effortlessly to made no effort but reached

5. Author's Purpose
What is the author's purpose for writing this selection?

_____

_____

_____

_____

How do you know?

_____

_____

_____

_____

_____

6. Author's Viewpoint
Reread paragraph 1. Underline the text that states the author's viewpoint.

7. Details Reread section 1. Highlight the details the author uses to support his viewpoint. Why does the author choose these particular details to support his viewpoint?

_____

_____

_____

_____

_____

_____

_____

_____

8. Word Choice Circle the sentence with the repeated words "much, much" in paragraph 5. Why does the author repeat these words?

_____

_____

_____

_____

_____

_____

9. Word Choice Find and underline other repeated words in section 2. Discuss and write about how the words help support the author's viewpoint.

_____

_____

_____

_____

_____

_____

_____

_____

_____

_____

_____

Nor could they find any "grinds," people who worked harder than everyone else, yet just didn't have what it takes to break the top ranks. Their research suggested that once a musician has enough ability to get into a top music school, the thing that distinguishes one performer from another is how hard he or she works. That's it. And what's more, the people at the very top don't work just harder or even much harder than everyone else. They work much, *much* harder.

6   The idea that excellence at performing a complex task requires a critical minimum level of practice surfaces again and again in studies of expertise. In fact, researchers have settled on what they believe is the magic number for true expertise: ten thousand hours.

7   "The emerging picture from such studies is that ten thousand hours of practice is required to achieve the level of mastery associated with being a world-class expert—in anything," writes the **neurologist** Daniel Levitin. "In study after study, of **composers**, basketball players, fiction writers, ice skaters, concert pianists, chess players, master criminals, and what have you, this number comes up again and again. Of course, this doesn't address why some people get more out of their practice sessions than others do. But no one has yet found a case in which true world-class expertise was accomplished in less time. It seems that it takes the brain this long to **assimilate** all that it needs to know to achieve true mastery."

...the magic number for true expertise: ten thousand hours.

8   This is true even of people we think of as prodigies. Mozart, for example, famously started writing music at six. But, writes the psychologist Michael Howe in his book *Genius Explained,*

9   by the standards of mature composers, Mozart's early works are not outstanding. The earliest pieces were all probably written down by his father, and perhaps improved in the process. Many of Wolfgang's childhood compositions, such as the first seven of his concertos for

In Other Words
neurologist brain doctor
composers people who write music
assimilate put together, combine

piano and orchestra, are largely arrangements of works by other composers. Of those concertos that only contain music original to Mozart, the earliest that is now regarded as a masterwork (No. 9, K. 271) was not composed until he was twenty-one: by that time Mozart had already been composing concertos for ten years.

10   The music critic Harold Schonberg goes further: Mozart, he argues, actually "developed late," since he didn't produce his greatest work until he had been composing for more than twenty years.

11   To become a chess **grandmaster** also seems to take about ten years. (Only the legendary Bobby Fischer got to that elite level in less than that amount of time: it took him nine years.) And what's ten years? Well, it's roughly how long it takes to put in ten thousand hours of hard practice. Ten thousand hours is the magic number of greatness.

12   Even Mozart—the greatest musical **prodigy** of all time—**couldn't hit his stride** until he had his ten thousand hours in. Practice isn't the thing you do once you're good. It's the thing you do that makes you good.

13   The other interesting thing about that ten thousand hours, of course, is that ten thousand hours is an *enormous* amount of time. It's all but impossible to reach that number all by yourself by the time you're a young adult. You have to have parents who encourage and support you. You can't be poor, because if you have to hold down a part-time job on the side to help make ends meet, there won't be time left in the day to practice enough. In fact, most people can reach that number only if they get into some kind of special program—like a hockey all-star squad—or if they get some kind of extraordinary opportunity that gives them a chance to put in those hours. ❖

In Other Words

grandmaster champion
prodigy genius
couldn't hit his stride didn't become an expert musician

Reread and Analyze

10. Word Choice   Reread paragraph 6. The words "magic number for true expertise" help reinforce the author's viewpoint. Explain why you think the author chose those words.

_____

_____

_____

_____

_____

_____

_____

11. Word Choice   Highlight other strong words in section 2. Discuss and write about how the words help support the author's viewpoint.

_____

_____

_____

_____

_____

_____

_____

_____

_____

_____

Discuss

12. Synthesize With the class, list some of the details and word choices that the author uses to support his viewpoint. Discuss why the author chooses them.

Detail or Word Choice	Why the Author Chose it

Then, with the class, discuss how authors choose words deliberately to reinforce a viewpoint. Make notes.

_____

_____

_____

13. Write Use your notes from question 12 to write about the ways that authors use details and word choices to support viewpoints. Use the questions below to organize your thoughts. If you need more space, continue your writing on another piece of paper.

- What is the author's viewpoint?

- What details does the author use to support his viewpoint?

- Evaluate the author's details: Why does he choose these details to support his viewpoint?

- Evaluate the author's word choice: How does the author's choice of words help reinforce his viewpoint?

- Do the author's details and choice of words make a persuasive argument? Explain.

_____

_____

_____

_____

_____

Connect with the **EQ** Do We Find or Create Our True Selves?

Explore the notion of talent.

14. Opinion Reread paragraph 12. Does the author believe that we find or create our true selves? How do you know?

_____

_____

_____

_____

_____

_____

_____

15. Theme What is the writer's message about identity?

_____

_____

_____

_____

_____

_____

_____

_____

Key Vocabulary Review

A. Read each sentence. Circle the word that best fits into each sentence.

1. When you achieve a difficult (**category** / **goal**), you feel proud.

2. It is a (**tradition** / **freedom**) in many families to eat turkey on Thanksgiving Day.

3. Many schools offer (**distorted** / **advanced**) classes.

4. When you know something well, you (**transform** / **understand**) it.

5. A skilled magician relies on (**appearance** / **illusion**) to entertain an audience.

6. Wearing a swimsuit at the beach is (**normal** / **serious**) behavior.

7. Some people can trace their (**program** / **roots**) through many generations.

8. It is exciting when you (**realize** / **claim**) what you want to do in the future.

B. Use your own words to write what each Key Vocabulary word means. Then write a synonym for each word.

Key Word	My Definition	Synonym
1. category		
2. depressed		
3. freedom		
4. ideals		
5. implore		
6. potential		
7. solution		
8. transform		

advanced	• depressed	ideals	poet	roots	• tradition
appearance	• distorted	illusion	• potential	serious	• transform
• category	freedom	implore	program	solution	understand
claim	• goal	• normal	realize	struggle	weight

• **Academic Vocabulary**

C. Answer the questions using complete sentences.

1. Who is your favorite **poet** and why?

_____

_____

2. Describe your **appearance**.

_____

_____

3. When is it important to be **serious**?

_____

_____

4. How might you recognize **distorted** facts?

_____

_____

5. What are some ways to maintain a healthy **weight**?

_____

_____

6. Describe the most recent **program** you attended or watched.

_____

_____

7. How would you feel if someone decided to **claim** your belongings as his or her own?

_____

_____

8. Which academic subject do you **struggle** with the most?

_____

_____

Prepare to Read

▶ Enabling or Disabling?
▶ This I Believe

Key Vocabulary

A. How well do you know these words? Circle a rating for each word. Check your understanding of each word by circling *yes* or *no*. Then write a definition. If you are unsure of a word's meaning, refer to the Vocabulary Glossary, page 792, in your student text.

Rating Scale	
1	I have never seen this word before.
2	I am not sure of the word's meaning.
3	I know this word and can teach the word's meaning to someone else.

Key Word	Check Your Understanding	Deepen Your Understanding
1 agony (**a**-gu-nē) *noun* **Rating:** 1 2 3	When people are in **agony,** they smile, laugh, and tell jokes. **Yes No**	My definition: _____ _____ _____ _____ _____
2 avoid (u-**void**) *verb* **Rating:** 1 2 3	People wear sunscreen and hats to **avoid** sunburn. **Yes No**	My definition: _____ _____ _____ _____ _____
3 consequence (**kon**-su-kwens) *noun* **Rating:** 1 2 3	A **consequence** of a severe thunderstorm might be fallen power lines and floods. **Yes No**	My definition: _____ _____ _____ _____ _____
4 dependent (di-**pen**-dunt) *adjective* **Rating:** 1 2 3	Pets are **dependent** on their owners for food and water. **Yes No**	My definition: _____ _____ _____ _____ _____

Key Word	Check Your Understanding	Deepen Your Understanding
5 enable (i-**nā**-bul) *verb* **Rating:** 1 2 3	Airplanes **enable** people to travel quickly from one place to another. **Yes** **No**	My definition: _____ _____ _____ _____ _____
6 relationship (ri-**lā**-shun-ship) *noun* **Rating:** 1 2 3	Your **relationship** with your friends is the same as your relationship with your family. **Yes** **No**	My definition: _____ _____ _____ _____ _____
7 rescue (**res**-kyū) *verb* **Rating:** 1 2 3	Sometimes search dogs are used to **rescue** people lost in the wilderness. **Yes** **No**	My definition: _____ _____ _____ _____ _____
8 responsibility (ri-spon-su-**bi**-lu-tē) *noun* **Rating:** 1 2 3	A **responsibility** is something a person should not do. **Yes** **No**	My definition: _____ _____ _____ _____ _____

B. Use one of the Key Vocabulary words to write about a helpful relationship you have had. Why was it helpful?

_____

_____

Before Reading Enabling or Disabling?

LITERARY ANALYSIS: Analyze Development of Ideas

Authors use text features to help them develop and connect ideas. These text features also help readers understand the text. Titles tell what the text is about. Section heads tell the main idea of an entire section. Each paragraph tells about a single idea. Visuals give more information or explain the text.

A. Read the passage below. Find the nonfiction text feature and write it in the diagram below. Then, write the main idea and details of the paragraph in the diagram.

Look Into the Text

The Enabler

Jerry had a hectic week, so hectic that he didn't have time to study for Friday's social studies test . . .

"Ma," he said, "please call me in sick. If I don't get some extra time to study I'm going to flunk."

So Mom called him in sick on Friday, and he got a C when he took the test on Monday. Jerry gave her a big hug and called her his chief helper. Another description would also fit: his chief enabler. If that sounds like a compliment, it's not.

Main-Idea Diagram

Text Feature:
Main Idea:

Detail:
Detail:

B. How did the text feature help you find the main idea and details?

_____

_____

FOCUS STRATEGY: Identify Main Ideas

HOW TO UNCOVER MAIN IDEAS IN NONFICTION

1. **Form a Question** Turn the section head into a question.

2. **Make a Web** Write your question in the center.

3. **List Details** Find information to answer your question.

4. **Write a Main Idea Statement** Review the question and the details. The answer to your question is the main idea.

A. Read the passage. Use the strategies above to uncover the main idea. Complete the web with a question and details from the passage. Then answer the questions.

Look Into the Text

Alcoholism—and Beyond

Enabling is a term that's been used for a long time as it relates to alcoholism. The term refers to family and friends who smooth the way for alcoholics so that they never have to face the consequences of their behavior. The term *enabler* has been broadened to include anyone who enables a person to continue with destructive behavior.

Details Web

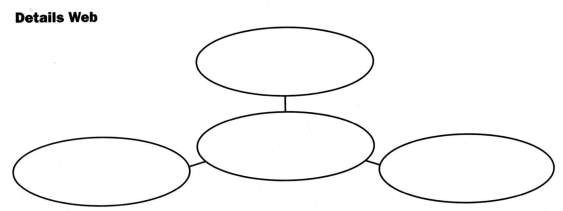

1. Write a main idea statement for this passage.

   _____

   _____

2. How did the strategies help you find the main idea?

   _____

Selection Review Enabling or Disabling?

EQ **How Much Should People Help Each Other?**
Read about helpful and harmful relationships.

A. In "Enabling or Disabling?" you read about how people who are trying to help one another can have harmful relationships. Complete the chart with the enablers' behavior and why it is harmful.

Enablers and Their Relationship	What the Enabler Does	Why the Behavior is Harmful
Jerry and his mom		
Jenny and her dad		
Janey and Frank		

B. Use the information in the chart to answer the questions.

   1. How were the people discussed in this selection enablers?

   _____

   _____

   2. Why does an enabler make it their responsibility to fix someone else's problem? Use **responsibility** in your response.

   _____

   _____

   3. Choose one of the relationships in the chart. How could the individuals turn a harmful relationship into a helpful one?

   _____

   _____

Connect Across Texts

*You learned about harmful **relationships** in "Enabling or Disabling?" In this essay, Isabel Allende writes about a beautiful relationship.*

This I Believe

by Isabel Allende

I have lived my life with passion and in a hurry, trying to accomplish too many things. I never had time to think about my beliefs until my 28-year-old daughter Paula fell ill . . .

Key Vocabulary
relationship *n.*, the way that people are connected to each other

▲ Isabel Allende was a journalist in Chile but left the country in 1975 after her uncle, the president, was killed. Since then, she has written many short stories, articles, and novels.

1. Development of Ideas
Nonfiction selections may be illustrated with photos that tell you what the text is about. Look at the photo and read the caption. How do they help you understand what the text is about?

_____

_____

_____

_____

_____

_____

_____

_____

_____

2. Interpret
What is the author's attitude toward life despite the death of her daughter? Circle sentences on this page that give you clues.

_____

_____

_____

_____

_____

_____

_____

_____

_____

_____

_____

She was **in a coma** for a year and I took care of her at home, until she died in my arms in December of 1992.

During that year of **agony** and the following year of **grieving**, everything stopped for me. There was nothing to do—just cry and remember. However, in that experience I discovered there is consistency in my beliefs, my writing and the way I lead my life. I have not changed: I am still the same girl I was fifty years ago, and the same young woman I was in the 1970s. I still lust for life. I am still **ferociously** independent. I still crave justice. And I fall madly in love easily.

Paralyzed and silent in her bed, my daughter Paula taught me a lesson that is now **my mantra**: You only have what

Paula was living in Madrid, Spain, when she became sick from a rare blood disease. Allende was by her daughter's side until Paula died.

you give. It's by spending yourself that you become rich.

Paula led a life of service. She worked as a volunteer helping women and children eight hours a day, six days a week. She never had any money, but she needed very little. When she died she had nothing and she needed nothing.

During her illness I had to let go of everything: her laughter, her voice, her grace, her beauty, her company and finally her spirit. When she died I thought I had lost everything. But then I realized I still had the love I had given her. I don't even know if she was able to receive that love. She could not respond in any way—her eyes were **somber** pools that reflected no light. But I was full of love and that love keeps growing, and multiplying, and giving fruit.

Key Vocabulary
agony *n.*, great suffering and worry

In Other Words
in a coma not aware and not moving
grieving being very sad and missing her
ferociously very, extremely
Paralyzed Not able to move
my mantra what I try to do, my motto
somber dark and sad

The pain of losing my child meant I had to **throw overboard all excess baggage** and keep only what is essential. Because of Paula, I don't **cling** to anything anymore. Now I like to give much more than to receive. I am happier when I love than when I am loved. I adore my husband, my son, my grandchildren, my mother, my dog, and frankly I don't know if they even like me. But who cares? Loving them is my joy.

Give, give, give—what is the point of having experience,

> ## I don't cling to anything anymore.

3. Interpret
Do you agree that you can be happier loving your family and friends than feeling loved by them? Why or why not?

_____
_____
_____
_____
_____
_____
_____
_____

4. Relate Main Ideas and Details
Summarize the main idea of this page. Circle and list two details from the text that support it.

_____
_____
_____
_____
_____
_____
_____
_____
_____
_____
_____
_____

Desperate for a story to tell her sick daughter, Allende wrote a letter that became a best-selling memoir, *Paula*. Allende remembers, "I was not thinking of publishing. My only goal was to survive."

In Other Words
throw overboard all excess baggage
  get rid of things I didn't need
cling hold on tightly

5. Interpret

Highlight a sentence that shows the author's viewpoint. Describe the way Allende feels about giving.

_____

_____

_____

_____

_____

_____

knowledge or talent if I don't give it away? Of having stories if I don't tell them to others? Of having wealth if I don't share it? I don't intend to be cremated with any of it! It is in giving that I connect with others, with the world, and with the divine.

It is in giving that I feel the spirit of my daughter inside me, like a soft presence. ❖

Selection Review This I Believe

A. Allende wrote a book about her daughter Paula. Read the title and the question, then find the main idea and two details that support it in the essay.

Title:	**Paula**
Question:	**Why does Allende write about Paula?**

1. Detail 1: _____

2. Detail 2: _____

3. Main Idea: _____

B. Answer the questions.

1. How did the nonfiction text features (photos and captions) help you understand the essay?

_____

_____

2. What is something the author learned about people who help others?

_____

_____

Reflect and Assess

► **Enabling or Disabling?**
► **This I Believe**

WRITING: Write About Literature

A. What kind of help should parents give their teenagers? Plan your writing. List evidence from both selections.

How Parents Can Help	How Parents Should Not Help

B. What did you conclude about the kinds of help parents should or should not give their teenagers? Write a journal entry explaining your beliefs. Support your beliefs with evidence from both texts.

_____

_____

_____

_____

_____

_____

_____

_____

_____

Integrate the Language Arts

LITERARY ANALYSIS: Analyze Style

Authors think about their topic, purpose, and audience before writing. Then they choose language that will best express their ideas. This language is the author's **style**.

A. Answer the questions about "This I Believe."

   1. What is the topic of the essay?

   _____

   _____

   2. Why do you think the author wrote this essay?

   _____

   _____

   3. Who might be the intended audience for this essay?

   _____

   _____

B. Read the excerpt from "This I Believe." Find three words or phrases that affect you the most, and list them in the chart. Explain how the author's choice of words makes you feel.

> *I still lust for life. I am still ferociously independent. I still crave justice. And I fall madly in love easily.*

Word or Phrase	How It Makes Me Feel

C. Write a paragraph about someone who has taught you an important lesson. Choose language that will best express your ideas.

_____

_____

_____

_____

_____

_____

VOCABULARY STUDY: Multiple-Meaning Words

Many English words have multiple meanings. You can use context clues near an unfamiliar word to figure out the correct meaning of the word.

A. Read the sentences in the chart below. Use context clues to figure out the meaning of each underlined word.

Sentence	Meaning of Underlined Word
I only wear one kind of shoe.	
The politician made a good pitch for lowering taxes.	
Every row in the theater was filled with people.	
It's my dream to become a movie star.	
You should never park your car next to a fire hydrant.	

B. Write another meaning for each of the underlined words from the chart above. Use a dictionary to confirm each meaning.

kind _____

pitch _____

row _____

star _____

park _____

C. Each word below has more than one meaning. Write a sentence for each meaning.

match

1. _____

2. _____

turn

1. _____

2. _____

Prepare to Read

▶ Brother Ray
▶ Power of the Powerless: A Brother's Lesson

Key Vocabulary

A. How well do you know these words? Circle a rating for each word. Check your understanding for each word by circling *yes* or *no*. Then complete the sentences. If you are unsure of a word's meaning, refer to the Vocabulary Glossary, page 792, in your student text.

Rating Scale	
1	I have never seen this word before.
2	I am not sure of the word's meaning.
3	I know this word and can teach the word's meaning to someone else.

Key Word	Check Your Understanding	Deepen Your Understanding
1 advice (ud-**vīs**) *noun* **Rating:** 1　2　3	It is sometimes helpful for a person to seek **advice** when making a difficult decision. **Yes**　　　**No**	Good advice I have given is _____ _____ _____ _____ _____ .
2 communicate (ku-**myū**-nu-kāt) *verb* **Rating:** 1　2　3	People can **communicate** with each other with their cell phones. **Yes**　　　**No**	My favorite way to communicate is _____ _____ _____ _____ _____ .
3 condition (kun-**di**-shun) *noun* **Rating:** 1　2　3	A healthy baby usually has a serious medical **condition**. **Yes**　　　**No**	A medical condition I am familiar with is _____ _____ _____ _____ _____ .
4 disabilities (dis-u-**bi**-lu-tēz) *noun* **Rating:** 1　2　3	Some people with **disabilities** use special equipment to help them. **Yes**　　　**No**	Two examples of how my school and community support people with disabilities are _____ _____ _____ _____ .

Key Word	Check Your Understanding	Deepen Your Understanding
5 **discipline** (**di**-su-plun) *noun* **Rating:** 1 2 3	Most parents believe that **discipline** is unhealthy for their children. **Yes** **No**	An example of effective discipline in school is _____ _____ _____ _____ _____ .
6 **hero** (**hear**-ō) *noun* **Rating:** 1 2 3	A **hero** runs away from danger because he is scared. **Yes** **No**	Someone I consider to be a hero is _____ _____ _____ _____ _____ .
7 **outlook** (**owt**-look) *noun* **Rating:** 1 2 3	If you are positive, you have a good **outlook** on life. **Yes** **No**	If I want to change my outlook, I _____ _____ _____ _____ _____ .
8 **presence** (**pre**-zuns) *noun* **Rating:** 1 2 3	To feel someone's **presence**, you have to be in the same room as the person. **Yes** **No**	I like to be in the presence of _____ _____ _____ _____ _____ .

B. Use one of the Key Vocabulary words to tell how you have helped a family member in a special time of need.

_____

_____

LITERARY ANALYSIS: Analyze Text Structure: Chronology

Authors tell their own life stories in autobiographies. They usually tell about the events in **chronological order**, or the order the events happened.

A. Read the passage below. Find the important events in Ray's life by focusing on time-order words and phrases. Write the events in the Sequence Chain, in the order in which they happened.

Look Into the Text

> Mama always wanted me to learn things. Even though she didn't have much education herself, she taught me all she knew— the numbers, the alphabet, the way to spell, how to add and subtract. So when I started going blind, she began to look into schools for me. I was the only blind person in Greenville; people just didn't know what to do with me.
>
> Mama sought out advice. She asked Miss Lad who worked at the post office. She talked to the banker and to Mr. Reams who owned the general store. Soon everyone in town learned about my plight.

Sequence Chain

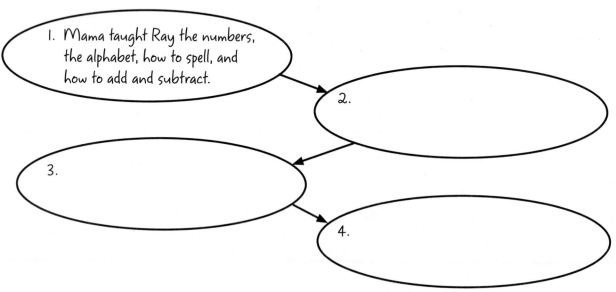

1. Mama taught Ray the numbers, the alphabet, how to spell, and how to add and subtract.
2.
3.
4.

B. Complete the sentence.

Everyone in town learned about Ray's blindness after _____

_____ .

FOCUS STRATEGY: Summarize Nonfiction

Focus Strategy

HOW TO SUMMARIZE NONFICTION

1. **Identify the Topic** Look for key words. What is the paragraph mostly about?

2. **Find the Important Information** What is the most important idea?

3. **Summarize the Paragraph** Use your own words to tell about the topic and important information.

A. Read the passage. Use the strategies above to summarize. Answer the questions below.

Look Into the Text

> Mama was a country woman with a whole lot of common sense. She understood what most of our neighbors didn't—that I shouldn't grow dependent on anyone except myself. "One of these days I ain't gonna be here," she kept hammering inside my head. Meanwhile, she had me scrub floors, chop wood, wash clothes, and play outside like all the other kids. She made sure I could wash and dress myself. And her discipline didn't stop just 'cause I was blind. She wasn't about to let me get away with any foolishness.

1. What was Mama's attitude toward raising a blind child?

_____

_____

2. In your own words, what is the most important idea?

_____

_____

3. Which of the three strategies did you use to answer question 1?

_____

_____

B. Return to the passage above and circle the words or sentences that gave you the answer to the first question.

Selection Review Brother Ray

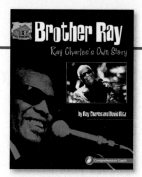

EQ ## How Much Should People Help Each Other?
Learn what families do for each other in special situations.

A. In "Brother Ray," you learned how Mama helped Ray the most by encouraging his independence. In the map, list three things that Ray did to be independent. Then write the outcome of his actions.

Goal-and-Outcome Map

> **Goal:**
> Mama wanted Ray to be independent.

↓

> **Action 1:**

↓

> **Action 2:**

↓

> **Action 3:**

↓

> **Outcome:**

B. Use the information in the map to answer the questions.

1. Why did Mama feel it was so important to make Ray independent?

_____

_____

2. How did Mama help Ray with his disability? Use **disability** in your answer.

_____

_____

3. Why might it have been hard for Mama to do the things she did?

_____

_____

Power of the Powerless: A Brother's Lesson

by Christopher de Vinck

Connect Across Texts

In "Brother Ray," Ray Charles tells what happened when he became blind. In this memoir, de Vinck tells about a boy with many **disabilities**.

I grew up in the house where my brother was on his back in his bed for almost 33 years, in the same corner of his room, under the same window, beside the same yellow walls. Oliver was blind, **mute**. His legs were twisted. He didn't have the strength to lift his head nor the intelligence to learn anything.

Today I am an English teacher, and each time I introduce my class to the play about **Helen Keller**, "The Miracle Worker," I tell my students about Oliver. One day, during my first year teaching, a boy in the last row raised his hand and said, "Oh, Mr. de Vinck. You mean he was **a vegetable**."

I **stammered** for a few seconds. My family and I fed Oliver. We changed his diapers, hung his clothes and bed linen on the basement line in winter, and spread them out white and clean on the lawn in the summer. I always liked to watch the grasshoppers jump on the pillowcases.

We bathed Oliver. Tickled his chest to make him laugh. Sometimes we left the radio on in his room. We pulled the shade down over his bed in the morning to keep the sun from burning his tender skin. We listened to him laugh as we watched television downstairs.

Interact with the Text

1. Summarize
Highlight the important information the author tells you about Oliver and his family. Write a sentence that summarizes this relationship.

_____

_____

_____

_____

_____

_____

Key Vocabulary
disabilities *n.*, problems that can limit what a person does

In Other Words
mute not able to speak
Helen Keller a famous blind and deaf woman
a vegetable someone who can't move or talk (slang)
stammered was not able to speak clearly

2. Interpret

Despite the problems that Oliver had, and the effort it took to care for him, how did the author and his family feel about Oliver?

_____

_____

_____

_____

_____

_____

_____

_____

_____

3. Analyze Text Structure: Chronology

Underline time-order words and phrases. Explain how using words and phrases like this and describing the events in order is effective.

_____

_____

_____

_____

_____

_____

_____

_____

_____

_____

_____

_____

_____

We listened to him rock his arms up and down to make the bed squeak. We listened to him cough in the middle of the night.

"Well, I guess you could call him a vegetable. I called him Oliver, my brother. You would have liked him."

One October day in 1946, when my mother was pregnant with Oliver, her second son, she **was overcome by fumes** from a leaking coal-burning stove. My oldest brother was sleeping in his crib, which was quite high off the ground so the gas didn't affect him. My father pulled them outside, where my mother **revived** quickly.

On April 20, 1947, Oliver was born. A healthy looking, plump, beautiful boy. One afternoon, a few months later, my mother brought Oliver to a window. She held him there in the sun, the bright good sun, and there Oliver looked and looked directly into the sunlight, which was the first moment my mother realized that Oliver was blind. My parents, the true **heroes** of this story, learned, with the passing months, that blindness was only part of the problem. So they brought Oliver to Mt. Sinai Hospital in New York for tests to determine the extent of his **condition**.

The doctor said that he wanted to make it very clear to both my mother and father that there was absolutely nothing that could be done for Oliver. He didn't want my parents to **grasp at false hope**.

> # I called him Oliver, my brother. You would have liked him.

Key Vocabulary

hero _n._, someone whom others admire; someone who acts with courage to help others

condition _n._, a problem with a person's health

In Other Words

was overcome by fumes lost consciousness because of the strong gas

revived woke up and felt better

grasp at false hope hope for something that would not happen

▲ Critical Viewing: Character How do you think the mother in this painting feels about her child? Explain how this relates to Oliver's mother.

4. Interpret
Underline the words that show how the author's parents felt about Oliver after finding out about his disabilities. How do you think their outlook influenced their decision? Use **outlook** in your answer.

"You could place him in an institution," he said. "But," my parents replied, "he is our son. We will take Oliver home of course." The good doctor answered, "Then take him home and love him."

5. Analyze Text Structure: Chronology

Highlight time-order words and phrases that show that the author shifts back to the present. Why does the author do this?

Patterned Landscape, 1999, Anne Rothenstein. Oil on canvas, private collection, England & Co. Gallery, London, The Bridgeman Art Library.

▲ **Critical Viewing: Design** Notice the colors and patterns in this painting. How do they make you feel? How does that feeling compare with the feeling of Oliver's home?

Oliver grew to the size of a 10-year-old. He had a big chest, a large head. His hands and feet were those of a 5-year-old, small and soft. We'd wrap a box of baby cereal for him at Christmas and place it under the tree; pat his head with a damp cloth in the middle of a July heat wave. His baptismal certificate hung on the wall above his head. A bishop came to the house and **confirmed** him.

Even now, years after his death from pneumonia on March 12, 1980, Oliver still remains the weakest, most helpless human being I ever met, and yet he was one of the most powerful human beings

In Other Words

confirmed performed a religious ceremony for

I ever met. He could do absolutely nothing except breathe, sleep, eat, and yet he was responsible for action, love, courage, insight. When I was small my mother would say, "Isn't it wonderful that you can see?" And once she said, "When you go to heaven, Oliver will run to you, **embrace** you, and the first thing he will say is 'Thank you.'" I remember, too, my mother explaining to me that we were blessed with Oliver in ways that were not clear to her at first.

So often parents are faced with a child who is severely retarded, but who is also **hyperactive**, demanding or wild, who needs constant care. So many people have little choice but to place their child in an institution. We were fortunate that Oliver didn't need us to be in his room all day. He never knew what his condition was. We were blessed with his **presence**, a true presence of peace.

When I was in my early 20s I met a girl and fell in love. After a few months I brought her home to meet my family. When my mother went to the kitchen to prepare dinner, I asked the girl, "Would you like to see Oliver?" for I had told her about my brother. "No," she answered.

Soon after, I met Roe, a lovely girl. She asked me the names of my brothers and sisters. She loved children. I thought she was wonderful. I brought her home after a few months to meet my family. Soon it was time for me to feed Oliver. I remember **sheepishly asking** Roe if she'd like to see him. "Sure," she said.

> We were blessed with his presence, a true presence of peace.

6. Summarize
Circle the information that shows what this paragraph is mostly about. Summarize the information in your own words.

Key Vocabulary
presence *n.*, the fact or feeling that someone is there

In Other Words
embrace hug
hyperactive overly active
sheepishly asking feeling unsure as I asked

7. Interpret

What does the phrase, "power of the powerless" mean in the second paragraph?

_____

_____

_____

_____

_____

_____

_____

_____

I sat at Oliver's bedside as Roe watched over my shoulder. I gave him his first spoonful, his second. "Can I do that?" Roe asked with ease, with freedom, with compassion, so I gave her the bowl and she fed Oliver one spoonful at a time.

The power of the powerless. Which girl would you marry? Today Roe and I have three children. ❖

> **Key Vocabulary**
> **advice** *n.*, ideas about how to solve a problem; suggestions

Selection Review Power of the Powerless: A Brother's Lesson

A. Choose one important event from the story. Summarize the event in two or three sentences.

| Event 1: | Oliver's effect on his family |
| Event 2: | Roe's experience meeting Oliver |

Event: _____

Summary: _____

_____

B. Answer the questions.

1. How did recognizing time-order words help you understand the chronology of the story?

_____

_____

2. What advice could the author give to parents who have children with disabilities?

_____

_____

Reflect and Assess

WRITING: Write About Literature

A. What did Ray Charles's and Christopher de Vinck's mothers teach them? List examples in the chart.

Ray Charles's Mother	Christopher de Vinck's Mother
She taught Ray the importance of education by sending him away to school.	She taught Christopher loyalty by refusing to put Oliver in an institution.

B. Write a paragraph that summarizes what Ray Charles's and Christopher de Vinck's mothers taught their sons. Support your summary with examples from both selections.

_____

_____

_____

_____

_____

_____

_____

_____

_____

Integrate the Language Arts

▶ **Brother Ray**
▶ **Hard Times**
▶ **Power of the Powerless: A Brother's Lesson**

LITERARY ANALYSIS: Compare Literature and Film

Novels and short stories have inspired many popular films. Filmmakers sometimes make movies based on nonfiction texts, too.

A. Read the excerpt from "Brother Ray." Imagine you saw this same scene in the film version of Ray Charles's story.

> Take my bicycle. Somehow—I can't remember the exact circumstances—I was given one. Couldn't have been much older than ten or eleven. Riding was something I learned to do quickly. I loved the feeling of motion, and being blind wasn't gonna stop me from enjoying the bike.
> Now most mamas would die rather than let a blind child scoot around on a bike. . . . She let me stray, little by little, further and further away from her. And once she saw I was capable of maneuvering this bike, she became less afraid.

Describe how this scene might be different in the film version.

_____

_____

_____

_____

B. Answer the questions about the film version of the same scene.

 1. Do you think the film version would include everything from the excerpt? Explain.

 _____

 _____

 2. How would your feelings about the scene change if you heard background music?

 _____

 _____

C. Think of a book or a short story you have read. Describe a scene from the story. How would your feelings about the events change if you saw a film version?

_____

_____

_____

_____

160 Unit 4: Give and Take

VOCABULARY STUDY: Context Clues

When you don't know what a word means, you can look for **context clues** in nearby words and sentences to figure out the meaning.

A. Read the sentences from "Brother Ray." Then write what you think the underlined words mean in each sentence.

Sentence	What I Think the Word Means
She wasn't about to let me get away with any foolishness.	
Somehow—I can't remember the exact circumstances—I was given one. Couldn't have been much older than ten or eleven.	
Folks started worrying about me. No one knew what to do.	

B. What context clues did you use to figure out the meanings of the words in the chart above?

1. foolishness _____

2. circumstances _____

3. folks _____

C. Write a sentence for each of the words above.

1. _____

_____

2. _____

_____

3. _____

_____

Prepare to Read

▶ **He Was No Bum**
▶ **miss rosie**

Key Vocabulary

A. How well do you know these words? Circle a rating for each word. Check your understanding of each word by circling the synonym. Then complete the sentences. If you are unsure of a word's meaning, refer to the Vocabulary Glossary, page 792, in your student text.

Rating Scale

1 I have never seen this word before.

2 I am not sure of the word's meaning.

3 I know this word and can teach the word's meaning to someone else.

Key Word	Check Your Understanding	Deepen Your Understanding
❶ arrange (u-**rānj**) *verb* **Rating:** 1 2 3	To **arrange** something is to _____ it. ignore organize	I like to arrange _____ _____ _____ _____ _____ .
❷ destruction (di-**struk**-shun) *noun* **Rating:** 1 2 3	If you see **destruction**, you see _____. wreckage creation	Examples of destruction from a tornado are _____ _____ _____ _____ _____ .
❸ dignity (**dig**-nu-tē) *noun* **Rating:** 1 2 3	If you have **dignity**, you have _____. anxiety self-respect	A situation when you should act with dignity is _____ _____ _____ _____ _____ .
❹ guardian (**gar**-dē-un) *noun* **Rating:** 1 2 3	A **guardian** is a _____. protector competitor	Having a guardian is important when _____ _____ _____ _____ _____ .

Key Word	Check Your Understanding	Deepen Your Understanding
5 **intervene** (in-tur-**vēn**) *verb* **Rating:** 1 2 3	To **intervene** is to get _____. involved overlooked	A reason to intervene in a friend's life is _____ _____ _____ _____ _____ .
6 **survive** (sur-**vīv**) *verb* **Rating:** 1 2 3	To **survive** a disaster is to _____. live die	When you survive a difficult experience, you _____ _____ _____ _____ _____ .
7 **veteran** (**ve**-tu-run) *noun* **Rating:** 1 2 3	To be a war **veteran** is to be _____. an ex-volunteer an ex-soldier	This country can honor a war veteran by _____ _____ _____ _____ .
8 **willingly** (**wi**-ling-lē) *adverb* **Rating:** 1 2 3	If you respond **willingly**, you act _____. gracefully readily	Something I do willingly is _____ _____ _____ _____ _____ .

B. Use one of the Key Vocabulary words to write about a time you helped someone who could barely survive on their own.

_____

_____

Before Reading He Was No Bum

LITERARY ANALYSIS: Analyze Text Structure

The author's purpose in writing a eulogy is to honor the memory of a person who has died by writing about the person's life. The author usually tells about events in time order, or **chronological order**.

A. Read the passage below. Find the events in Arthur Joseph Kelly's life, and plot them in the Sequence Chain.

> **Look Into the Text**
>
> A bum died. That's what it seemed like. They found his body in a flophouse on West Madison Street, Chicago's Skid Row. White male, approximately fifty-five years old. A bum died.
>
> They didn't know.
>
> He was no bum. And his story . . . well, let his story tell itself.
>
> The man's name was Arthur Joseph Kelly. Growing up, he wanted to be a firefighter. When he was a child he would go to the firehouse at Aberdeen and Washington, the home of Engine 34. His two sisters would go with him sometimes. The firefighters were nice to the kids. This was back in the days when the neighborhood was all right.

Sequence Chain

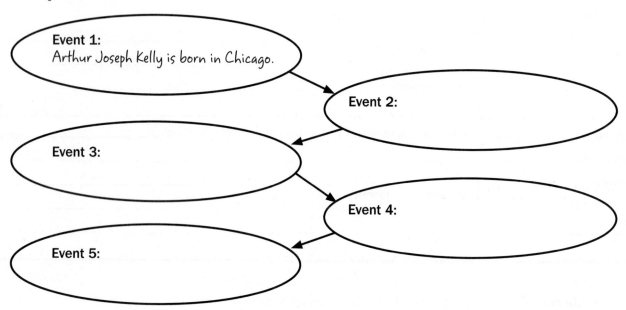

Event 1:
Arthur Joseph Kelly is born in Chicago.

Event 2:

Event 3:

Event 4:

Event 5:

B. Answer the question about Arthur Joseph Kelly.

How does the author honor Arthur Joseph Kelly? _____

_____

FOCUS STRATEGY: Determine What's Important

HOW TO DETERMINE WHAT'S IMPORTANT

1. **Identify the Topic** Note what the author is talking about.

2. **Find Important Details** Choose key details about the topic.

3. **Make Personal Connections** Find personal connections that help you understand the text.

A. Read the passage. Use the strategies above to determine what's important as you read. Answer the questions below.

Look Into the Text

> Arthur Joseph Kelly became a teenager, and then a man, and he never quite had what it takes to be a firefighter. He didn't make it. He did make it into the Army. He was a private in World War II, serving in the European Theater of Operations. He didn't make out too well. He suffered from shell shock. It messed him up pretty badly.
>
> He was placed in a series of military hospitals, and then, when the war was over, in veterans' hospitals. Whatever had happened to him in the service wasn't getting any better.

1. What event changed Kelly's life?

_____

_____

2. Underline a detail in the passage above that you can relate to. Explain how making the connection might help you understand this person's life.

_____

_____

B. Circle the words or sentences in the passage above that give important details about Kelly.

Selection Review He Was No Bum

EQ **How Much Should People Help Each Other?**
Read about people who can barely survive on their own.

A. In "He Was No Bum," you found out how a group of firefighters helped a veteran in need. Write details about how they helped Kelly in the Details Web below.

Details Web

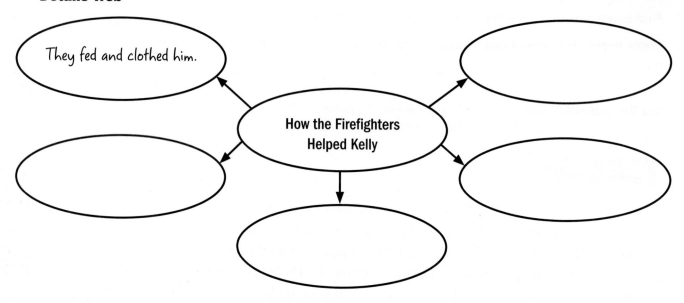

They fed and clothed him.

How the Firefighters Helped Kelly

B. Use the information in the Details Web to answer the questions.

1. What is the most important thing the firefighters did to help Kelly? Explain why you think so.

_____

_____

2. How did the firefighters help Kelly to survive? Use **survive** in your answer.

_____

_____

_____

3. A eulogy honors the memory of a person who has died. What do you think is the most important thing people should remember about Kelly?

_____

_____

Connect Across Texts
In "He Was No Bum," firefighters **intervened** *to help Arthur Joseph Kelly* **survive**. *Who helps a needy woman in this poem?*

miss rosie

by Lucille Clifton

when i watch you
wrapped up like garbage
sitting, surrounded by the smell
of too old potato peels

5   or
when i watch you
in your old man's shoes
with the little toe cut out
sitting, waiting for your mind

10   like next week's grocery
i say
when i watch you
you wet brown bag of a woman
who used to be the best looking gal in georgia

15   used to be called the Georgia Rose
i stand up
through your destruction
i stand up

Old Woman, 2005, Maia Stefana Oprea. Acrylics, watercolor and ink, private collection of Ortansa Van Der Wateren, London.

▲ Critical Viewing: Design Study the lines in this painting. How do they add to the work? Compare the feeling of the art to the feeling of the poem.

Interact with the Text

1. Simile and Metaphor
Underline the simile that tells what Rosie is wrapped up like. What image do you have of Rosie when you read this comparison?

_____

_____

_____

_____

_____

_____

Key Vocabulary
● **intervene** *v.*, to get involved
● **survive** *v.*, to live, to last
  destruction *n.*, ruin, wreckage

In Other Words
peels skins
the Georgia Rose a beautiful woman whom everyone loves

2. Determine Importance
On page 167, highlight the details that tell how Miss Rosie used to be. Why do you think these details are important?

_____

_____

_____

_____

_____

All that may be needed is that the injustice in the world be mentioned so that nobody can ever say, "Nobody told me."

—*Lucille Clifton*

Key Vocabulary
dignity *n.*, self-respect

Selection Review miss rosie

A. Read the phrases from the poem and write what they mean to you.

1. "waiting for your mind" (line 9) _____

_____

2. "wet brown bag" (line 13) _____

_____

3. "i stand up / through your destruction / i stand up" (lines 16–18) _____

_____

B. Answer the questions.

1. How does the figurative language, like similes and metaphors, help you understand the poem?

_____

_____

2. What type of help do you think Miss Rosie needs? Brainstorm three ways to help her. Who might give her this help?

_____

_____

_____

_____

2   I did and I didn't leave her behind, because I'm still thinking and now writing about this scene, **reviling** my own **cowardice**. Reader, can you believe I did what I did? Does it seem certain that I am heartless?

3   Let me give some more details of the scene, not because I hope to be forgiven. I ask only that all of us try to find ourselves in this weird landscape. It was the United States of America. I was at a busy intersection, in a car. The woman had the leathery, lined face and tattered-looking hair of a person

▲ **Critical Viewing: Effect** Why do you think the artist chose to cover part of the woman's face? What effect does it have on the feeling you get from the art?

who lives her whole life outdoors beneath the sun. So did her attacker. Both of them wore the clothes that make for an instantly recognizable uniform: shirts and pants weathered by hard daily wear to a neutral color and texture. Her possessions, and his, were stuffed into two bulky backpacks that leaned against a signpost in a median dividing six lanes of city traffic. I was in the middle lane of traffic on one side. All of the other people in this crowd were also in automobiles, on either side of me, opposite me, ahead and behind, most of them with their windows rolled up, listening to the radio or talking on cell phones. From what I could tell, no one else was watching this woman get beaten up and chased across three, then six, then nine separate lanes of traffic in the intersecting streets. I considered how I could get out of my car (should I leave it **idling**? lock it? what?) and run toward this woman and man, shouting at him to stop, begging the other drivers to use their phones to call the police.

> **Reader, can you believe I did what I did?**

In Other Words
reviling harshly judging
cowardice lack of bravery
idling running

Reread and Analyze

Text Structure: Chronology Reread paragraph 1. Underline the time order words that show the chronology, or sequence of events. Then circle the verbs in paragraph 1. When are these actions happening?

Now reread paragraph 2. Underline the time order words and notice the verbs. When are these actions happening?

6. Text Structure: Chronology Reread paragraph 3. Highlight clues that show how these events relate to the events in paragraphs 1 and 2. What happens to the sequence of events?

7. Determine Importance
Reread paragraphs 4, 5, 6, and the first half of paragraph 7. Underline details that the author includes to define and develop her ideas about *home*. What is the main idea about home?

_____

_____

_____

_____

_____

_____

_____

_____

8. Determine Importance
Reread paragraph 4 and the second half of paragraph 7. Double underline the details that the author uses to describe *homelessness*. What is the main idea about homelessness?

_____

_____

_____

_____

_____

_____

_____

_____

And then, after I had turned over this scenario in my mind for eight or nine seconds, the light changed and every car but mine began to move, and I had to think instead about the honking horns, the blocked traffic, the public **nuisance** I was about to become, and all the people who would shake their heads at my do-gooder foolishness and inform me that I should stay away from these rough-looking characters because this was obviously a domestic dispute.

4   But that could not have been true. It was not domestic. *Domestic* means "of the home," and these people had no home. That was the problem—theirs, mine, everybody's. These people were beneath or somehow outside the laws that govern civil behavior between citizens of our country. They were homeless.

5   In his poem "Death of a Hired Man," Robert Frost captured in just a few words the most perfect definition of home I've ever read:

6   *Home is the place where, when you have to go there,*
        They have to take you in.

7   I wish I could ever have been so **succinct**. I've spent hundreds of pages, even whole novels, trying to explain what home means to me. Sometimes I think it's the only thing I ever write about. Home is place, geography, and psyche; it's a matter of survival and safety, a **condition** of attachment and self-definition. It's where you learn from your parents and repeat to your children all the stories of what it means to belong to the place and people **of your ken**. It's a place of safety—and that is one of the most real and pressing issues for those who must live without it. For homeless women and men, the probability of being sexually assaulted or physically attacked is so great that it's a matter not of *if* but of *when*. Homelessness is the loss first of community and finally of the self. It seems **fatuous** that I could spend so much time contemplating the **subtle nuances** of home (let alone buy a magazine devoted to home remodeling

Key Vocabulary
condition *n.*, situation

In Other Words
nuisance problem
succinct exact
of your ken you know
fatuous foolish
subtle nuances small details

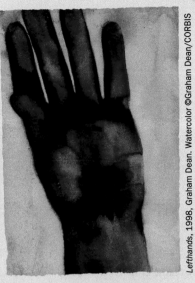
Lefthands, 1998, Graham Dean. Watercolor ©Graham Dean/CORBIS

🔺 Critical Viewing: Effect What do you notice about the two hands in this painting? What do you think the author of the essay would notice about them?

or decor) when there are people near me—sometimes only a few feet away from me—who don't have one, can't get one, aren't even in the picture.

8   I wish I could go back to that afternoon that haunts me and do what I know I should have done: get out of my car, make a scene, stop traffic, stop a violent man if I could. Home is the place where, when you have to go there, they have to take you in. My car might have been the place she had to go, with no other earthly alternatives left to her, and so it may be that I have to take her in, take that risk, get **criticized or tainted** by the communicable disease of **shame** that is homelessness. In some sense she did come in, for she is still with me. I **rehearse** a different scene in my mind. If I meet her again I hope I can be ready.

9   It's a **tenuous** satisfaction that comes from rationalizing problems away or **banning them from** the sidewalk. Another clean definition I admire, as succinct as Frost's for the complexities of home, is Dr. Martin Luther King Jr.'s explanation of peace: True peace, he said, is not merely the absence of tension. It's the **presence** of justice. ❖

9. Development of Ideas
Reread paragraph 8. Highlight the author's conclusions about *home*. Why does the author connect these ideas with the events at the beginning of the narrative?

_____

_____

_____

_____

_____

_____

10. Development of Ideas
Reread paragraph 9. Underline Dr. Martin Luther King Jr.'s definition of true peace. Why do you think the author concludes her essay with this definition?

_____

_____

_____

_____

_____

_____

_____

_____

_____

Key Vocabulary
presence *n.*, being, the fact or feeling that something is there

In Other Words
criticized or tainted judged or dirtied
shame embarrassment and disgrace
rehearse replay
tenuous weak
banning them from not allowing them on

CLOSE READING Household Words

Discuss

11. **Synthesize** With the class, list the text structure and details that the author uses to develop her ideas. Discuss why the author chose them.

	Why the Author Chose It
Text structure (paragraphs 1 and 2):	
Main ideas about *home* and *homelessness* (paragraphs 4–7):	
Supporting details (paragraphs 4–7):	
Conclusion (paragraphs 8 and 9):	

Then, with the class, discuss how authors deliberately choose specific text structures and details to develop their ideas. Make notes.

_____

_____

_____

12. **Write** Use your notes from question 11 to write about the ways that authors uses text structures and details to develop their ideas. Use the questions below to organize your thoughts. Write your answer on a separate sheet of paper.

- · What text structure did the author use to make her point?

- · What are the author's main ideas?

- · Evaluate the author's use of supporting details: Why did the author choose these details to help support her main ideas?

- · Why does the author end her essay as she does?

Connect with the **EQ**   How Much Should People Help Each Other?

Think about why people choose not to help others.

13. Opinion Reread paragraph 8. To what extent would the author say we should help others? How do you know?

_____

_____

_____

_____

_____

_____

_____

_____

14. Theme What is the writer's message about why people choose not to help others? What is her message about our obligations to others?

_____

_____

_____

_____

_____

_____

Key Vocabulary Review

A. Use the words to complete the paragraph.

destruction	hero	relationship	survive
enable	outlook	rescue	willingly

The firefighter _____ (1) went into the burning house and was able to _____ (2) the baby. He became the family's _____ (3). Even though the fire resulted in the complete _____ (4) of their home, they were grateful to _____ (5) the tragedy. They knew that their loving _____ (6) would _____ (7) them to keep a positive _____ (8) about the future.

B. Use your own words to write what each Key Vocabulary word means. Then write a synonym for each word.

Key Word	My Definition	Synonym
1. advice		
2. agony		
3. condition		
4. consequence		
5. dignity		
6. guardian		
7. presence		
8. veteran		

Unit 4 Key Vocabulary

advice	• communicate	destruction	• enable	outlook	responsibility
agony	condition	dignity	guardian	presence	• survive
arrange	consequence	disabilities	hero	relationship	veteran
avoid	dependent	discipline	• intervene	rescue	willingly

• **Academic Vocabulary**

C. Complete the sentences.

1. Pets are **dependent** on their owners for _____

   _____.

2. One way to **arrange** books and CDs is to organize them by_____

   _____.

3. One **responsibility** I have is _____

   _____.

4. I think the easiest way to **communicate** with someone is by _____

   _____.

5. It is a good idea to **intervene** if _____

   _____.

6. People with physical **disabilities** might use a _____

   _____.

7. One thing I try to **avoid** is _____

   _____.

8. Parents may **discipline** their children when _____

   _____.

Prepare to Read

▶ **Jump Away**
▶ **Showdown with Big Eva**

Key Vocabulary

A. How well do you know these words? Circle a rating for each word. Check your understanding of each word by circling *yes* or *no*. Then complete the sentences. If you are unsure of a word's meaning, refer to the Vocabulary Glossary, page 792, in your student text.

Rating Scale	
1	I have never seen this word before.
2	I am not sure of the word's meaning.
3	I know this word and can teach the word's meaning to someone else.

Key Word	Check Your Understanding	Deepen Your Understanding
1 attitude (**a**-tu-tüd) *noun* **Rating:** 1 2 3	Your **attitude** can affect the way other people perceive you. **Yes** **No**	I have a good attitude about _____ _____ _____ _____ .
2 bully (**boo**-lē) *noun; verb* **Rating:** 1 2 3	A **bully** is someone who would defend a younger student. **Yes** **No**	A bully makes me feel _____ _____ _____ _____ .
3 challenge (**cha**-lunj) *verb* **Rating:** 1 2 3	A boxer might **challenge** his opponent to another match. **Yes** **No**	People who challenge me to reach my goals are _____ _____ _____ _____ .
4 confront (kun-**frunt**) *verb* **Rating:** 1 2 3	Parents might **confront** their children if they stay out too late. **Yes** **No**	You should confront friends if _____ _____ _____ _____ .

Key Word	Check Your Understanding	Deepen Your Understanding
5 intimidate (in-**ti**-mu-dāt) *verb* **Rating:** 1 2 3	High school seniors often **intimidate** freshmen. **Yes**　　**No**	Some things that intimidate me in my life are _____ _____ _____ _____ _____ .
6 reform (ri-**form**) *verb* **Rating:** 1 2 3	When a person makes a mistake, it is impossible to **reform.** **Yes**　　**No**	A person needs to reform if he or she _____ _____ _____ _____ _____ .
7 revelation (re-vu-**lā**-shun) *noun* **Rating:** 1 2 3	A famous philosopher would keep a **revelation** to himself. **Yes**　　**No**	It was a revelation to me when I found out that _____ _____ _____ _____ _____ .
8 sympathetic (sim-pu-**the**-tik) *adjective* **Rating:** 1 2 3	Friends who listen to your problems are **sympathetic.** **Yes**　　**No**	It's easy for me to be sympathetic to others who _____ _____ _____ _____ _____ .

B. Use one of the Key Vocabulary words to tell about an experience you had when someone treated you badly. What did you do?

_____

_____

Before Reading Jump Away

LITERARY ANALYSIS: Analyze Theme

The **topic** is what the story is about, and the **theme** is the author's message about that topic. Authors usually don't tell you the theme, so take notes about the characters' thoughts, words, and actions, as well as the story's ending, for clues about a story's theme.

A. Read the passage below. Write notes about the theme in the chart.

> ### Look Into the Text
>
> Fenny wasn't scared that way. He wasn't bothered by heights. That's not why he was clinging to the bridge railing. He just didn't want to go in before Mike said so. That'd mean certain trouble for him at school. Today was their turn. Six or seven of them, all the oddballs on campus, challenged to jump from Jensen's Bridge to prove themselves to Mike and the rest of his crew of strong-arms.

Type of Clue	Text Clue
Topic	being bullied
Characters' Thoughts, Words, and Actions	

B. Complete the sentence about the paragraph's theme.

The theme of this paragraph could be _____

_____

_____ .

FOCUS STRATEGY: Make Connections

HOW TO MAKE CONNECTIONS

1. **Text to Self** Does this detail remind you of your own life? Explain.

2. **Text to Text** Does this detail remind you of another story or text? Explain.

3. **Text to World** Does this detail relate to issues in the world? Explain.

A. Read the passage. Use the strategies above to make connections as you read. Then answer the questions below.

Look Into the Text

. . . Mike glared at him. "I said go on three. My three. Not two, not two and a half. And definitely not your three. That too difficult a plan for you?" See, things hadn't changed much. Mike was still a jerk.

"Easy enough plan. Your three, not mine. You were just taking your sweet time, though. Like you were having a hard time figuring what came after two."

Fenny saw the others tilt their heads up and in his direction. One or two of them leaned up on an elbow. Mike inched his way up to Fenny with his chest sticking out, his slicked-back hair shining in the sun. "What'd you say?" Now the two were up on each other, face to face, breathing heavy.

"I know you just didn't speak out of turn. And I know you didn't just say what I think I heard you say. Right?"

1. If you were Fenny, how would you respond to Mike? Explain.

_____

_____

2. Which strategy did you use to answer question 1?

_____

B. Use a different strategy above to make connections. Explain how you used it.

_____

_____

Selection Review Jump Away

 EQ **Do People Get What They Deserve?**
Find out how people deal with bullies.

A. In "Jump Away," you read how Fenny and the others react to being bullied. In the Character Description Map, write what the characters do and what their actions show about them.

Character Description Map

Character	What the Character Does	What This Shows About the Character
Fenny		
Mike		
The "oddballs" from campus		

B. Use the information in the map to answer the questions.

1. What is the theme of "Jump Away"? How did making notes about the characters help you figure out the theme?

_____

_____

2. Do Fenny and his friends deserve to have Mike intimidate them into jumping off the bridge? Explain. Use **intimidate** in your answer.

_____

_____

3. How would this story have been different if Fenny had decided not to jump? Explain.

_____

_____

Connect Across Texts

In "Jump Away," Fenny figures out how he will deal with a threat from Mike. In this personal narrative, a student tells how she dealt with a **bully**.

SHOWDOWN WITH
BIG EVA
by Laila Ali

I saw my sophomore year as a new beginning. I was looking forward to going to a new high school and was happy to be starting out fresh . . .

Key Vocabulary

bully *n.*, a person who is repeatedly mean to others

▲ The author, Laila Ali, became a professional boxer like her famous father, Muhammad Ali.

1. Interpret
Look at the photo of the author on page 185. Make a prediction about how Laila will choose to deal with her bully.

_____

_____

_____

_____

_____

2. Make Connections
Circle the words and phrases that show what Laila wanted as she began high school. What does this remind you of? What kind of connection did you make?

_____

_____

_____

_____

3. Theme
Underline the words and phrases that show what Big Eva and Laila do that could be clues to the theme. What do their words and actions tell you?

_____

_____

_____

_____

_____

_____

I even got a new hairdo, a short cut that made me feel more mature. It was a clean look; I was looking for a clean start.

My older sister, Hana, and my best friend, Alice, had been going to Hamilton High, where they seemed to be having fun. I knew there were cliques, but I figured I'd find my own place.

Hana Ali (left), Muhammad Ali, and Laila. This photo was taken many years after Hana and Laila met Big Eva

I was at Alice's house a month before school started when I felt the first twinge of trouble. Alice was on the phone with a girl **reputed** to be the roughest sister at Hamilton. For some reason this girl had **attitude** about me and was **talking mess**. She was telling Alice how she had every intention of kicking my butt. "If she's talking about me," I said, "let her say it to me."

I got on the phone.

"I hear you think you're **all that**," said the girl I'll call Big Eva.

"I don't think anything."

"Well, don't think you can just stroll over to Hamilton and be cool. Because you can't. I don't want you there. If you show up that first day, I'll **whup you**."

"Tell you what," I said, "not only will I show up that first day, but I'll personally come over and introduce myself to you. That way you don't have to go looking for me."

"You don't know who you talking to."

"I **ain't** talking to anyone." And with that, I hung the phone up in her ear.

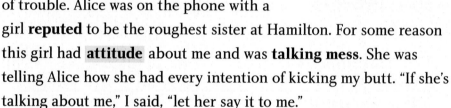

Key Vocabulary
● **attitude** _n._, **1**: a way of feeling about or looking at the world **2**: unfriendly or negative feelings toward someone or something

In Other Words
reputed known, said
talking mess saying bad things about me
all that really great
whup you hit you, beat you up
ain't am not

When the first day of school came around, I was ready. Because Hana had preceded me at Hamilton, no one quite knew what to make of me. Hana was sweet; I was fire. Hana was friendly; I was **reserved**. **I gave off a don't-mess-with-me vibe.** And I wasn't interested in joining any clique. I've always gone my own way. Alice and Hana were my only friends—and that was enough. In fact, I was with Alice and Hana when I had my first "encounter." We were heading toward the school's main entrance.

A group of seven or eight tough-looking girls were hanging out on the steps. They all had attitudes. The biggest among them had a deep cut across her face. I wouldn't call her pretty.

"That's Big Eva," whispered Alice. I had figured as much.

I walked over to Big Eva and stood right in front of her, toe to toe.

"I'm Laila."

Big Eva started rolling her neck, chewing gum and scowling like she wanted to fight. I still didn't know why and I didn't care. I wasn't budging.

"I told you I'd introduce myself," I said. "So here I am."

"Girl," she said, "you don't know who you're messing with."

Her girls **closed ranks** and started moving in on me. I still didn't budge. That's when the bell rang.

"After school," said Big Eva. "I'll be looking for you."

"I'll save you the trouble. I'll meet you right here."

Word got out. The whole school was **buzzing with anticipation**.

I walked over to Big Eva and stood right in front of her...

In Other Words
reserved quiet
I gave off a don't-mess-with-me vibe. People thought that they should stay away from me.
closed ranks stepped close together
buzzing with anticipation excited

4. Make Connections
Underline the words and phrases that describe Laila and Hana. How are they similar to people you have read about or know personally? What strategy did you use to answer?

_____

_____

_____

_____

_____

_____

5. Theme
Highlight the words or phrases that show how Laila solved her problems with Big Eva. Why did Laila act this way? Explain.

_____

_____

_____

_____

_____

_____

_____

_____

_____

6. Make Connections
Underline the details that describe the scene. How do these details help you as you read the narrative? How did you make a connection?

_____

_____

_____

_____

_____

_____

_____

7. Interpret
What is your opinion about how Laila handled the situation at Taco Bell?

_____

_____

_____

_____

_____

_____

_____

_____

_____

_____

_____

_____

Big Eva, who wouldn't back down, and Laila Ali, who wouldn't be **intimidated**, were going head to head.

When the final bell rang at 3:30, I was back on the steps, waiting for Big Eva, with a crowd gathering round. Everyone wanted action, and I was ready for _whatever_. When Eva didn't show up, I was half-relieved, half-disappointed. I started walking to Taco Bell, and a large group walked with me. After a few steps, I looked across the street and saw Big Eva and her girls, heading for the same place. A large group also trailed them. It was a scene straight out of _Grease_.

...I was ready for _whatever_.

When we got to Taco Bell, I ordered, then found a seat on one side of the restaurant. Eva's gang sat on the other. I wasn't sure what she wanted to do, but I was going to let her make the first move because she was the one who had the problem with me.

Hana, Alice, and I sat there for a good half hour. By then the place was packed with Hamilton students waiting for a **brawl**. I felt a hundred eyes on me, but I just sat and ate my taco. When I was finished, I got up, slowly walked past Eva's table and, without saying a word, dumped my garbage in the trash. Eva kept rolling her neck, but she never made a move. Nothing happened—until the next day.

I was in the girls' room when Big Eva showed up. "**You're all show and no go**," she said.

"Fine," I said. "Let's go."

She shoved me hard. I shoved her back harder. And just as we were about to **get cracking**, a teacher walked through the door. A few seconds later we were sitting in the principal's office.

Key Vocabulary
intimidate _v._, to make someone feel unimportant or afraid

In Other Words
Grease a musical about teens in the 1950s
brawl fight
You're all show and no go You talk a lot, but you don't do anything
get cracking really start fighting

The principal started a long speech about the **futility** of fighting. I interrupted her.

"Look," I said directly to Big Eva, "I'm not interested in fighting. I never was. I just wasn't about to be **bullied**. What makes you think you can go around here bullying everybody?"

I expected Eva to start talking more mess. Instead, something amazing happened. Big Eva started crying. I mean, big tears. Maybe it was because the door was closed and we were alone in that office; maybe because she'd been holding it in so long; or maybe because she sensed that I wasn't really angry at her. Whatever the reason, in between tears she **let loose** all the reasons she'd been acting the bully. All her tears and fears came spilling out—how she hated being overweight, how she felt ugly inside, how she never got any attention at home, how the only way she beat back bad feelings was by intimidating others, how deep down she really hated herself and the **ugly front she had created** to scare off the world.

I was shocked by Big Eva's gut-honest **revelations**. And also moved—so moved that I shed a few tears myself. I knew she was being honest; I could feel all the hurt this girl had suffered. I even put my arms around her and let her cry in my arms—both of us sobbing. Two girls who twenty minutes earlier were ready to fight were now acting like long-lost sisters. It was crazy, but in its own way, it was beautiful.

Laila uses her fighting spirit in her boxing. In 2002, she won a best female athlete award from Black Entertainment Television.

Interact with the Text

8. Interpret
Highlight the words and phrases that show how Laila showed support for Big Eva. What do these actions show you about Laila?

Key Vocabulary
bully v., to threaten
● **revelation** n., something that is revealed, or made known

In Other Words
futility uselessness
let loose started to talk about
ugly front she had created mean way she acted

9. Interpret

Read the events in the time line. Do you think the experience with Big Eva led Laila to her decision to be a professional boxer? Why or why not?

_____

_____

_____

_____

_____

_____

_____

_____

I'm not saying Big Eva **reformed** and joined the Girl Scouts, but **the chip was off her shoulder**. From that day on, Big Eva and I were cool. ❖

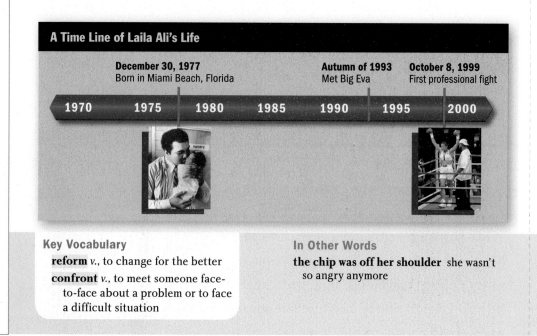

A Time Line of Laila Ali's Life

December 30, 1977
Born in Miami Beach, Florida

Autumn of 1993
Met Big Eva

October 8, 1999
First professional fight

1970   1975   1980   1985   1990   1995   2000

Key Vocabulary
reform v., to change for the better
confront v., to meet someone face-to-face about a problem or to face a difficult situation

In Other Words
the chip was off her shoulder she wasn't so angry anymore

Selection Review Showdown with Big Eva

A. Make connections to "Showdown with Big Eva" using the three strategies. Write your connections below.

Text to Self: _____

Text to Text: _____

Text to World: _____

B. Answer the questions.

1. How did knowing how the characters changed help you figure out the theme of the story? What is the theme?

_____

_____

2. How would Big Eva and Laila answer the question, "Do people get what they deserve?" Would they answer it differently? Why or why not?

_____

_____

_____

Reflect and Assess

WRITING: Write About Literature

A. Plan your writing. The selections present different views of how a bully reacts when confronted. List examples from the selections that show how each bully reacts.

Jump Away	Showdown with Big Eva

B. Which narrative do you think is more realistic in showing how bullies react? Why? Write an opinion statement. Use examples from both texts to support your opinion.

_____

_____

_____

_____

_____

_____

_____

_____

_____

_____

Integrate the Language Arts

LITERARY ANALYSIS: Analyze Mood and Tone

The **mood** of a story is the feeling you get when you read it. The **tone** is the author's attitude toward the characters and the topic.

A. Read the sentences from "Jump Away." Describe how these sentences make you feel. Then write what you think the author's attitude might be.

Sentence	How It Makes Me Feel	Author's Attitude
He let go with one hand to brush back his hair.		
Fenny swung his arm up over his body in a perfect arc and sliced his hand into the water.		
Fenny saw the others tilt their heads up and in his direction.		

B. Use the information in the chart above to answer the questions.

1. How would you describe the mood of this story? Give examples. _____

_____

2. How would you describe the story's tone? _____

_____

C. Imagine that Fenny's actions do change his relationship with Mike. Write a new ending to the story. Show your feelings and attitude.

_____

_____

_____

_____

_____

_____

_____

VOCABULARY STUDY: Relate Words

One strategy to learn new words is to put them in groups, or categories. For example, the words *intimidate* and *confront* are both related to things that bullies do.

A. Think of words that describe a brave person. Use a thesaurus to find synonyms, or words with similar meanings. List them in the web.

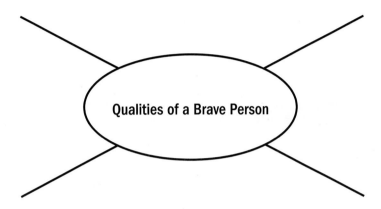

Qualities of a Brave Person

B. Relate the words you wrote in the web to what you know about the meaning of the word *brave*. Write what you think each word means. Use a dictionary to confirm your definitions.

1. _____
2. _____
3. _____
4. _____

C. Write a sentence using each word in your web.

1. _____

_____

2. _____

_____

3. _____

_____

4. _____

_____

Unit 5
Pages 396–417

Prepare to Read

▶ **Fear**
▶ **Violence Hits Home**

Key Vocabulary

A. How well do you know these words? Circle a rating for each word. Check your understanding of each word by marking an *X* next to the correct definition. Then complete the sentences. If you are unsure of a word's meaning, refer to the Vocabulary Glossary, page 792, in your student text.

Rating Scale	
1	I have never seen this word before.
2	I am not sure of the word's meaning.
3	I know this word and can teach the word's meaning to someone else.

Key Word	Check Your Understanding	Deepen Your Understanding
❶ defiant (di-**fī**-unt) *adjective* **Rating:** 1 2 3	☐ resistant or challenging ☐ clear and exact	Children are defiant when _____ _____ _____ _____ .
❷ intruder (in-**trüd**-ur) *noun* **Rating:** 1 2 3	☐ an invited guest ☐ an unwelcome visitor	Things people do to protect their homes from an intruder are _____ _____ _____ .
❸ motivate (**mō**-tu-vāt) *verb* **Rating:** 1 2 3	☐ to move toward action ☐ to move away from an object	My friends motivate me to _____ _____ _____ _____ .
❹ positive (**po**-zu-tiv) *adjective* **Rating:** 1 2 3	☐ good or helpful ☐ critical	I expect to have a positive experience when I _____ _____ _____ _____ .

194   Unit 5: Fair Play

Key Word	Check Your Understanding	Deepen Your Understanding
5 **reaction** (rē-**ak**-shun) *noun* **Rating:** 1 2 3	☐ an action that is quick ☐ an action that is a response	When I make a mistake, my reaction is to _____ _____ _____ _____.
6 **response** (ri-**spons**) *noun* **Rating:** 1 2 3	☐ a reply or an answer ☐ a kind of invitation	When I hear a song I like, my response is to _____ _____ _____ _____.
7 **revenge** (ri-**venj**) *noun* **Rating:** 1 2 3	☐ retaliation or payback ☐ discipline or order	An action that might cause someone to seek revenge would be _____ _____ _____ _____.
8 **violence** (**vī**-luns) *noun* **Rating:** 1 2 3	☐ physical exercise ☐ physical force	A possible way to end violence is to _____ _____ _____ _____.

B. Use one of the Key Vocabulary words to write about a time you had to respond to a violent situation. What did you do?

_____

_____

LITERARY ANALYSIS: Analyze Theme

Theme is the main message in a story. Look for clues in the title, setting, and the thoughts, actions, and problems of the characters.

A. Read the passage below. Find the clues that will help you determine the theme of the story and write them in the chart.

Look Into the Text

Alphonso "Zo" Driggers is fourteen years old. He is taller than a lot of kids his age in the neighborhood, taller and thinner. He has lived in the same place since he was born. Two weeks ago, his mother, who lives alone with Zo in their small clapboard house, finally decided to install security bars on the windows and expensive security doors on both the front and back.

Type of Clue	Text Clue
Title	"Fear"
Setting	
Actions of characters	

B. Complete the sentence about the theme of the story. Then describe what problem you think the characters will face.

I think the theme of the story "Fear" will be _____

_____

_____

_____

_____

_____

FOCUS STRATEGY: Make Connections

HOW TO MAKE CONNECTIONS

Focus Strategy

1. **Read** with a partner.

2. **Share Ideas** Think about how the story connects to your life, other stories, or the world.

3. **Discuss** Talk to a partner about how your connections help you understand the setting, characters, and plot of the story.

A. Read the passage. Use the strategies above to make connections. Write the details and your connections in the chart.

Look Into the Text

It is a school night, a Tuesday, in early February. Zo's mother, who works as a checker in a grocery store, has an evening shift—something that doesn't happen very often. Zo is home alone. ... It's a dark night; a winter breeze is blowing along the street outside—not cold, but not warm either. There is a dark feeling to the evening ... suddenly Zo hears something. ... Somebody outside is messing with the window in the spare bedroom at the back of the house ... Zo freezes.

Detail	Connection
Zo is home alone.	Being home alone can be scary.

1. What do you think Zo is feeling? Explain.

_____

2. How does making connections help you understand the character?

_____

_____

B. Return to the passage above and circle the words or sentences that gave you the answer to the first question.

Selection Review Fear

 Do People Get What They Deserve?
Find out how people respond to violence in their communities.

A. In "Fear," you found out how a young boy finds the courage to react to violence in his home. Complete the map below.

Problem and Solution Map

Problem:
Zo is left home alone.

↓

Event 1:
Event 2:
Event 3:

↓

Solution:

B. Use the information in the Problem and Solution Map to answer the questions.

1. How does Zo find courage to stand up to the intruders?

_____

_____

2. How does Zo frighten the intruders? Use **intruder** in your answer.

_____

_____

3. Do you think Zo should have called the police? Why or why not?

_____

_____

_____

Violence Hits Home

by Denise Rinaldo

Connect Across Texts

*In "Fear," Zo faces **intruders** who are trying to break into his house. In this magazine article, a teen struggles against **violence** in his own community.*

A Bad Situation

Growing up in Oakland, California, Antonio Bibb knew about violence. His community **has been plagued by** murders, battles between gangs, and robberies. So when Antonio heard about an anti-violence program for high school students called Teens on Target, he was **intrigued**. He was in the seventh grade at the time, but promised himself that when he got to high school, he'd join the group.

Antonio knew lots of kids who had lost family members to violence. He felt lucky he hadn't, and he wanted to do something **positive** . "I felt like there was no way to stop violence, but I hoped I might be able to change things a bit," Antonio, now 18, says.

He also wanted to show others that he was on the side of peace. "Pretty much every adult on my dad's side of the family has been in jail, including my dad," Antonio says. "Even when I was young, people were starting to judge me and categorize me because of that."

Positive Start

In his freshman year, Antonio joined Teens on Target. By tenth grade, he was doing well in school and had become a leader in the program. He got to travel to Maryland for an anti-violence conference. "It was more than **an extracurricular activity to me**," Antonio says. "I really felt like I was helping to stop younger kids from making the same mistakes adults in their families might be making."

Interact with the Text

1. Make Connections
Circle a phrase that explains how people treated Antonio. Describe a time when you felt that someone judged you before they got to know you. How does this help you understand Antonio?

_____

_____

_____

_____

_____

_____

_____

_____

Key Vocabulary

intruder *n.*, someone who goes where he or she should not go

violence *n.*, physical action that is very rough, harmful, and mean

• **positive** *adj.*, good, helpful, favorable

In Other Words

has been plagued by has had many
intrigued very interested
an extracurricular activity to me something I did outside of school

2. Development of Ideas
Read the caption on this page. Explain how the photo and caption help you understand Antonio's feelings.

_____

_____

_____

_____

_____

_____

_____

_____

3. Interpret
Underline a sentence in the second column that tells how Antonio reacted to his uncle's death. How would responding with revenge change everything he had worked for with Teens on Target?

_____

_____

_____

_____

_____

_____

Antonio stands on the street where his uncle was killed. "I kept thinking of my little cousin growing up without a father," the teen says.

Then, one day during his junior year, Antonio received terrible news. Antonio's Uncle Michael, with whom he had been extremely close, was shot and killed on a street, **in a case of mistaken identity**.

"My father told me and I didn't believe it," Antonio says. "It didn't really **sink in** until I flipped on the news and I saw another one of my uncles on the air talking about it."

Antonio says that he walked through the next several months feeling a combination of disbelief and sadness. His family was **in turmoil**. "They were broken," he says. Sometimes, Antonio had thoughts of **revenge** —of turning to violence himself and **tracking down** his uncle's killer. "I kept thinking of my little cousin growing up without a father," he says.

Key Vocabulary
revenge _n._, the act of hurting someone who has hurt you

In Other Words
in a case of mistaken identity by a killer who thought the uncle was someone else
sink in seem real
in turmoil upset and confused
tracking down finding

Teen in Turmoil

Experts say Antonio's **reaction** was normal for a teen who has lost a close family member to violence.

"Revenge fantasies are common," says Kenneth J. Doka, a professor of psychology at the College of New Rochelle in New York and an expert in **grief** and dying. "The key, of course, is helping people not act out on those feelings."

Thanks to his work with Teens on Target, Antonio understood that and did not seek revenge. The memory of his uncle, who Antonio says was "a very powerful and positive man," also helped.

In the fall of his senior year, Antonio was starting to feel like his old self. Then, tragedy struck again. "I lost my best friend in a gang-related shooting," he says. Antonio **snapped** back into revenge mode, and this time it was worse.

"I was ready to quit Teens on Target," he says. "I felt like I had to get back at somebody. There was no reason for my uncle and my friend to die, and I was going to do something about it."

After his best friend was killed, Antonio really struggled with thoughts of revenge.

Key Vocabulary
• **reaction** *n.*, what you think or do because of something else

In Other Words
grief deep sadness
snapped went

4. Development of Ideas
Read the heading of this section. Explain what you think this section of the article will be about. What other features of a magazine article does this page display?

To the Rescue

Who kept Antonio from **snapping**? A woman named Teresa Shartell. Teresa is the Teens on Target program coordinator with whom Antonio had been working since his freshman year. She was his teacher, counselor, and friend.

"Teresa reminded me that lots of kids we work with were going through the same situation I was, and that now I was in an even better position to **motivate** them," Antonio says. "She said they'd see how I was reacting to my situation and that would really help them out."

Antonio says he "took what Teresa said and **ran with it**. I realized that we're all going to go through pain. It's what you choose to do with it that makes you the person you are."

The teen **threw himself into his work** with Teens on Target with more passion than ever. He also **vowed to serve as an inspiration for** his now-fatherless cousin. "A lot of kids turn to violence because they see it at school and at home; they don't have strong role models," Antonio says. "I'm trying to be that role model for my cousin."

Teresa Shartell (right) helped Antonio channel his anger over losing his uncle and friend into helping others keep the peace.

Key Vocabulary
- **motivate** *v.*, to give reason to, to inspire, to stimulate

In Other Words
snapping doing the wrong thing
ran with it really used it, really applied it
threw himself into his work decided to work intensely
vowed to serve as an inspiration for promised to act the right way to help

Root Causes

WHAT CAUSES VIOLENCE? HOW CAN VIOLENCE BE AVOIDED?	**FEAR.** If someone is afraid to walk down a street, he or she may carry a weapon for protection. A better idea is to talk to someone like a parent, teacher, or counselor who can help resolve a tense situation peacefully. **STEREOTYPING.** Violence can result when people are judged by their looks, dress, or whom they hang out with. A better idea is to get to know people before you decide how you feel about them. **BAD ROLE MODELS.** If kids grow up surrounded by violence, they're going to **emulate** it. Providing positive role models and teaching kids to act peacefully can prevent future violence.

A Life's Work

Antonio plans to **devote** his life to the fight against violence. That includes making sure as few people as possible have to go through the kind of losses he's experienced. One of his goals is to reduce the number of guns on the street. "If it hadn't been so easy to get guns, I think my uncle would still be living," Antonio says.

Now a high school graduate, Antonio has continued to work with Teens on Target and is shopping around for a college to attend. "My life is pretty blessed right now," he says. "I'm doing

In Other Words
emulate copy
devote dedicate

5. Interpret
Underline the idea in the first column on page 202 that caused Antonio to become a better role model. Explain how he can be a better role model now.

_____

_____

_____

6. Development of Ideas
Explain how the text box on this page adds important information to the magazine article. Summarize its main points.

_____

_____

_____

_____

_____

_____

7. Make Connections
Circle phrases that tell you about Antonio's goals. What kind of connection can you make to Antonio's goals?

_____

_____

_____

_____

_____

8. Interpret
Underline three phrases or sentences that show some of Antonio's advice. Explain his message in your own words.

_____

_____

_____

_____

_____

exactly what I want to do." Antonio is used to giving advice to kids. "Be a leader. Stop following everyone else," he says. "It doesn't matter if you can't buy the stuff you think is cool from movies

and videos—**some Phat Farm or some Sean John** or whatever it is. Just be yourself. The more you shine for yourself, the more you can shine in front of everybody else." ❖

In Other Words
some Phat Farm or some Sean John popular clothes or shoes

Selection Review Violence Hits Home

A. Choose one story detail below and make a connection. Identify the connection as Text to Self, Text to Text, or Text to World.

Story Detail 1: Antonio knows at a young age that he wants to work for peace.

Story Detail 2: Antonio chooses to do what is right and does not seek revenge.

Connection: _____

B. Answer the questions.

1. What features of the magazine article helped you understand what the writer was saying?

_____

_____

2. If you wrote an email to Antonio, what would you tell him about revenge?

_____

_____

Reflect and Assess

WRITING: Write About Literature

A. Plan your writing. Read the opinion statement below. Decide if you agree or disagree with it. List examples from both selections to support your choice.

Opinion: The government should provide money to groups like Teens on Target.

Fear	Violence Hits Home

B. What is your opinion? Use another sheet of paper and write a letter to the editor of a school or local newspaper. Support your opinion with information from both texts.

Integrate the Language Arts

LITERARY ANALYSIS: Analyze Suspense

Suspense is a feeling of uncertainty or excitement about what will happen next. Authors create suspense by putting a character in a dangerous situation, creating a struggle for a character, or having a character face an important decision.

A. Think of examples of how the authors of "Fear" and "Violence Hits Home" create suspense. List your examples in the web.

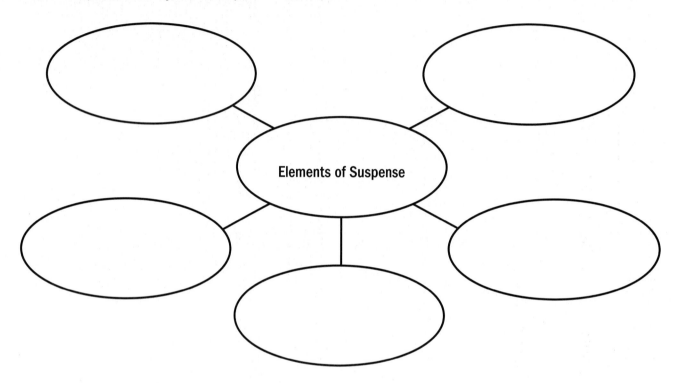

B. Answer the questions.

1. How does the author create suspense in "Fear"?

_____

_____

2. Was the author's technique for creating suspense in "Violence Hits Home" different from the technique used in "Fear"? Explain.

_____

_____

C. Write a fictional scenario including elements of suspense.

_____

_____

_____

_____

VOCABULARY STUDY: Relate Words

Synonyms are words that have a similar meaning. **Antonyms** are words that have opposite meanings.

A. Use a thesaurus to find a synonym and an antonym for each word in the chart below.

Word	Synonym	Antonym
calm		
inspire		
positive		
powerful		
tragedy		

B. Each set of words below contains two synonyms and one antonym. Underline the antonym in each set.

1. resist, fight, allow
2. fear, calmness, panic
3. powerful, weak, strong
4. good, positive, bad
5. blessing, tragedy, disaster

C. Read each sentence below. Replace each underlined word with a synonym.

1. Antonio wants peace in his community.

   _____

2. The intruders believe Zo's terror will make him open the door.

   _____

3. By threatening to call the police, Zo was able to fight the intruders.

   _____

4. Antonio's uncle is a strong influence in his life.

   _____

5. Antonio decides that his experience can be a good example for other young people to follow.

   _____

Prepare to Read

▶ **Abuela Invents the Zero**
▶ **Karate**

Key Vocabulary

A. How well do you know these words? Circle a rating for each word. Check your understanding of each word by circling *yes* or *no*. Then complete the sentences. If you are unsure of a word's meaning, refer to the Vocabulary Glossary, page 792, in your student text.

	Rating Scale
1	I have never seen this word before.
2	I am not sure of the word's meaning.
3	I know this word and can teach the word's meaning to someone else.

Key Word	Check Your Understanding	Deepen Your Understanding
❶ assume (u-**süm**) *verb* **Rating:** **1 2 3**	You can **assume** a tall person plays basketball. **Yes No**	I assume that the life of a movie star is _____ _____ _____ _____ .
❷ compromise (**kom**-pru-mīz) *noun* **Rating:** **1 2 3**	A person who makes a **compromise** will not give up. **Yes No**	I made a compromise when _____ _____ _____ _____ .
❸ existence (ig-**zis**-tuns) *noun* **Rating:** **1 2 3**	A scientist might think about the **existence** of life on other planets. **Yes No**	An animal that has disappeared from existence is _____ _____ _____ _____ .
❹ ignore (ig-**nor**) *verb* **Rating:** **1 2 3**	A professional football player might **ignore** a minor injury and play through the pain. **Yes No**	I do not want to ignore _____ _____ _____ _____ .

Key Word	Check Your Understanding	Deepen Your Understanding
5 **inconvenient** (in-kun-**vē**-nyunt) *adjective* **Rating:** 1 2 3	An **inconvenient** traffic jam might make you late to a movie. Yes No	A power outage is inconvenient when _____ _____ _____ _____ .
6 **insult** (in-**sult**) *verb* **Rating:** 1 2 3	Name-calling can **insult** people. Yes No	I was insulted when _____ _____ _____ _____ .
7 **ridiculous** (ru-**di**-kyu-lus) *adjective* **Rating:** 1 2 3	An elephant might look **ridiculous** wearing a bathing suit. Yes No	The most ridiculous thing I ever saw was _____ _____ _____ _____ .
8 **value** (**val**-yū) *verb* **Rating:** 1 2 3	A business owner probably does not **value** his or her customers. Yes No	The two qualities I value most in a friendship are _____ _____ _____ _____ .

B. Use one of the Key Vocabulary words to write about a personal experience where you were insulted. How did you react?

_____

_____

Before Reading Abuela Invents the Zero

LITERARY ANALYSIS: Analzye Theme

The **theme** of a story is its message. These story elements give clues to the story's theme:

- The **title** can indicate the **topic**. The topic gives clues about the theme.
- The **setting** and **plot** help you understand the **characters**.

A. Read the passage below. Look for the clues that tell you about the theme. Then, complete the map.

> **Look Into the Text**
>
> "You made me feel like a zero, like a nothing," she says in Spanish, *un cero, nada.* She is trembling, an angry little old woman lost in a heavy winter coat that belongs to my mother. And I end up being sent to my room, like I was a child, to think about my grandmother's idea of math.
>
> It all began with Abuela coming up from the Island for a visit. It was her first time in the United States. My mother and father paid her way here so that she wouldn't die without seeing snow. If you asked me, and nobody has, the dirty slush in this city is not worth the price of a ticket. But I guess she deserves some kind of award for having had ten kids and survived to tell about it.

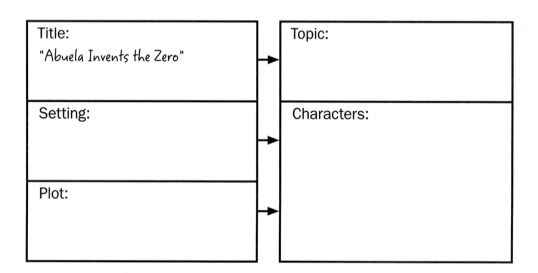

Title:
"Abuela Invents the Zero"   →   Topic:

Setting: →   Characters:

Plot: →

B. Use the information in the map to complete the sentence.

The theme of this story might be _____

_____

_____.

FOCUS STRATEGY: Make Connections

HOW TO MAKE CONNECTIONS

1. **Use a Double-Entry Journal** Copy a quote and page number. Write a comment to explain the connection.

2. **Follow Up on Your Comments** As you read more of the story, add new ideas based on what you learn.

A. Read the passage. On a separate piece of paper, write a journal entry using the strategies above. Answer the questions below.

Look Into the Text

So since she's only four feet eleven inches tall, she walks around in my mother's big black coat looking ridiculous. I try to walk far behind them in public so that no one will think we're together. I plan to stay very busy the whole time she's with us so that I won't be asked to take her anywhere, but my plan is ruined when my mother comes down with the flu and Abuela absolutely *has* to attend Sunday mass or her soul will be eternally damned. She's more Catholic than the Pope. My father decides that he should stay home with my mother and that I should escort *la abuela* to church. He tells me this on Saturday night as I'm getting ready to go out to the mall with my friends.

"No way," I say.

1. How does the narrator feel about her grandmother? Explain how the connection helps you understand the text.

_____

_____

2. How did your journal entry help you answer question 1?

_____

_____

B. Return to the passage above and circle the phrases or sentences that helped you make a connection and answer the first question.

Unit 5: Fair Play   211

Selection Review Abuela Invents the Zero

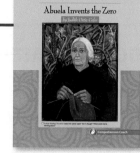

EQ **Do People Get What They Deserve?**
Find out what happens to people who insult others.

A. In "Abuela Invents the Zero," you learn how Connie changes after she insults her grandmother. Complete the Flow Chart below.

Flow Chart

What she does:
Connie ignores her lost grandmother at church. Her grandmother cannot find her way back to her seat.

↓

Why she does it:

↓

What she learns:

↓

Theme:

B. Use the information in the chart to answer the questions.

1. How does Connie change from the beginning of the story to the end?

_____

_____

2. Why does Connie assume her grandmother is a foolish old woman?
Use **assume** in your answer.

_____

_____

_____

3. How might Connie's relationship with her grandmother change in the future?

_____

_____

Karate
by Huynh Quang Nhuong

Connect Across Texts

In "Abuela Invents the Zero," Connie is unkind to her grandmother. In this personal narrative, find out what happens when someone is unkind to the author's grandfather.

My grandmother had married a man whom she loved with all her heart, but who was totally different from her. My grandfather was very shy. He never laughed loudly, and he always spoke very softly. And physically he was not as strong as my grandmother. But he excused his lack of physical strength by saying that he was a "**scholar**."

About three months after their marriage, my grandparents were in a restaurant. A **rascal** began to **insult** my grandfather because he looked weak and had a pretty wife. At first he just made insulting remarks, such as, "Hey! Wet chicken! This is no place for a weakling!"

This story takes place in a restaurant in Vietnam, the country where the author was born and grew up.

Interact with the Text

1. Make Connections
Reread the second paragraph. Think about a time when you felt similarly insulted. Use that connection to describe how the narrator's grandparents must have felt after the insult.

_____

_____

_____

_____

_____

_____

Key Vocabulary
insult *v.*, to say or do something mean to someone

In Other Words
scholar person who studies a lot
rascal mean person

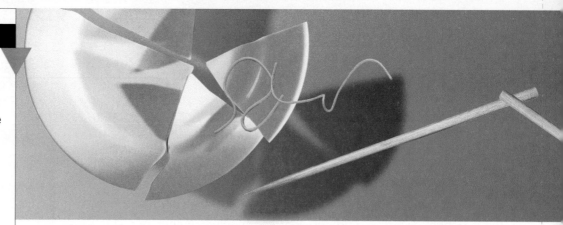

3. Irony
Highlight the phrases that show why this scene is ironic. Explain the situation in your own words.

My grandfather wanted to leave the restaurant even though he and my grandmother had not yet finished their meal. But my grandmother pulled his shirtsleeve and signaled him to remain seated. She continued to eat. She looked as if nothing had happened.

Tired of yelling insults without any result, the rascal got up from his table and moved over to my grandparents' table. He grabbed my grandfather's chopsticks. My grandmother immediately **wrested** the chopsticks from him and struck the rascal on his cheekbone with her elbow. The blow was so quick and powerful that he lost his balance and fell on the floor. Instead of finishing him off, as any street fighter would do, my grandmother let the rascal recover from the blow. But as soon as he got up again, he kicked over the table between him and my grandmother. Food and drink flew all over the place. Before he could do anything else, my grandmother kicked him on the chin. The kick was so **swift** that my grandfather didn't even see it. He only heard a heavy thud. Then he saw the rascal tumble backward and collapse on the ground.

> She looked as if nothing had happened.

In Other Words
wrested pulled, grabbed
swift quick

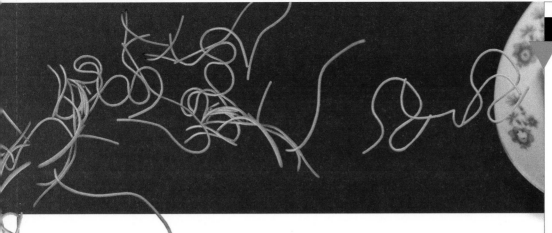

All the onlookers were surprised and delighted, especially the owner of the restaurant. Apparently the rascal, one of the best karate fighters of our area, came to his restaurant every day and left without paying for his food or drink. The owner was too afraid to confront him.

While the rascal's friends tried to **revive him**, everyone else surrounded my grandmother. They asked her who had taught her karate. She said, "Who else? My husband!"

After the fight at the restaurant people **assumed** that my grandfather knew karate very well, but refused to use it for fear of killing someone. In reality, my grandmother had received special training in karate from my great-great uncle from the time she was eight years old.

What is **karate?**

Karate is a form of self-defense that developed long ago in Asia. Traditionally, karate students do not use any weapons. They use their arms and legs to hit and kick opponents.

Key Vocabulary
● **assume** *v.*, to think that something is true

In Other Words
revive him wake him up

6. Interpret
What happened as a result of the author's grandmother telling everyone that her husband was one of the best karate fighters? Circle the words and phrases that helped you answer the question.

_____

_____

_____

_____

_____

Anyway, after that incident, my grandfather never had to worry again. Any time he had some business downtown, people treated him very well. And whenever anyone happened to bump into him on the street, they bowed to my grandfather in a very respectful way. ❖

Selection Review Karate

A. Choose one story detail below and explain how using your prior knowledge to make a connection helped you understand the text.

Detail 1: All the onlookers were surprised and delighted to see the grandmother kick the rascal.

Detail 2: Everyone assumed the grandfather was an expert in karate, and they treated him with respect.

Detail: _____

Prior Knowledge: _____

_____

B. Answer the questions.

1. How did understanding irony help you appreciate and enjoy this story?

_____

_____

2. Who got what they deserved in this narrative? Explain.

_____

_____

Reflect and Assess

WRITING: Write About Literature

A. Plan your writing. How did the characters in each selection respond to insults? List examples in the chart.

Abuela Invents the Zero	Karate
Abuela points her finger at Connie like a judge passing a sentence on a criminal.	

B. How would you advise a good friend to respond to an insult? Write a letter of advice to your friend. Support your views with examples from both texts.

_____

_____

_____

_____

_____

_____

_____

_____

_____

Integrate the Language Arts

LITERARY ANALYSIS: Analyze Flashback

A **flashback** is a break in the action of a story. It takes the reader back in time to tell about something that already happened. It is used to provide background information about a character or an event.

Example: *It all began with Abuela coming up from the Island for a visit.*

A. Describe the events in "Abuela Invents the Zero" that show a shift in time.

Abuela Invents the Zero
Present: Connie remembers when Abuela said Connie made her feel like a zero.
Flashback:
Present:

B. List three things that the author's use of flashback in "Abuela Invents the Zero" helped you understand about Connie and her grandmother.

1. _____

2. _____

3. _____

C. Describe how the reader's opinion of Abuela might be different if the author had not used a flashback.

_____

_____

_____

_____

VOCABULARY STUDY: Antonyms

Antonyms are words that mean the opposite, or nearly the opposite, of each other. Some antonyms are formed by adding a prefix such as *in-*, *ir-*, or *un-*. For instance, the opposite of *common* is *uncommon*.

A. Read the prefixes in the chart below and write a word you know that contains the prefix.

Prefix	Words I've Used
dis-	
in-	
ir-	
un-	

B. Write the words from the chart above and each word's antonym.

Word	Antonym

C. Use the words you came up with or the word's antonym to write sentences about the characters or events in "Abuela Invents the Zero" or "Karate."

1. _____

2. _____

3. _____

4. _____

Read for Understanding

1. Genre What kind of text is this passage? How do you know?

_____

_____

_____

2. Topic Write a topic sentence to tell what the text is mostly about.

_____

_____

_____

_____

_____

Reread and Summarize

3. Key Ideas In each section, circle three words or phrases that express the key ideas in that section. Note next to each word or phrase why you chose it.

· Section 1: paragraphs 1–10
· Section 2: paragraphs 11–21

4. Summary Use your topic sentence and notes from item 3 to write a summary of the selection.

_____

_____

_____

_____

_____

_____

Why We Must Never Forget

BY NORMAN Y. MINETA

February 15, 1992

1   I am proud to join you here today. Very proud. . . . The fact that our nation—the United States of America—has now apologized to us for our **internment** fifty years ago tells me how much this nation has changed, and that the changes have been for the better. With those changes have come understanding, reflection, and the recognition that basic human rights either apply to us all—or they belong to no one. *However*, there is no escaping another truth: that the **specter** of racism is lurking in us all. . . .

2   It was here in California and the West Coast fifty years ago that our life as a community was forever transformed by an attack that struck at the heart of the U.S. Constitution. This was an attack not of our making. But three thousand miles away in Washington, D.C., the government of the United States—our government—decided that Americans of Japanese ancestry were a categorical threat to the United States.

3   No matter that these threats were unproven, or that we were either American citizens or permanent resident aliens. All were **tarred** with the same indiscriminate brush of racial hatred and fear.

4   We were all scared, those of us who were alive at the time. The entire world was at war. The United States had been brought into this war—the Second World War—after the Empire of Japan had attacked Pearl Harbor, Hawaii, on December 7, 1941. One of the first **casualties** of that attack was faith and trust within our American nation.

5   America quickly saw little value in distinguishing between the attackers that Sunday morning and loyal Japanese Americans who were every bit as much the target of that dawn air raid in Hawaii. All too much effort was invested, instead, in **expedience**. And the search was on for **scapegoats**. . . .

In Other Words

internment imprisonment
specter danger
tarred painted
casualties losses
expedience fast action
scapegoats people to blame

Historical Background

During World War II, U.S. citizens of Japanese ancestry were unfairly forced to live in internment camps. In 1988, Congressman Norman Y. Mineta helped pass a bill requiring the U.S. government to apologize.

6   One by one, Japanese American communities along the West Coast disappeared: removed into stark, barren camps scattered throughout some of the most inhospitable regions of the United States. The myth that this forced relocation was being done for our protection was a lie exposed by the first sight of camp guard towers with their machine guns pointed in at us, instead of out.

7   Tens of thousands of us spent up to four long years in these camps. The vast majority of us cooperated with our government, determined to prove our loyalty **in the long run** by sacrificing peacefully **in the short run** our most basic rights as Americans. And we served this country well. Far above and beyond **the call of duty**. . . .

One by one, Japanese American communities along the West Coast disappeared…

8   Internment drained and **crippled** many Japanese American families. Homes, farms, and businesses were lost. Lives were ruined. . . .

9   The result was that once the war had ended and the camps were closed, we tried to forget the internment.

10   Parents never spoke of it to their children. But here there was an inescapable contradiction: How can you prove your loyalty once and for all, as we had tried to do, if you allow personal justice denied to stand silently in a specter of shame? The answer is, you can't.

Manzanar Internment Camp, Manzanar, California, circa 1943, Bill Manbo. Photograph, Takao Bill Manbo.

In Other Words

in the long run over time
in the short run at that moment
the call of duty what was expected
crippled permanently harmed

Reread and Analyze

5. Theme Circle the title of the speech. What clue does Congressman Mineta's title give to his theme?

_____

_____

_____

_____

_____

6. Theme Reread paragraph 1. Underline the sentence identifying a change the congressman believes is for the better. What detail does it add to the clues in the title?

_____

_____

_____

_____

_____

7. Theme Find and underline other clues to his theme that the author gives in section 1.

8. Irony Double underline the reason given for why people were put in camps. Then, highlight the words that show the irony. How does this show irony?

_____

_____

_____

_____

9. Theme A statement of opinion can be a strong clue to the author's theme. Reread paragraph 11. Highlight the sentence that begins "And the lesson I learned...."

10. Theme Highlight statements of opinion in paragraphs 12 and 21. How do the author's statements of opinion in section 2 add to the author's message?

_____

_____

_____

_____

_____

_____

_____

_____

_____

_____

_____

11   And the lesson I learned was that wronged individuals must stand up and fight for their rights if our nation is to be true to its principles, without exception. That's what our successful effort to **redress** the internment was meant to do.

Dorothea Lange, 1942.

U.S. Army medic Ted Miyata (right) was sent home in 1942 to help his mother (left) prepare for internment.

Miyata's daughter stands where her grandmother and father were photographed sixty-five years before.

12   For me, that ten-year struggle in Congress won back for us our **dignity**. In the Civil Liberties Act of 1988 . . . it says, and I quote:

13   *The Congress recognizes that, as described by the Commission on Wartime Relocation and Internment of Civilians, a grave injustice was done to both citizens and permanent resident aliens of Japanese ancestry by the evacuation, relocation, and internment of civilians during World War II.*

14   *As the Commission documents, these actions were carried out without adequate security reasons and without any acts of **espionage or sabotage** documented by the Commission, and were **motivated** largely by racial prejudice, wartime **hysteria**, and a failure of political leadership.*

15   *The excluded individuals of Japanese ancestry suffered enormous damages, both material and intangible, all of which resulted in significant human suffering for which appropriate **compensation** has not been made.*

16   *For these fundamental violations of the basic civil liberties and constitutional rights of these individuals of Japanese ancestry, the Congress apologizes on behalf of the Nation.*

Key Vocabulary
- **motivate** *v.*, to give reason; to inspire; to stimulate

In Other Words
redress provide compensation for
dignity self-worth
espionage or sabotage spying or disloyalty
hysteria panic
compensation payment

17   That last sentence means more to me than perhaps any other in law, for it represents everything that our government is designed to do when it works at its best. And today, fifty years after **Executive Order 9066** was signed, the successful effort to redress that wrong stands as a reminder of what ultimate accountability can and should mean in the United States.

Dorothea Lange, 1942.

Paul Kitagaki, Jr., 2006.

Labeled with identification tags, Fumiko Hayashida and baby Natalie leave their farm.

Sixty-four years later, mother and daughter stand at their Washington farm.

18   It should mean truth. It should mean justice. And it should mean universality of the rights guaranteed by the U.S. Constitution.

19   But today, we must remain vigilant to ensure that these truths hold true for our children and grandchildren. The most recent wave of **Japan-bashing and America-bashing** holds for us a special danger. Those who prefer not to learn from the mistakes of the past, those who prefer **a jingoism** of hate, those who prefer to seek scapegoats continue to pose a threat.

20   The war in the Middle East last year demonstrated how genuine a concern this is for every minority community. In 1942, Japanese Americans were threatened and interned. But in 1991, when Arab Americans were threatened, there were voices within government and without to **bear witness**. We helped stop history from repeating itself.

21   None of us can predict who might next fall target to hysteria, racism, and weak political leadership. But with our strength of conviction and witness to history, I do believe that we can ensure that such a tragedy as our internment never befalls anyone ever again here in the United States. ❖

Today a monument marks the spot where the Manzanar Internment Camps were.
Manzanar National Historic Site/Park and Recreation

In Other Words

Executive Order 9066 the law that ordered the Japanese internment
Japan-bashing and America-bashing cruel comments about Japan and America
a jingoism an extreme culture
bear witness call attention to it

11. Irony Underline words in paragraph 18 that tell what one should expect of the U.S. government. Tell why its treatment of Japanese people during World War II represented situational irony.

_____

_____

_____

_____

12. Theme Double underline the sentences that tell what kept Arab Americans from being mistreated. How do these details help you understand the author's theme?

_____

_____

_____

_____

13. Theme Consider all of the clues the author has given you. How would you sum up the author's message about life?

_____

_____

_____

_____

_____

Discuss

14. Synthesize With the class, list some of the clues the author gives to his theme as he develops it. Discuss why the author chooses them.

Clue	Why the Author Included It

Then, with the class, discuss how authors deliberately choose clues to help them develop their theme. Make notes.

_____

_____

_____

15. Write Use your notes from question 14 to write about the ways authors communicate a theme. Use the questions below to organize your thoughts. For more space, continue your writing on another piece of paper.

- What details and other clues does the author use to develop his theme?
- How do these work together to help him get across his message?
- Why is it helpful to include historical details when communicating a message about how to act in our time?
- How helpful is irony in getting across ideas?
- How does the author use all these things to communicate his theme?

_____

_____

_____

_____

Connect with the EQ — Do People Get What They Deserve?
Think about the power of an apology.

16. **Opinion** How would the author respond to the Essential Question: Do people get what they deserve? How does the text support your assumption about the author's answer?

_____

_____

_____

_____

_____

_____

_____

_____

17. **Theme** Does the theme of Congressman Mineta's speech support the ideas expressed by Martin Luther King, Jr., or by the Hopi proverb on page 364? Use evidence from the speech to support your answer.

_____

_____

_____

_____

_____

_____

_____

_____

Key Vocabulary Review

A. Read each sentence. Circle the word that best fits into each sentence.

1. Someone who is always mean to people is a (**bully / intruder**).

2. If you have a (**positive / sympathetic**) outlook, you see the world in a good way.

3. When you (**insult / confront**) someone, you discuss a problem face-to-face.

4. When people send invitations, they often ask for a (**response / reaction**).

5. Waving signs and cheering is one way to help (**challenge / motivate**) a team.

6. Someone who is behaving in a goofy or silly manner is being (**ridiculous / defiant**).

7. When you do not pay attention to something, you (**reform / ignore**) it.

8. Most plants need water and sunlight for their (**existence / attitude**).

B. Use your own words to write what each Key Vocabulary word means. Then write a synonym for each word.

Key Word	My Definition	Synonym
1. assume		
2. attitude		
3. challenge		
4. defiant		
5. inconvenient		
6. insult		
7. intimidate		
8. sympathetic		

Unit 5 Key Vocabulary

• assume	compromise	ignore	intruder	reform	ridiculous
• attitude	confront	inconvenient	• motivate	• response	sympathetic
bully	defiant	insult	• positive	• revelation	value
• challenge	existence	intimidate	• reaction	revenge	violence

• **Academic Vocabulary**

C. Complete the sentences.

1. I show my **reaction** to good news by _____
   _____ .

2. My school handles student **violence** by _____
   _____ .

3. If I watched a television show about an **intruder**, it would make me feel _____
   _____ .

4. One thing I am willing to make a **compromise** about is _____
   _____ .

5. The relationship I **value** most in my life is _____
   _____ .

6. One thing I would choose to **reform** is _____
   _____ .

7. A movie character might seek **revenge** because _____
   _____ .

8. I was surprised by the **revelation** that _____
   _____ .

Prepare to Read

▶ **16: The Right Voting Age**
▶ **Teen Brains Are Different**

Key Vocabulary

A. How well do you know these words? Circle a rating for each word. Check your understanding of each word by circling the correct synonym. Then complete the sentences. If you are unsure of a word's meaning, refer to the Vocabulary Glossary, page 792, in your student text.

Rating Scale
1 I have never seen this word before.
2 I am not sure of the word's meaning.
3 I know this word and can teach the word's meaning to someone else.

Key Word	Check Your Understanding	Deepen Your Understanding
❶ **establish** (i-**sta**-blish) *verb* **Rating:** **1 2 3**	To **establish** something is to _____ it. create destroy	Things that I can establish include _____ _____ _____ _____ .
❷ **generation** (je-nu-**rā**-shun) *noun* **Rating:** **1 2 3**	A **generation** is an age _____. restriction group	An experience that I think I will have that my grandparents' generation did not is _____ _____ _____ _____ .
❸ **judgment** (**juj**-munt) *noun* **Rating:** **1 2 3**	If you make a **judgment**, you make an _____. effort evaluation	A person needs to use good judgment when they are _____ _____ _____ _____ .
❹ **mature** (mu-**choor**) *adjective* **Rating:** **1 2 3**	A **mature** decision is a _____ decision. grown-up childish	I show that I am mature by _____ _____ _____ _____ _____ .

Key Word	Check Your Understanding	Deepen Your Understanding
5 participate (par-**ti**-su-pāt) *verb* **Rating:** 1 2 3	To **participate** in something is to _____ it. do avoid	I would like to participate in _____ _____ _____ _____ _____ .
6 politics (**pah**-lu-tiks) *noun* **Rating:** 1 2 3	If you talk about **politics**, you are talking about the _____. entertainment government	People who are involved in politics include _____ _____ _____ _____ _____ .
7 qualified (**kwah**-lu-fīd) *adjective* **Rating:** 1 2 3	A **qualified** person is _____. experienced untrained	I can become better qualified for a job by _____ _____ _____ _____ _____ .
8 vote (vōt) *verb* **Rating:** 1 2 3	To **vote** is to _____. ignore choose	I want to vote in order to _____ _____ _____ _____ _____ .

B. Use one of the Key Vocabulary words to tell about a responsibility you look forward to having in the future.

_____

_____

LITERARY ANALYSIS: Analyze Viewpoint: Argument and Evidence

In a **persuasive argument**, the writer states a **claim** and uses **evidence**, facts or data, to support it. The writer tries to convince readers to agree with his or her claim.

A. Read the passage below. Write the evidence that supports the writer's claim in the web.

Look Into the Text

☑Youths Need the Right to Vote

The National Academies, scientists who write reports for the government, state that 80% of 16- and 17-year-olds work before graduation. The *Houston Chronicle* reports that 61% of teenagers work during the school year. Taxes are taken from these teens' paychecks. But these teens have no say about the ways that tax money is spent.

Details Web

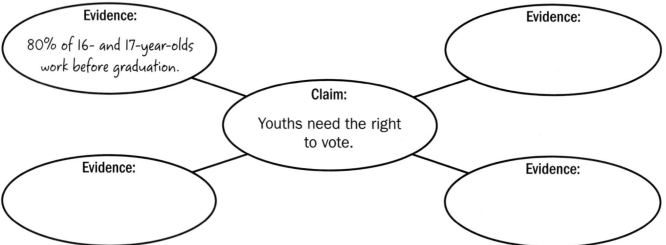

Evidence:
80% of 16- and 17-year-olds work before graduation.

Evidence:

Claim:
Youths need the right to vote.

Evidence:

Evidence:

B. Complete the sentence about the writer's argument.

The writer's argument is strong because _____

_____.

FOCUS STRATEGY: Draw Conclusions

HOW TO DRAW CONCLUSIONS

Focus Strategy

1. **Identify the Writer's Claim** Is the claim based on factual evidence?

2. **Analyze the Evidence** Are the sources reliable? Is the evidence relevant?

3. **Decide If the Claim Is Valid** Does the evidence support the writer's claim?

A. Read the passage. Use the strategies above to draw conclusions as you read. Then answer the questions below.

Look Into the Text

☑Youths Have Political Knowledge

Young people are learning more about politics than adults. For example, some teens participated in the "We the People" education program. Then they were tested in the areas of government and politics. The results of the testing showed that teens knew as much as or more than adults.

According to the Voting Rights Act of 1965, high school students are qualified to vote. This law states that a sixth-grade education is sufficient for voting. If most 16-year-olds have a tenth-grade education, then they are definitely qualified to vote.

1. What claim does the writer make about teenage voters?

_____

_____

2. Is the writer's claim supported? Explain why you agree or disagree with the writer's opinion.

_____

_____

_____

_____

B. Return to the passage above, and circle the words and sentences that helped you answer the first question.

Selection Review 16: The Right Voting Age

EQ **What Rights and Responsibilities Should Teens Have?**
Decide whether teens are mature enough to vote.

A. In "16: The Right Voting Age," you read a persuasive argument that stated why teenagers should have more rights and responsibilities. Complete the diagram with the evidence.

Main-Idea Diagram

> **Writer's Main Argument:**
> The voting age should be lowered to 16.

> Evidence:
>
> Evidence:
>
> Evidence:
>
> Evidence:

B. Use the information in the diagram to answer the questions.

1. Why did the writer include facts and statistics about young people?

_____

_____

2. How might lowering the voting age to 16 affect the next generation's rights and responsibilities? Use **generation** in your answer.

_____

_____

3. Do you think 16-year-old teens should be allowed to vote? Explain.

_____

_____

Teen Brains Are Different

by Lee Bowman

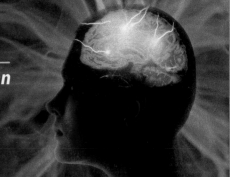

Connect Across Texts

The National Youth Rights Association uses evidence to support its claim that teens are **mature** and ready for responsibilities. This expository nonfiction presents research to support another view.

Have you ever seen a movie in which a teenager got trapped inside an adult body? Maybe you think the teen can really think and act like an adult. The answer may surprise you.

Teen and Adult Brains

The latest brain research strongly shows that teen brains are very different from adult brains. In teens, parts of the brain related to emotions, **judgment**, and "thinking ahead" are not fully operating. This is one reason why teens show less maturity and control than adults.

Dr. Ruben Gur is a professor of psychology who studies brain behavior. He points out that **impulse control** comes last to the brain and is often the first to leave as people **age**.

How the Brain Matures

Until recently, most brain experts thought that the brain stopped growing by the time a person was about 18 months old. They also thought that the brain **had almost all of its neurons** by age three.

In fact, **the brain's gray matter** has a final period of growth around

According to research, teenagers cannot control their emotions and behavior as well as adults because teens' brains are still growing.

Interact with the Text

1. Text Structure: Main Idea and Details
Underline the main idea in column 1. Write one detail that the writer includes to support this main idea.

_____

_____

_____

_____

_____

2. Draw Conclusions
Highlight one detail Dr. Ruben Gur gives about impulse control. Think about what you know. Explain what you believe about controlling impulses.

_____

_____

_____

_____

_____

_____

_____

Key Vocabulary
• **mature** *adj.*, like a grown-up
  judgment *n.*, the ability to make good decisions

In Other Words
impulse control being able to think before acting
age get older
had almost all of its neurons was almost developed
the brain's gray matter part of the brain

3. Interpret
What does this diagram show? Why do you think the author included it?

_____

_____

_____

_____

_____

_____

_____

_____

4. Text Structure: Main Idea and Details
Underline the main idea in column 2. How does it support the main idea of the article?

_____

_____

_____

_____

_____

_____

_____

_____

_____

_____

_____

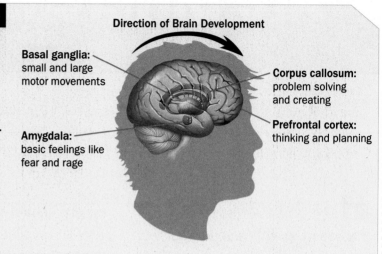

Inside a Teen Brain

Direction of Brain Development

The brain grows rapidly before birth and for the first few years of life. A second growth spurt starts around age 12. It lasts through the teen years, when the brain develops gradually from back to front.

Basal ganglia: small and large motor movements

Amygdala: basic feelings like fear and rage

Corpus callosum: problem solving and creating

Prefrontal cortex: thinking and planning

⚠ Interpret the Diagram According to this diagram, which part of the brain develops last?

the ages of 11 to 13. This occurs in the front of the brain, an important area for thinking and planning.

These new brain cells do not start working right away, though. It seems to take most of the teen years for them to link to the rest of the brain and to **establish** millions of connections. Only then do the cells allow their owners to think and behave like adults.

At the same time, **adolescent hormones** activate other areas of the brain. The flow of hormones especially affects the amygdala.

This is a simple part of the brain that controls basic feelings like fear and rage.

Different Responses

The result is that teens look at things differently than adults. In a recent study, Deborah Yurgelun-Todd of Harvard Medical School and McClean Hospital noted how teens and adults respond differently to the same pictures. The **subjects** were shown photos of people who looked afraid. The adults named the correct emotion, but the teens seldom did.

Key Vocabulary
• **establish** v., to set up, to create

In Other Words
adolescent hormones natural chemicals in teens' bodies
subjects teens and adults in the study

Yurgelun-Todd and her team repeated the test. This time they **scanned** the subjects' brains. They discovered that the adults and teens used different parts of the brain. Adults used both the advanced front part and the **more primitive** amygdala to process what they had seen. Younger teens used only the amygdala. Older teens **showed a shift toward using** the front part of the brain.

Yurgelun-Todd says that teens may be physically mature. But that does not mean that they can make evaluations as well as adults. "Good judgment is learned," she adds. "But you can't learn it if you don't have the necessary hardware."

Brain Hardware: Use It or Lose It

The development of teen brains involves a process called *myelinization*. During this process, layers of fat cover wire-like nerve fibers that connect parts of the brain. Over time, this helps the brain operate in a more precise and efficient way. It doesn't just affect thinking and problem solving, though. It also impacts body movement and mastery of skills, from throwing a baseball to playing a horn.

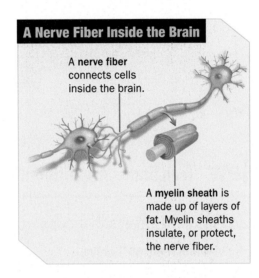

A Nerve Fiber Inside the Brain

A **nerve fiber** connects cells inside the brain.

A **myelin sheath** is made up of layers of fat. Myelin sheaths insulate, or protect, the nerve fiber.

If you don't use your brain cells, they die off. Brain cells that aren't being used don't hook up to other parts of the brain and usually get killed off. "If they're not on the network, they die and their place is taken up with **cerebral fluid**. This goes on well beyond age eighteen," said Dr. David Fassler, a psychiatrist at the University of Vermont.

In Other Words
scanned used special equipment to see
more primitive simpler
showed a shift toward using were different because more of them used
cerebral fluid liquid in and around the brain

Interact with the Text

5. Text Structure: Main Idea and Details
Underline the definition and effects of myelinization. Why does the writer include these important details in the article?

_____

_____

_____

_____

_____

_____

_____

6. Draw Conclusions
Circle what happens to brain cells if they are not used. Use details from the text and what you know from your own experience to draw a conclusion about why this happens.

_____

_____

_____

_____

_____

_____

_____

_____

Dr. Jay Giedd studies brains at the National Institute of Mental Health. He thinks the new understanding of teen brains "argues for doing a lot of things as a teenager. You are **hardwiring** your brain in adolescence," Dr. Giedd says. "Do you want to hardwire it for sports and playing music and doing mathematics, or for lying on the couch in front of the television?" ❖

In Other Words
hardwiring setting up permanent patterns for

Selection Review Teen Brains Are Different

A. Read the main idea, and list three details that support it.

Main Idea:	Teen brains are different from adult brains.

1. _____

_____

2. _____

_____

3. _____

_____

B. Answer the questions.

1. Choose one of the details you listed above. Then draw a conclusion about the text based on that detail and what you know.

_____

_____

2. Based on what you just read, what are two rights and responsibilities younger teens should not have? Why not?

_____

_____

Reflect and Assess

WRITING: Write About Literature

A. Plan your writing. List reasons from each selection that show why you think teens should or should not be able to vote.

16: The Right Voting Age	Teen Brains Are Different

B. What characteristics do you think make someone a good voter? Review the information you gathered in the chart above, then write a short analysis explaining your answer. Include examples from both texts.

_____

_____

_____

_____

_____

_____

_____

_____

_____

_____

_____

Integrate the Language Arts

16: The Right Voting Age
Teen Brains Are Different

LITERARY ANALYSIS: Evaluate the Author's Purpose and Viewpoint

The **purpose** of a persuasive text is to persuade readers to think or take action. Usually, the author has an agenda, or goal. An author of persuasive texts chooses facts that illustrate his or her **viewpoint.**

A. "16: The Right Voting Age" was written by the National Youth Rights Association. Write your ideas about the authors' purpose. Then list the facts given to support the authors' claim that teens should be able to vote.

Author's Purpose	Supporting Facts

B. Answer the questions.

1. Who is the intended audience for "16: The Right Voting Age"? Why? _____

_____

_____

2. How did you identify the intended audience? _____

_____

_____

C. Think about another persuasive text you have recently read. Describe the topic. What was the author's purpose and viewpoint? Who was the intended audience? What agenda do you think the author had?

_____

_____

_____

_____

_____

_____

238   Unit 6: Coming of Age

VOCABULARY STUDY: Specialized Vocabulary

Specialized vocabulary words are words that relate to a specific area of study. You can use a dictionary to learn more about the words.

A. The specialized vocabulary words below all relate to brain development. Write what each word means. Check the dictionary for the correct definition, if necessary.

Word	Specialized Definition
adolescent	
cell	
hormones	
neuron	

B. The sentences below contain words that relate to the government. Write the specialized definition and the part of speech for each underlined word. Use a dictionary if you need to.

1. American citizens have the <u>right</u> to vote in elections. _____

   _____

2. When the man lost his case, he made an <u>appeal</u> to the Supreme Court. _____

   _____

3. The election of five new members to the <u>House</u> resulted in a majority
   of Democrats. _____

   _____

4. The Supreme Court is the highest <u>court</u> in the country. _____

   _____

C. Write a new sentence using each of the specialized words in Activity B, but use the word with a different meaning.

right_____

appeal _____

House _____

court _____

Prepare to Read

▶ **Should Communities Set Teen Curfews?**
▶ **Curfews: A National Debate**

Key Vocabulary

A. How well do you know these words? Circle a rating for each word. Check your understanding of each word by circling *yes* or *no*. Then write a definition. If you are unsure of a word's meaning, refer to the Vocabulary Glossary, page 792, in your student text.

Rating Scale	
1	I have never seen this word before.
2	I am not sure of the word's meaning.
3	I know this word and can teach the word's meaning to someone else.

Key Word	Check Your Understanding	Deepen Your Understanding
1 accountable (u-**kown**-tu-bul) *adjective* **Rating:** 1 2 3	Parents are **accountable** for their young children. Yes No	My definition: _____ _____ _____ _____ _____
2 authority (u-**thor**-u-tē) *noun* **Rating:** 1 2 3	A student has the **authority** to suspend another student from school. Yes No	My definition: _____ _____ _____ _____ _____
3 discrimination (dis-kri-mu-**nā**-shun) *noun* **Rating:** 1 2 3	**Discrimination** is about treating everyone fairly. Yes No	My definition: _____ _____ _____ _____ _____
4 impose (im-**pōz**) *verb* **Rating:** 1 2 3	Teachers **impose** classroom rules that students must follow. Yes No	My definition: _____ _____ _____ _____ _____

Key Word	Check Your Understanding	Deepen Your Understanding
5 neglect (ni-**glekt**) *noun* **Rating:** 1 2 3	A clean house shows a homeowner's **neglect**. **Yes** **No**	My definition: _____ _____ _____ _____ _____
6 prohibit (prō-**hi**-but) *verb* **Rating:** 1 2 3	Laws **prohibit** drivers from driving past the speed limit. **Yes** **No**	My definition: _____ _____ _____ _____ _____
7 restriction (ri-**strik**-shun) *noun* **Rating:** 1 2 3	A **restriction** limits a person's activity or freedom. **Yes** **No**	My definition: _____ _____ _____ _____ _____
8 violate (**vī**-u-lāt) *verb* **Rating:** 1 2 3	People are rewarded if they **violate** the law. **Yes** **No**	My definition: _____ _____ _____ _____ _____

B. Use one of the Key Vocabulary words to write about a right you think teens should have.

_____

_____

LITERARY ANALYSIS: Evaluate Evidence

A writer presents an argument by stating a claim and supporting that claim with evidence. Evidence can include background information, an account of an event, a quote from an expert, and facts. Sometimes a writer makes more than one claim.

A. Read the passage below. Complete the chart with evidence that supports the writer's claims.

Look Into the Text

The Importance of Curfews

Once upon a time, parents weren't afraid to set guidelines or impose restrictions on their children's behavior. They understood that loving their children required setting limits and saying no.

That time is gone. Too many of today's parents just don't want to be responsible for their children.

A case in point: A parent dropped a 12-year-old child off in downtown Orlando at 8 o'clock one morning. At 2 o'clock the following morning, the child was still downtown. That's neglect, plain and simple.

Author's Claim	Evidence
In the past, parents were strict.	
Parents don't want to be responsible for their children.	

B. Complete the sentence about the writer's claims.

To support her claims, the writer uses evidence such as _____

_____.

FOCUS STRATEGY: Compare Arguments

HOW TO COMPARE ARGUMENTS

1. **Read** the text.
2. **Identify** the claim.
3. **Look at evidence** to decide if it supports the claim.

A. Read the passage. Use the strategies above to write about the claim and evidence as you read. Then answer the questions below.

Look Into the Text

> So far, I think the curfew is working. The downtown area is safer for kids. Kids aren't being harassed. In fact, the curfew hasn't caused much trouble at all.
>
> The police are doing a very good job. They've been taught how to deal with situations and problems without becoming confrontational. They issue warnings and give kids a certain amount of time to leave. If the kids won't go, police officers pick them up and call their parents.

1. What claim is the author making in this passage?

   _____

   _____

2. What evidence does the author give to support her claim?

   _____

   _____

B. Return to the passage, and reread the evidence. Is the evidence strong enough to support the claim that curfews are working? Explain.

   _____

   _____

Selection Review Should Communities Set Teen Curfews?

A. In "Should Communities Set Teen Curfews?" you read the argument for supporting curfew laws. Complete the web below with evidence from the article, including from the graph.

Details Web

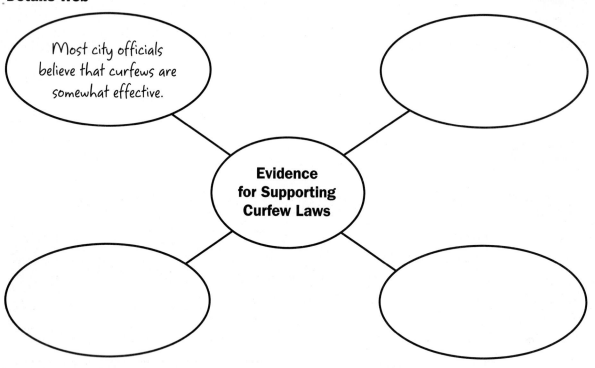

Most city officials believe that curfews are somewhat effective.

Evidence for Supporting Curfew Laws

B. Use the information in the web to answer the questions.

1. Why does the writer believe curfew laws are necessary?

_____

_____

2. How do curfew laws make parents and teens accountable for a teen's actions? Use **accountable** in your answer.

_____

_____

3. Are you convinced that curfew laws make teens safer? Why or why not?

_____

_____

Curfews:
A National Debate

Connect Across Texts

You read arguments in favor of curfews in "Should Communities Set Teen Curfews?" Read the opposite point of view in this persuasive commentary.

In the summer of 1995, the District of Columbia passed a law **imposing** a curfew on teenagers. The law requires everyone under the age of 17 to be home by 11:00 p.m. on weekdays and midnight on weekends. Then they have to stay put until 6:00 a.m. the next morning. The law also **prohibits** drivers under 18 from driving in the District after midnight. Teenagers face punishment if caught in public after curfew. Their parents could be **prosecuted** as well.

In passing this law, Washington, D.C., joined what has become a trend. According to a report in the *American Journal of Police*, 146 of the country's 200 major cities impose curfews of some sort on minors. That's almost 75% of the cities.

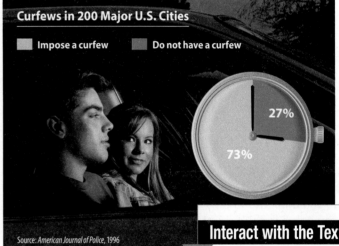

Curfews in 200 Major U.S. Cities

☐ Impose a curfew   ☐ Do not have a curfew

27%
73%

Source: *American Journal of Police*, 1996

Interact with the Text

1. Word Choice
Underline the words and phrases that appeal to your emotions. Explain how these words make you feel about the topic.

_____

_____

_____

_____

_____

_____

_____

Key Vocabulary
- **impose** *v.*, to establish, to apply
- **prohibit** *v.*, to keep people from doing something, to prevent

In Other Words
prosecuted charged by police with breaking the law

3. Interpret
Why do you think the writer used the graph in the article? Is it effective?

Curfews are one of many **misguided** anti-crime strategies. Laws like these **divert** attention from the real causes of crime. The fact is that such laws are **empty political gestures**. They will do nothing to make our streets safer. It is absurd to think that any teenager who is selling drugs or carrying a gun would rush home at 11:00 p.m. to avoid **violating** curfew. Or that this same teenager won't have a false **ID**.

Juvenile Violent Crime

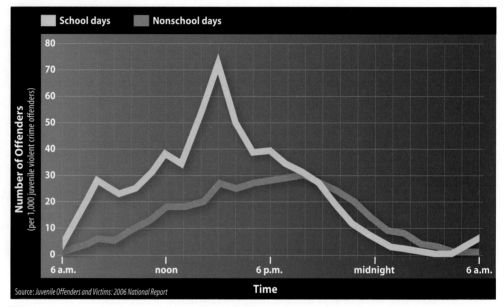

Interpret the Graph At what time during a school day is juvenile crime most likely to occur?

Certainly any crime that would be committed after midnight can just as easily be committed earlier. In fact, the most active period for juvenile crimes is from noon to 6:00 p.m. on school days.

What curfews will do is **wreak havoc with** the constitutional right to freedom of movement. Curfew laws punish the innocent instead of

Key Vocabulary
● **violate** v., to go against

In Other Words
misguided incorrect, unwise
divert shift
empty political gestures passed so the
    government looks as if it is being helpful
ID identification card
wreak havoc with ruin, destroy

the guilty. They put law-abiding teenagers under house arrest every night of the week. But it's not because they have done anything wrong. It is because of the crimes committed by others.

Curfews criminalize normal and otherwise lawful behavior. Teenagers can't walk the dog or go for an early morning run during curfew hours. Curfew laws **usurp** the rights of parents to raise their children as they think best. It becomes a crime for parents to allow their teenagers to go to the theater or a jazz club. This law **injects** the government where it doesn't belong.

There is also no evidence that curfews work. In Houston, a curfew was introduced, and youth crime went down by 22%. But in New York, where no curfew exists, youth crime went down 30%. In Detroit and New Orleans, youth crime increased after curfews were introduced. And in San Francisco, youth crime went down after a curfew was **repealed**.

Crime and Curfews

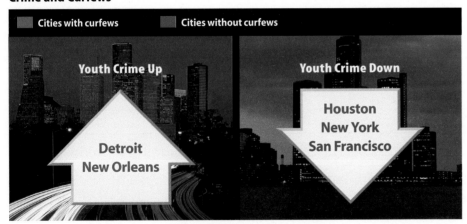

▲ Interpret the Graphic Which cities have curfews? Does crime always go down when a city has a curfew? How can you tell?

In Other Words
usurp take away
injects puts
repealed removed

4. Interpret
Underline the phrases that the writer uses to support the argument that a curfew is like a house arrest. Is this evidence reliable? Why or why not?

5. Compare Arguments
What argument is the writer trying to make about the relationship between curfews and crime rates? What is your opinion about this argument?

6. Word Choice

Underline words or phrases about discrimination that appeal to your emotions. Explain why the writer may have included these loaded words.

_____

_____

_____

_____

_____

Curfews also **squander** police resources that should be used to fight real crime. That is why many police chiefs oppose them.

And inevitably, curfews result in **discrimination**. Studies have consistently found that curfew laws are **disproportionately** enforced in minority communities.

In sum, while curfews may give the appearance of bold action, in reality they do far more harm than good. ❖

Key Vocabulary
- **discrimination** *n.*, treating people unfairly

In Other Words
squander waste
disproportionately unfairly

Selection Review Curfews: A National Debate

A. List three examples of ways the author used loaded words and examples to convince readers. Use evidence from the text. Explain whether these choices were effective and why.

1. _____

_____

2. _____

_____

3. _____

_____

B. Answer the questions.

1. Compare this writer's argument with the writer's argument from "Should Communities Set Teen Curfews?" Which argument do you agree with? Why?

_____

_____

_____

2. Do you think that curfews interfere with teens' rights, or do they help teens become more responsible? Explain.

_____

_____

Reflect and Assess

WRITING: Write About Literature

A. Plan your writing. Read the opposing opinions. Put an *X* next to the opinion you agree with. Then list examples from each text that support the opinion or oppose it.

☐ **Opinion 1:** Curfews are a good idea.

☐ **Opinion 2:** Curfews are a bad idea.

Should Communities Set Teen Curfews?	Curfews: A National Debate

B. What is your opinion? Write an argument with details from your own experience and evidence from the text.

_____

_____

_____

_____

_____

_____

_____

_____

_____

Integrate the Language Arts

LITERARY ANALYSIS: Analyze Persuasive Techniques

Persuasive techniques are ways writers persuade readers to believe or to do something. Writers use a variety of persuasive techniques to influence their readers—some can be deceptive, or misleading.

A. Complete the T Chart with ways that each selection tries to persuade readers to believe certain ideas.

T Chart

Should Communities Set Teen Curfews?	Curfews: A National Debate
makes claims, which may or may not be true, that towns with curfews are safer	quotes studies and uses statistics to make claims believable

B. Answer the questions.

1. Which selection do you think was most effective in persuading readers to believe a claim? Why? _____

_____

_____

2. Did either of the selections use deceptive techniques to persuade readers? Explain. _____

_____

_____

C. Write a brief paragraph to persuade someone to buy what you believe is a great product. Choose a persuasive technique used in one of the selections.

_____

_____

_____

_____

VOCABULARY STUDY: Analogies

An **analogy** is a comparison between two pairs of things. Analogies can show many different relationships, such as objects and their uses, or ideas and their opposites.

A. Read each analogy in the chart below. Then write the type of relationship between the two pairs.

Analogy	Type of Relationship
Blue is to *sky* as *yellow* is to *sun*.	
Lion is to *mammal* as *lizard* is to *reptile*.	
Laughter is to *happiness* as *tears* are to *sadness*.	
Blocks are to *toys* as *couch* is to *furniture*.	
Black is to *white* as *tall* is to *short*.	

B. Complete the analogy.

1. *Dog* is to *bark* as *bird* is to _____ .

2. *Car* is to *road* as *boat* is to _____ .

3. *Farmer* is to *plow* as *firefighter* is to _____ .

4. *Legs* are to *walking* as *eyes* are to _____ .

5. *Earrings* are to *ears* as *shoes* are to _____ .

C. Create your own analogies below. Each analogy pair is started for you.

1. *Clown* is to *joke* as _____ .

2. *Winter* is to *summer* as _____ .

3. *Short stories* are to *fiction* as _____ .

4. *Food* is to *hungry* as _____ .

5. *Golf clubs* are to *golfing* as _____ .

Prepare to Read

▶ What Does Responsibility Look Like?
▶ Getting a Job

Key Vocabulary

A. How well do you know these words? Circle a rating for each word. Check your understanding of each word by circling *yes* or *no*. Then complete the sentences. If you are unsure of a word's meaning, refer to the Vocabulary Glossary, page 792, in your student text.

Rating Scale
1 I have never seen this word before.
2 I am not sure of the word's meaning.
3 I know this word and can teach the word's meaning to someone else.

Key Word	Check Your Understanding	Deepen Your Understanding
1 afford (u-**ford**) *verb* **Rating:** 1 2 3	Many teens have jobs in order to **afford** things they want to buy. Yes No	Some things I can afford are _____ _____ _____ _____ _____.
2 dropout (**drop**-owt) *noun* **Rating:** 1 2 3	A **dropout** is someone who graduates from high school. Yes No	I do not want to be a dropout because _____ _____ _____ _____ _____.
3 experience (ik-**spear**-ē-uns) *noun* **Rating:** 1 2 3	**Experience** as a volunteer can help you gain new skills. Yes No	I learned a lot from an experience I had when _____ _____ _____ _____.
4 income (**in**-kum) *noun* **Rating:** 1 2 3	A student might support his family's **income** by working at a store on weekends. Yes No	One way a teenager can earn an income is by _____ _____ _____ _____.

Key Word	Check Your Understanding	Deepen Your Understanding
5 **independent** (in-du-**pen**-dunt) *adjective* **Rating:** **1 2 3**	An **independent** person depends on other people to survive. Yes No	I will be independent when _____ _____ _____ _____ _____ .
6 **position** (pu-**zi**-shun) *noun* **Rating:** **1 2 3**	Anyone can be appointed to the **position** of president of a company. Yes No	In the future, I would like to be appointed to the position of _____ _____ _____ _____ .
7 **reality** (rē-**a**-lu-tē) *noun* **Rating:** **1 2 3**	**Reality** is how things are at the present moment, not how you want things to be. Yes No	One reality many teenagers face is _____ _____ _____ _____ .
8 **reckless** (**re**-klus) *adjective* **Rating:** **1 2 3**	A **reckless** driver is someone who knows the traffic laws and follows them. Yes No	I think a reckless person is someone who _____ _____ _____ _____ .

B. Use one of the Key Vocabulary words to write about a responsibility that you currently have.

_____

_____

Before Reading   What Does Responsibility Look Like?

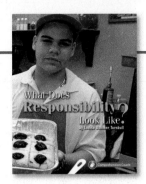

LITERARY ANALYSIS: Evaluate Argument and Reasons

Writers state claims and then supply reasons to persuade you to agree with them. Writers base their reasons on evidence.

A. Read the passage below. In the Main-Idea Tree, write the writer's claim and the reasons given to support it.

Look Into the Text

> Your plans, you say, are to find a job, get a place of your own, and live your own life. These are understandable goals, but completely unattainable for a 16-year-old dropout.
>
> Buy a copy of today's newspaper and turn to the help-wanted section. Circle the jobs for which you qualify. Notice that high-paying positions require college degrees. Other employers want a high school graduate or GED equivalent. Few bosses will hire those under 18 except as babysitters, ushers, dog-walkers, clerks, or fast-food workers. These jobs pay minimum wage with no benefits and little chance for advancement.

Main-Idea Tree

Writer's Claim

Reasons   Evidence

B. Explain how the writer uses reasons to support her argument.

_____

_____

_____

FOCUS STRATEGY: Form Generalizations

HOW TO FORM GENERALIZATIONS

Focus Strategy

1. **Note details** from the text.

2. **Add examples** about the ideas from your own experience or knowledge.

3. **Make a generalization** that applies to many examples.

4. **Read on** to form more generalizations.

A. Read the passage, and use the strategies above to form generalizations. Then complete the chart.

Look Into the Text

> In addition, landlords demand references. They also want first and last months' rent and a hefty damage deposit before you move in. Many will not rent to minors unless a responsible adult guarantees payment. . . .

Generalization Chart

Details from the Text: Landlords want references, first and last months' rent, a damage deposit, and a guarantee from an adult if you are a teen.
My Experience:
Generalization:

B. Explain how using the strategies helped you to form a generalization.

_____

_____

Selection Review   What Does Responsibility Look Like?

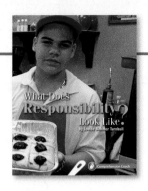

 What Rights and Responsibilities Should Teens Have?
Read about the reality of adult responsibilities.

A. In "What Does Responsibility Look Like?" you found out what it takes to be independent and responsible. Complete the chart with reasons the writer gives for staying in school. Then summarize the writer's argument.

Reason:	Reason:	Reason:
Only minimum wage jobs are available to high school dropouts.		

Writer's Argument:

B. Use the information in the chart to answer the questions.

1. How does the writer use reasons to convince the reader to believe her argument? Is her use of reasons successful?

_____

_____

2. Do you think teenagers who leave school are reckless? Why or why not? Use **reckless** in your answer.

_____

_____

3. Do you think all dropouts face the same problems that the writer presented? Why or why not? Write a paragraph.

_____

_____

_____

_____

_____

_____

_____

_____

_____

Getting a Job

Connect Across Texts

"What Does Responsibility Look Like?" advises teens about the **realities** of taking on responsibilities. Read the following functional documents that relate to getting a job.

(817) 902-3426. Ask for La...
Experienced only.

RESTAURANT
F/T Servers needed for downtown restaurant in Lander's Hotel. Dinner shift. Exp req'd. Fax resume and cover to (817) 555-2408 or email landers@towntalk.com

NOW HIRING

187 Meadow Road
Grapevine, TX 76051
March 6, 2014

Dear Sir or Madam:

I was very interested to see your advertisement in yesterday's *Daily Gazette*. I am interested in a career in hotel and restaurant management and would like the opportunity to work in a restaurant like yours.

Although I cannot work full-time right now, I hope that you will still consider me for a job. I have been working for more than a year as a server during the dinner shift. My current **position** has given me a chance to acquire excellent serving skills, and I am eager to develop them more.

I would also value the **experience** of working with your management team and hope that you would consider training me to work with them eventually.

My resume and a letter of recommendation are attached for your consideration.

Sincerely,

Ken Wauneka

Ken Wauneka

Interact with the Text

1. Author's Tone and Purpose
Highlight words and phrases that show the author's tone and purpose. Explain the tone and purpose of this cover letter.

Key Vocabulary

reality *n.*, the sum of everything real
position *n.*, a specific job
experience *n.*, something you have done, or skills you have learned

Cultural Background

The word *resume* is French. It is often spelled *résumé*, but you may see it without the accents in newspaper ads.

KEN WAUNEKA
187 Meadow Road
Grapevine, TX 76051
(817) 555-3965

Position Desired: *Part-Time Server*

• Dependable • Intelligent • Honest • Hardworking

Career Goal:

Hotel and restaurant management

Paid Work Experience:

Server, Jan. 2013–present
• Work dinner shifts part-time at Green Creek Cafe.

Dishwasher, Busser, Sept. 2012–Dec. 2012
• Worked at El Rancho Restaurant after school and on weekends.

Kitchen Helper, Summers 2010–2012
• Helped clean and **run errands** in my uncle's restaurant, The Desert Diner.

Education:

Will graduate from high school in June 2014.

References:

• *Rita Sando*, Green Creek Cafe manager   (817) 555-4861
• *Lee Wauneka*, owner of The Desert Diner   (817) 555-2699

In Other Words
run errands do small jobs to help

Cultural Background
Every business and area of work has its own jargon, or special vocabulary. Jargon includes words used in a particular way. In the workplace, a *shift* is the full period of time someone works. A *busser* is a worker who sets and clears tables.

GREEN CREEK CAFE

64 Baylord Street
Grapevine, TX 76051
(817) 555–4861

March 1, 2014

To Whom It May Concern:

I manage the restaurant where Ken Wauneka has been working. He handles a large section of the restaurant during the dinner shift. I am impressed by his skills as a server during this busy, demanding time.

Ken is not only an excellent server, but he has also **mastered** many other duties, such as assisting the cook and **bussing tables**. Ken is a great team player. He always helps his coworkers during **a crunch**.

We will be sorry to lose Ken, but we know that his goal is to become a manager at an establishment like yours. I think Ken would make a great addition to your staff and I highly recommend him.

Sincerely yours,

Rita Sando

Rita Sando
Manager

In Other Words
mastered learned
bussing tables clearing away dirty dishes
   and setting tables
a crunch the busy times

Interact with the Text

3. Author's Tone and Purpose
Underline words and phrases that show the author's purpose. Explain the purpose of this letter.

4. Form Generalizations
Highlight important details in this letter of recommendation. What type of information should this type of document always have?

5. Form Generalizations

Mark an *X* next to the most important details on this job application. Explain why you think this information is necessary to include on a job application.

Lander's

HOTEL AND RESTAURANT

JOB APPLICATION

Date __March 10, 2014__

Tell us about yourself.

Name __Ken Wauneka__

Street Address __187 Meadow Road__   Apt. _____

City __Grapevine__

State __Texas__   Zip __76051__

Phone __(817) 555-3965__

What position are you applying for? __server__

What hours and shifts are you interested in?

O Full-time   O Breakfast shift
Ø Part-time   O Lunch shift
                         Ø Dinner shift

Have you worked in a restaurant before?

Ø Yes   O No

If Yes, turn to page 2 of this application and describe where you worked and what you did. Begin with your most recent position.

— Page 1 —

Position/Duties:

I am a part-time dinner waiter at Green Creek
Cafe. I tell customers about the daily specials
and take and deliver their orders. At the end
of each shift, I help set up the dining room for
the next day.

Position/Duties:

I started as a dishwasher at El Rancho Restaurant.
When I was promoted to busser, I helped clear
and set tables.

Position/Duties:

I was a kitchen helper at The Desert Diner.
I cleaned equipment, swept the floors, and
ran errands for the cooks.

When can you start work? _March 24, 2014_

— Page 2 —

6. Author's Tone and Purpose
Highlight words that show Ken's duties at the Green Creek Cafe. What was Ken's purpose for including these details?

7. Interpret
Ken sent a resume. Why do you think the employer asks for applicants to fill out an application?

8. Author's Tone and Purpose

Underline words and phrases that show the author's tone. Explain her tone and purpose.

_____

_____

_____

_____

_____

> Ken,
>
> Ms. Park called from Lander's Restaurant. She said she enjoyed interviewing you. She called your references, and she wants you to start on Saturday! Congratulations! Call her back at 555-2408.
>
> — Mom

Selection Review Getting a Job

A. You read four types of job application documents. Each has a different purpose. Explain the purpose of each document.

1. Cover Letter: _____

2. Resume: _____

_____

3. Recommendation Letter: _____

_____

4. Application:_____

B. Answer the questions.

1. What should you always do when you apply for a job? List two generalizations.

_____

_____

2. Imagine that Ken asks you to write a letter of recommendation based on the information he provided on his resume and job application. What information would you include? Why?

_____

_____

WRITING: Write About Literature

A. Plan your writing. Think of a job you might want to apply for. What should a cover letter for a job application include? Using "Getting a Job" as a model, list how you want your cover letter to sound and the information you want to include.

Elements of a Cover Letter	My Cover Letter
Tone	
Desired Position	
Experience	
Skills	

B. Using the ideas in the chart above, write a persuasive cover letter to an imaginary employer that explains why they should hire you.

_____

_____

_____

_____

_____

_____

_____

_____

_____

_____

_____

_____

_____

_____

_____

Integrate the Language Arts

LITERARY ANALYSIS: Evaluate Functional Documents

Functional documents tell how to do something. The information should be clear and easy to follow. If any information is out of order, unclear, or missing, then the document could be useless.

A. In the chart below, explain how each feature of a resume provides important information about the applicant to a potential employer.

Feature	Information
Position Desired	tells the employer exactly which position the applicant wishes to apply for
Goal and Experience	
Education	
References	

B. Review the features in the chart. Why do you think the information is presented in this order? Is this order logical? Why or why not?

_____

_____

_____

_____

_____

C. Write a brief outline of your own resume.

_____

_____

_____

_____

_____

_____

_____

_____

_____

VOCABULARY STUDY: Multiple-Meaning Words

Many words in English have both an everyday meaning and a special meaning in a career field. These are **multiple-meaning words.**

A. Read each word below. Write its everyday meaning. Use a dictionary to confirm the meaning, if necessary.

Word	Everyday Meaning
benefit	help or useful aid
break	
fire	
graveyard	
play	

B. Read the sentences below. Each sentence contains a word from the chart in Activity A, but the word has a special meaning. Write the special meaning of each underlined word.

Sentence	Special Meaning
Temporary jobs often do not have health and retirement benefits.	
Most people eat lunch on their break.	
You might be fired from a job if you arrive late every day.	
People who work during the graveyard shift often sleep during the day.	
I went to see my friend act in a play.	

C. For each word below, write a sentence with an everyday meaning and a specialized meaning.

shift _____

_____

pay _____

_____

Read for Understanding

1. Genre   What kind of text is this passage? How do you know?

_____

_____

_____

2. Topic   Write a topic sentence to tell what the text is mostly about.

_____

_____

_____

_____

_____

Reread and Summarize

3. Key Ideas   In each section, circle three words or phrases that express the key ideas in the section. Note next to each word or phrase why you chose it.

· Section 1: paragraphs 1–8
· Section 2: paragraphs 9–16

4. Summary   Use your topic sentence and notes from item 3 to write a summary of the selection.

_____

_____

_____

_____

_____

_____

Trashing Teens

An Interview with Psychologist Robert Epstein

by Hara Estroff Marano

Psychologist Robert Epstein spoke to Psychology Today's *Hara Estroff Marano about the legal and emotional constraints on American youth.*

2 **Q.**   Why do you believe that adolescence is an artificial extension of childhood?

3 **A.**   In every mammalian species, immediately upon reaching **puberty**, animals function as adults, often having offspring. We call our offspring "children" well past puberty. The trend started a hundred years ago and now extends childhood well into the 20s. The age at which Americans reach adulthood is increasing—30 is the new 20—and most Americans now believe a person isn't an adult until age 26.

4   The whole culture **collaborates** in artificially extending childhood, primarily through the school system and **restrictions** on **labor**. The two systems evolved together in the late 19th-century; the advocates of **compulsory**-education laws also pushed for child-labor laws, restricting the ways young people could work, in part to protect them from the abuses of the new factories. The juvenile justice system came into being at the same time. All of these systems isolate teens from adults, often in problematic ways.

Key Vocabulary
● **restriction** *n.*, something that limits activity

In Other Words
puberty physical maturity
collaborates works together
labor work
compulsory required

5   Our current education system was created in the late 1800s and early 1900s, and was modeled after the new factories of the industrial revolution. Public schools, set up to supply the factories with a skilled labor force, **crammed** education into a relatively small number of years. We have tried to pack more and more in while extending schooling up to age 24 or 25, for some segments of the population. In general, such an approach still reflects factory thinking—get your education now and get it efficiently, in classrooms in **lockstep** fashion. Unfortunately, most people learn in those classrooms to hate education for the rest of their lives.

6   **Q.** What are some likely consequences of extending one's childhood?

7   **A.** Imagine what it would feel like—or think back to what it felt like— when your body and mind are telling you you're an adult while the adults around you keep insisting you're a child. This infantilization makes many young people angry or depressed, with their distress carrying over into their families and contributing to our high divorce rate. It's hard to keep a marriage together when there is constant conflict with teens.

8   We have completely isolated young people from adults and created a peer culture. We stick them in school and keep them from working in any meaningful way, and if they do something wrong we put them in a pen with other "children." In most **nonindustrialized societies**, young people are integrated into adult society as soon as they are capable, and there is no sign of teen **turmoil**. Many cultures do not even have a term for adolescence. But we not only created this stage of life: We declared it inevitable. In 1904, American psychologist G. Stanley Hall said it was programmed by evolution. He was wrong.

We have completely isolated young people from adults. . .

Historical Background
The industrial revolution was the process of change from a farm-based economy to a factory-based economy that took place in England in the 1700s and then spread throughout most of the world.

Reread and Analyze

5. Author's Viewpoint What is Epstein's viewpoint in the interview?

_____

_____

_____

_____

_____

6. Word Choice Reread paragraph 5 and highlight the word *crammed*.

7. Word Choice Find and highlight other loaded words in section 1. Why does Epstein choose these words to express his viewpoint?

_____

_____

_____

_____

_____

8. Word Choice Reread paragraph 8. Find and underline the positive words Epstein uses in sentence 3. Why does he use these words?

_____

_____

_____

_____

9. Evidence Reread paragraph 10. Underline the information about the tests Dumas and Epstein administered. Is this evidence relevant and reliable?

9   **Q.** You believe in the inherent competence of teens. What's your evidence?

10   **A.** Dumas and I worked out what makes an adult an adult. We came up with 14 areas of competency—such as interpersonal skills, handling responsibility, leadership—and administered tests to adults and teens in several cities around the country. We found that teens were as competent or nearly as competent as adults in all 14 areas. But when adults estimate how teens will score, their estimates are dramatically below what the teens actually score.

11   Other long-standing data show that teens are at least as competent as adults. IQ is a **quotient** that indicates where you stand relative to other people your age; that stays stable. But raw scores of intelligence peak around age 14-15 and shrink thereafter. Scores on virtually all tests of memory peak between ages 13 and 15. Perceptual abilities all peak at that age. Brain size peaks at 14. Incidental memory—what you remember by accident, and not due to **mnemonics**—is remarkably good in early to mid teens and practically nonexistent by the '50s and '60s.

10. Evidence Reread paragraph 11. Find and underline other evidence Epstein uses to support his claim. Is this additional evidence reliable and relevant?

12   **Q.** If teens are so competent, why do they not show it?

13   **A.** What teens do is a small fraction of what they are capable of doing. If you mistreat or restrict them, performance suffers and is extremely misleading. The teens put before us as examples by, say, the music

A teenager plays the steel drums during the 2012 London Olympics.

In Other Words
competence ability
quotient number from a formula
mnemonics memory tricks

industry tend to be highly incompetent. Teens encourage each other to perform incompetently. One of the anthems of modern pop, "Smells Like Teen Spirit" by Nirvana, is all about how we need to behave like we're stupid.

14   Teens in America are in touch with their peers on average 65 hours a week, compared to about four hours a week in preindustrial cultures. In this country, teens learn virtually everything they know from other teens, who are in turn highly influenced by certain aggressive industries. This makes no sense. Teens should be learning from the people they are about to become. When young people exit the education system and are dumped into the real world, they have no idea what's going on and have to spend considerable time figuring it out.

15 **Q.** What can be done?

16 **A.** I believe that young people should have more options— the option to work, marry, own property, sign contracts, start businesses, make decisions about health care, live on their own—every right, privilege, or responsibility an adult has. I advocate a competency-based system that focuses on the abilities of the individual. For some it will mean more time in

I believe that young people should have more options...

school combined with work, for others it will mean that at age 13 or 15 they can set up an Internet business. Others will enter the workforce and become some sort of **apprentice**. The **exploitative factories** are long gone; competent young people deserve the chance to compete where it counts, and many will surprise us. ❖

In Other Words

apprentice assistant who is learning from an expert
exploitative factories workplaces that took advantage of young people

---

Reread and Analyze

11. Counterclaim Reread paragraphs 13 and 14. How does Epstein explain why teens seem to be incompetent? Is his evidence convincing?

_____

_____

_____

_____

_____

_____

12. Conclusion Reread paragraph 16. Double underline phrases that sum up Epstein's argument. Compare your underlines with a partner's and restate Epstein's viewpoint in your own words.

_____

_____

_____

_____

_____

_____

_____

CLOSE READING Trashing Teens

Discuss

13. **Synthesize** With the class, list specific ways that Epstein builds his argument, including loaded words and parts of an argument.

Word Choices		
Parts of the Argument		
Claim		
Evidence		
Counterclaim		
Rebuttal		
Conclusion		

Then, with the class, discuss how authors deliberately choose words and organize texts to make their arguments convincing. Make notes.

_____

_____

14. **Write** Use your notes from question 13 to write about the ways that authors use word choices and the structure of the argument to support and reinforce their viewpoints. Use the questions below to organize your thoughts. If you need more space, continue your writing on another piece of paper.

· What is Epstein's viewpoint?

· Evaluate Epstein's word choice: How does Epstein's choice of words help to advance, or reinforce, his viewpoint?

· Evaluate Epstein's use of structure: How does Epstein's organization of ideas help to advance, or reinforces his viewpoint?

· Do Epstein's word choices and structure add up to a convincing argument? Explain.

_____

_____

_____

_____

_____

Connect with the **EQ** What Rights and Responsibilities Should Teens Have?

Consider how society shapes teenage behavior.

15. **Opinion** Reread paragraph 16. What rights and responsibilities does Epstein think that teens should have? How do you know?

_____

_____

_____

_____

_____

_____

_____

16. **Theme** Reread the quotations on page 460. Would Epstein agree with Confucius? Would he agree with the Irish proverb? Use evidence from the text to support your answer. What is his message about teen competence and why it isn't always displayed?

_____

_____

_____

_____

_____

_____

_____

Key Vocabulary Review

A. Use the words to complete the paragraph.

accountable	**establish**	**neglect**	**restriction**
authority	**impose**	**prohibit**	**violate**

Principals and teachers have the _____ to _____ rules students must follow.
(1)   (2)

When students _____ these rules or _____ to follow them, they are held
(3)   (4)

_____ for their actions. Some rules may _____ certain behavior, like wearing
(5)   (6)

hats in class. Students may feel like these rules are a _____ of their rights, but principals
(7)

_____ most rules to keep students safe.
(8)

B. Use your own words to write what each Key Vocabulary word means.
Then write a synonym for each word.

Key Word	My Definition	Synonym
1. discrimination		
2. experience		
3. income		
4. mature		
5. participate		
6. politics		
7. position		
8. reckless		

Unit 6 Key Vocabulary

accountable	dropout	• impose	• mature	position	reckless
afford	• establish	• income	neglect	• prohibit	• restriction
• authority	experience	independent	• participate	qualified	• violate
• discrimination	• generation	judgment	politics	reality	vote

• **Academic Vocabulary**

C. Answer the questions using complete sentences.

1. If you could change one aspect of **reality**, what would you change and why?

_____

_____

2. Describe a time when you showed good **judgment**.

_____

_____

3. Do you think it is important to **vote**? Why or why not?

_____

_____

4. Describe a job you are **qualified** to perform.

_____

_____

5. What advice would you give to a high school **dropout**?

_____

_____

6. What makes someone **independent**?

_____

_____

7. What is one thing you wish you could **afford** to do?

_____

_____

8. How is your **generation** different from your parents' generation?

_____

_____

Prepare to Read
▶ Novio Boy: Scene 7, Part 1
▶ Oranges

Key Vocabulary

A. How well do you know these words? Circle a rating for each word. Check your understanding of each word by circling *yes* or *no*. Then complete the sentences. If you are unsure of a word's meaning, refer to the Vocabulary Glossary, page 792, in your student text.

Rating Scale

1	I have never seen this word before.
2	I am not sure of the word's meaning.
3	I know this word and can teach the word's meaning to someone else.

Key Word	Check Your Understanding	Deepen Your Understanding
❶ compliment (**kom**-plu-munt) *noun* Rating: 1 2 3	A person can give a **compliment** as a way to show appreciation and admiration. **Yes** **No**	One compliment I have received lately is _____ _____ _____ _____.
❷ conceal (kun-**sēl**) *verb* Rating: 1 2 3	The best way to **conceal** a secret is to tell everyone you know. **Yes** **No**	Famous people sometimes conceal their appearance by _____ _____ _____ _____.
❸ elegance (**e**-li-guns) *noun* Rating: 1 2 3	Dancers move with grace, beauty, and **elegance.** **Yes** **No**	When I think of elegance, I think of _____ _____ _____ _____ _____.
❹ nervous (**nur**-vus) *adjective* Rating: 1 2 3	A **nervous** person feels confident, assured, and eager. **Yes** **No**	One thing that makes me feel nervous is _____ _____ _____ _____.

Key Word	Check Your Understanding	Deepen Your Understanding
5 overprotective (ō-vur-pru-**tek**-tiv) *adjective* **Rating:** 1 2 3	Taking someone with a paper cut to the emergency room is an example of **overprotective** behavior. Yes No	Children of overprotective parents may react by _____ _____ _____ _____ _____ .
6 personality (pur-su-**na**-lu-tē) *noun* **Rating:** 1 2 3	Spending time with someone is a good way to find out what kind of **personality** they have. Yes No	I would describe my personality as _____ _____ _____ _____ .
7 reveal (ri-**vēl**) *verb* **Rating:** 1 2 3	When you **reveal** the truth, you keep it secret. Yes No	When I first meet someone, I don't like to reveal _____ _____ _____ _____ _____ .
8 romantic (rō-**man**-tik) *adjective* **Rating:** 1 2 3	**Romantic** movies are suspenseful and violent. Yes No	Romantic songs make me feel _____ _____ _____ _____ _____ .

B. Use one of the Key Vocabulary words to write about a situation where you made a good impression on someone.

_____

_____

Before Reading Novio Boy: Scene 7, Part 1

LITERARY ANALYSIS: Compare Representations: Script and Performance

We experience a play differently when we read it, as a script, and when we see it performed on stage. Some things may be clearer or less clear, more enjoyable or less enjoyable, in each medium.

A. Read the passage below. Complete the chart with examples of Patricia's and Rudy's dialogue and actions. In the last column, write whether you'd prefer a reading or a production of this part of the play. Tell why.

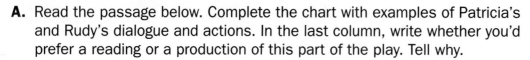

> **WAITER.** [*looking up happily*] Mademoiselle and monsieur. Please take this seat by the window. [*pulls chair out for* PATRICIA]
>
> **PATRICIA.** [*sniffs the flower on the table*] It's so romantic. So sophisticated, so charming, so . . . And look, a guitarist!
>
> [RUDY *sees that it's his* UNCLE JUAN, *who waves at him.* RUDY *shakes his head at his* UNCLE, *as if to say, Don't say anything.*]
>
> **PATRICIA.** It's a discriminating restaurant.
>
> **RUDY:** Do they discriminate against Latinos? If so, I ain't going to eat here. We'll go grub at Pollo Loco instead.

Dramatic Element	Example 1	Example 2	Script versus Production
Dialogue	"It's so romantic. So sophisticated, so charming, so . . . And look, a guitarist!"		
Stage directions			

B. Would you prefer reading this play or watching a performance of it? Explain your answer.

_____

_____

_____

FOCUS STRATEGY: Form Mental Images

HOW TO FORM MENTAL IMAGES

Focus Strategy

1. **Find Clues** Look for words that help you understand the characters and events.

2. **Visualize** Use the playwright's words to create pictures in your mind.

3. **Sketch** Draw pictures to show what is happening.

A. Read the passage. Use the strategies above to form mental images as you read. Answer the questions below.

Look Into the Text

[JUAN *starts playing his guitar and singing.* RUDY *and* PATRICIA *listen. Silly song, perhaps "Tort y Frijoles."*]

PATRICIA. He's really talented.

RUDY. He's OK.

WAITER. [*approaches with glasses of water*] Our special for the day is . . .
[*A "mooooo" sounds.*]

WAITER. [*continuing*] . . . tender veal. We have spotted cow, brown cow, black-and-white cow, and—
[*The mooing sounds again.*]

WAITER. I'll be back to get your order. I have to see about something in the kitchen. [*leaves, pulling a meat cleaver from belt*]

PATRICIA. The food's really . . .

PATRICIA. . . . fresh.

1. Which words and phrases help you understand the characters and events?

_____

_____

2. How do you visualize the scene in your mind?

_____

_____

_____

B. How did reading the dialogue and stage directions help bring the scene to life?

_____

_____

Selection Review Novio Boy: Scene 7, Part 1

 What Do You Do to Make an Impression?
Read about teens who are nervous on a first date.

A. In "Novio Boy: Scene 7, Part 1," Rudy and Patricia try to impress each other on their first date. In the Cause-and-Effect chart, write what the characters do and say and what effect their actions have.

Cause-and-Effect Chart

What the Characters Do and Say	What Impression They Make
Rudy takes Patricia to a nice restaurant.	Patricia is excited to be there and that Rudy would pick such a nice place.

B. Use the information in the chart on page 278 to answer the questions.

1. Based on their actions and words, what impression do you think Patricia and Rudy have of each other? Explain.

_____

_____

_____

_____

2. How would you describe Patricia's personality? Use **personality** in your answer.

_____

_____

_____

_____

3. Reread the part of the play where Rudy compliments Patricia. How do you visualize this scene? Make a sketch of the scene. Then describe it in your own words below.

_____

_____

_____

_____

_____

_____

Interactive

Connect Across Texts

In Part 1 of Novio Boy, *you read about the beginning of Rudy and Patricia's date. Read about another first date in this narrative poem.*

Oranges
by Gary Soto

The first time I walked
With a girl, I was twelve,
Cold, and weighted down
With two oranges in my jacket.
5 December. Frost cracking
Beneath my steps, my breath
Before me, then gone,
As I walked toward
Her house, the one whose
10 Porch light burned yellow
Night and day, in any weather.
A dog barked at me, until
She came out pulling
At her gloves, face bright
15 With rouge. I smiled,
Touched her shoulder, and led
Her down the street, across
A used car lot and a line
Of newly planted trees,

Classic Tiles Composition II, 2001, Ger Stallenberg.
Oil on canvas, private collection, the Netherlands.

▲ Critical Viewing: Effect How does the mood in this painting relate to the poem? How is it different from the poem?

In Other Words
rouge blush, red makeup

20 Until we were breathing
   Before a drugstore. We
   Entered, the tiny bell
   Bringing a saleslady
   Down a narrow aisle of goods.
25 I turned to the candies
   Tiered like bleachers,
   And asked what she wanted—
   Light in her eyes, a smile
   Starting at the corners
30 Of her mouth. I fingered
   A nickel in my pocket,
   And when she lifted a chocolate
   That cost a dime,
   I didn't say anything.
35 I took the nickel from
   My pocket, then an orange,
   And set them quietly on
   The counter. When I looked up,
   The lady's eyes met mine,
40 And held them, knowing
   Very well what it was all
   About.

       Outside,
   A few cars hissing past,

In Other Words
Tiered Placed, Arranged
fingered felt

Interact with the Text

1. Elements of Poetry
Underline words and phrases on page 280 that describe the setting. Describe the setting in your own words.

_____

_____

_____

_____

2. Mental Images
Circle details about the drugstore. Describe how you visualize the store.

_____

_____

_____

_____

_____

3. Elements of Poetry
Highlight how the boy pays for the candy and how the saleslady reacts. What does this tell you about the characters?

_____

_____

_____

_____

_____

_____

4. Elements of Poetry

Underline the actions of the characters. How does this narrative poem end?

_____

_____

_____

_____

_____

_____

45 Fog hanging like old
    Coats between the trees.
    I took my girl's hand
    In mine for two blocks,
    Then released it to let
50 Her unwrap the chocolate.
    I peeled my orange
    That was so bright against
        The gray of December
    That, from some distance,
55 Someone might have thought
    I was making a fire in my hands. ❖

Selection Review Oranges

A. Find descriptive details from the poem that helped you visualize, or picture, the setting and characters.

Details about the setting: _____

_____

Details about the characters: _____

_____

B. Answer the questions.

1. What story elements are in this narrative poem? Choose one and explain how it helped you understand the poem.

_____

_____

2. Do you think the boy made a good impression on his date? Why or why not?

_____

_____

Reflect and Assess

WRITING: Write About Literature

A. Plan your writing. Read the opposing opinions. Mark an *X* next to the claim you agree with. Then list examples from each text that support or oppose it.

- ☐ **Claim 1:**   It's necessary to spend a lot of money to impress a date.
- ☐ **Claim 2:**   You never have to spend a lot of money to impress a date.

Novio Boy: Scene 7, Part 1	Oranges

B. What is your opinion? State your opinion in a claim. Use evidence from both texts and your experience to support your claim.

_____

_____

_____

_____

_____

_____

_____

_____

_____

Integrate the Language Arts

LITERARY ANALYSIS: Compare Themes

Drama and poetry are two different **genres**, or types of literature. An author's choice of genre affects how the **theme**, or message, is expressed.

A. In a play, theme is frequently revealed through dialogue and action. Read the examples below and write the message that the lines reveal.

Dialogue	What It Reveals
RUDY. [*notices her jewelry*] That's a cute cat pin.	*Rudy says what's on his mind.*
PATRICIA. I mean, you're nicer than most boys, and not stupid, either.	
PATRICIA. Sounds weird, but I like my fries with mustard. **RUDY.** Yeah? Me, too.	
ALEX. Forget the notes. Speak from your heart.	

What is the theme? _____

B. Poets often choose words because of the images they create or because they have a particular sound. Answer the questions about "Oranges."

1. List two strong images from the poem.

_____

_____

2. What messages do these images communicate?

_____

_____

3. What is the theme of the poem?

_____

_____

C. Can you learn more about the theme from dialogue and action, or from description and word choice?

_____

_____

_____

VOCABULARY STUDY: Idioms

An **idiom** is a group of words that have a different meaning than the literal meaning. Context clues can help you figure out the meaning of an idiom.

A. Read the underlined idioms below. Use context clues to help you figure out the meaning of each idiom. Then write what you think the idiom means.

Idiom	What I Think It Means
Rudy hopes Patricia's parents do not come into the restaurant. If they do, he will be out of the frying pan and into the fire.	
Rudy doesn't order much food because everything on the menu costs an arm and a leg.	
Patricia thinks the cloth napkin is elegant, but Rudy could take it or leave it.	
Rudy wants to compliment Patricia, but he goes overboard when he reads lines from a notebook.	

B. Complete the following sentences with context clues. The underlined phrases are idioms.

1. I'm hungry enough to eat a horse because _____

2. She hoped no one was planning to spill the beans about _____

3. He was up the creek with no paddle when his computer_____

4. It was time to get the show on the road because_____

C. Write a short paragraph containing two idioms you know that do not appear above.

_____

_____

_____

_____

_____

_____

_____

_____

Prepare to Read

▸ **Novio Boy: Scene 7, Part 2**
▸ **Your World**

Key Vocabulary

A. How well do you know these words? Circle a rating for each word. Check your understanding of each word by circling the correct synonym. Then complete the sentences. If you are unsure of a word's meaning, refer to the Vocabulary Glossary, page 792, in your student text.

Rating Scale	
1	I have never seen this word before.
2	I am not sure of the word's meaning.
3	I know this word and can teach the word's meaning to someone else.

Key Word	Check Your Understanding	Deepen Your Understanding
❶ ashamed (u-**shāmd**) *adjective* **Rating:** 1 2 3	If you feel **ashamed**, you feel _____. guilty proud	I would feel ashamed if I _____ _____ _____ _____ _____ .
❷ conscious (**kon**-shus) *adjective* **Rating:** 1 2 3	If you make a **conscious** decision, you make a _____ decision. casual deliberate	An example of a time I made a conscious decision is when I _____ _____ _____ _____ .
❸ desire (di-**zīr**) *noun* **Rating:** 1 2 3	A **desire** is a _____. need wish	One desire I have for next year is _____ _____ _____ _____ .
❹ flirt (**flurt**) *verb* **Rating:** 1 2 3	To **flirt** is to act in a way that shows you _____ someone. like fear	In movies, people flirt with each other by _____ _____ _____ _____ _____ .

Key Word	Check Your Understanding	Deepen Your Understanding
5 **horizon** (hu-**rī**-zun) *noun* **Rating:** 1 2 3	If you see the **horizon**, you see the _____. **skyline** **stars**	The best place to see the horizon is _____ _____ _____ _____ .
6 **privacy** (**prī**-vu-sē) *noun* **Rating:** 1 2 3	Someone who values their **privacy** values their _____. **solitude** **openness**	You can respect someone's privacy by _____ _____ _____ _____ _____ .
7 **recover** (ri-**ku**-vur) *verb* **Rating:** 1 2 3	To **recover** something is to _____ it. **adapt** **regain**	If I wanted to recover as quickly as possible from a cold, I would _____ _____ _____ _____ .
8 **reluctant** (ri-**luk**-tunt) *adjective* **Rating:** 1 2 3	If you feel **reluctant**, you feel _____. **confident** **uncertain**	Something I am reluctant to try is _____ _____ _____ _____ _____ .

B. Use one of the Key Vocabulary words to write about what you do that gives you confidence.

_____

_____

Before Reading Novio Boy: Scene 7, Part 2

LITERARY ANALYSIS: Analyze Structure: Script

In a play, the playwright uses the structure of a script, including the **dialogue**, **set**, and **stage directions** to tell the story and reveal details about the **characters** and **plot**.

A. Read the passage below. Look for stage directions and dialogue that tell you about each character. Then complete the chart.

> **Look Into the Text**
>
> [RUDY, *straightening the collar of his shirt, returns to the table*;
>   PATRICIA *hurries to the table as well.*]
>
> **PATRICIA.** Is he a friend of yours?
>
> **RUDY.** Kind of. [*pause*] Patricia, you got a . . . complex personality.
>   I mean, you're not stuck-up. You're willing to go out with a boy
>   who . . .
>
> **PATRICIA.** What?
>
> **RUDY.** [*shyly*] Never mind.
>
> **PATRICIA.** Come on, tell me.
>
> **RUDY.** Who still has his G.I. Joes.
>
> **PATRICIA.** You're cute! [*pause*] You know, I saw you play baseball
>   before.

Character	What the Character Says and Does
Rudy	straightens his collar
Patricia	hurries to the table

B. Complete the sentence about Rudy and Patricia.

Rudy and Patricia _____

_____.

FOCUS STRATEGY: Identify Sensory Images

How to IDENTIFY SENSORY IMAGES

1. **Look for sensory images** or words that tell you how things look, sound, smell, taste, and feel.

2. **Imagine the scene** and what you see, hear, smell, taste, and touch.

A. Read the passage. Use the strategies above to identify sensory images as you read. Then answer the questions below.

Look Into the Text

> **ALEX.** *Mira*, she left a French fry. Here, Novio Boy. [*feeds it to* RUDY]
>
> **RUDY.** She wiped me out for the rest of ninth grade. But it beats doing nothing.
>
> [*At this,* JUAN *begins to play a song about "nothing."*]
>
> **RUDY.** Thanks for helping out, unc.
>
> **JUAN.** *No problema.* You're my only nephew. About the money . . . You can pay me back later.
>
> **ALEX.** But me first.
>
> [JUAN *returns to his stool and starts strumming his guitar softly.*]

1. What do you see, hear, smell, taste, and touch? Complete the chart with your responses to the text.

My Response to the Text	
I see: Alex, Juan, and Rudy talking. Alex feeds Rudy a fry. Juan plays the guitar. **I hear:**	**I smell:** **I taste:** **I feel:**

2. How do these sensory images help you experience the story?

_____

_____

B. Return to the passage above, and circle the words or sentences that helped you answer the first question.

Selection Review Novio Boy: Scene 7, Part 2

 What Do You Do to Make an Impression?
Read about people who gain confidence in themselves.

A. In Part 2 of "Novio Boy," Rudy's friends and family help him gain confidence in himself. Complete the chart with examples of dialogue and stage directions that give you new information about each of the characters.

Rudy	Patricia
pulls his notepad from his pocket and reads from it	

Rudy's Mom	Alex

B. Use the information in the chart to answer the questions.

1. Think about the characters' actions and dialogue. What new information do you learn about Rudy?

   _____

   _____

2. Rudy's mom asks if he is ashamed of her. Why do you think she asks him that? Use **ashamed** in your response.

   _____

   _____

3. How do you think Rudy would act if he goes out with Patricia again?

   _____

   _____

Connect Across Texts
In Part 2 of Novio Boy, *Rudy becomes more confident. Read this poem about another person who is **reluctant** at first but then changes.*

Your World

by Georgia Douglas Johnson

Your world is as big as you make it.
I know, for I used to abide
In the narrowest nest in a corner,
My wings pressing close to my side.

5   But I sighted the distant horizon
Where the skyline encircled the sea
And I throbbed with a burning desire
To travel this immensity.

I battered the cordons around me
10   And cradled my wings on the breeze
Then soared to the uttermost reaches
With rapture, with power, with ease!

Interact with the Text

1. Sensory Images
Underline the descriptive phrases that helped you experience what the poet is describing. How do they affect your understanding of the poem?

Key Vocabulary
• **reluctant** *adj.*, unsure, unwilling
  horizon *n.*, the line where the sky and land or water seem to meet
  desire *n.*, something that you want strongly; a wish

In Other Words
abide live
encircled went all around
immensity huge place
battered the cordons broke the ties
rapture happiness

Selection Review Your World

A. Complete the chart with sensory images from the poem and your experiences.

What I Read	What I Experience
"My wings pressing close to my side."	I feel like I'm trapped in a small space.

B. Answer the questions.

1. How did rhyme and rhythm help you understand the poem?

   _____

   _____

   _____

2. Describe what it would be like to meet the speaker in this poem. Use details from the poem to support your answer.

   _____

   _____

   _____

Reflect and Assess

WRITING: Write About Literature

A. Plan your writing. Read the first line of "Your World" below. Decide whether you agree or disagree with it. List evidence from both texts that supports your choice.

Your world is as big as you make it.

Novio Boy: Scene 7, Part 2	Your World

B. Write an explanation and comment about the first line of "Your World." Support your comment using your own opinion and evidence from both texts.

_____

_____

_____

_____

_____

_____

_____

_____

_____

_____

Integrate the Language Arts

LITERARY ANALYSIS: Rhythm and Meter

Rhythm is the pattern of beats that gives poetry its musical quality. The repetition of sounds is one form of rhythm. Another form is **meter**. Meter is a pattern of stressed and unstressed syllables in a line of poetry. A **foot** is a unit of stressed and unstressed syllables.

A. Read the lines below from "Your World" and mark each stressed syllable with a ´ and mark each unstressed syllable with a ˘.

> I battered the cordons around me
> And cradled my wings on the breeze
> Then soared to the uttermost reaches
> With rapture, with power, with ease!

B. In the lines below, mark each unstressed syllable with a ˘. Then mark each stressed syllable with a ´.

> Your world is as big as you make it.
> But I sighted the distant horizon.

What do you notice about the pattern of these two lines above?

_____

_____

C. Write a short poem with a specific rhythm and meter. You can use the same meter as "Your World," or make up a different pattern of stressed and unstressed syllables.

_____

_____

_____

_____

_____

_____

_____

_____

_____

_____

VOCABULARY STUDY: Idioms

Idioms mean something different from the literal, or exact, meanings of their words. To figure out the meaning of an unfamiliar idiom, you can study the context of the phrase, or predict the meaning, and then test your prediction.

A. Read the idioms that are underlined in the chart below. Write what you think each idiom means, then identify the strategy that you used to figure out the meaning.

Idiom	What I Think It Means	Strategy
Amanda was a <u>back-seat driver</u>, shouting out instructions along the way.	She was giving orders to the driver.	context
I had to stop dancing because I got a <u>Charley horse</u> in my left leg.		
It didn't matter which choice she made, they were both a <u>catch-22</u>.		
Lily's baby girl was as <u>cute as a kitten</u>.		

B. Read the excerpt from "Novio Boy." Write how you used each step to figure out the meaning of the underlined idiom.

> **RUDY.** How come you're spying on me?
> **MOTHER.** I'm not, m'ijo! Me and Estela came here to hear your uncle . . .
> **RUDY.** You're snooping! I know you are!
> **MOTHER.** <u>Cross my heart</u>. I didn't know, really.

1. Study the context of the phrase.

_____

2. Predict the meaning.

_____

3. Test your prediction.

_____

C. Complete the sentence containing the idiom "I wash my hands of it."

If my brother can't keep his room clean, I wash my hands of it because _____

_____

Prepare to Read

▸ To Helen Keller
▸ Marked/Dusting

Key Vocabulary

A. How well do you know these words? Circle a rating for each word. Check your understanding of each word by circling *yes* or *no*. Then write a definition. If you are unsure of a word's meaning, refer to the Vocabulary Glossary, page 792, in your student text.

Rating Scale
1 I have never seen this word before.
2 I am not sure of the word's meaning.
3 I know this word and can teach the word's meaning to someone else.

Key Word	Check Your Understanding	Deepen Your Understanding
❶ anonymous (u-**no**-nu-mus) *adjective* **Rating:** 1 2 3	An **anonymous** letter is unsigned. **Yes** **No**	My definition: _____ _____ _____ _____
❷ conquer (**kon**-kur) *verb* **Rating:** 1 2 3	You can sometimes **conquer** a fear by doing what you are afraid of. **Yes** **No**	My definition: _____ _____ _____ _____
❸ contribute (kun-**tri**-byūt) *verb* **Rating:** 1 2 3	A volunteer does not **contribute** time or effort. **Yes** **No**	My definition: _____ _____ _____ _____
❹ encouragement (in-**kur**-ij-munt) *noun* **Rating:** 1 2 3	Fans give their team **encouragement** by booing. **Yes** **No**	My definition: _____ _____ _____ _____

Key Word	Check Your Understanding	Deepen Your Understanding
5 imperfection (im-pur-**fek**-shun) *noun* **Rating:** 1 2 3	A used car never has an **imperfection**. **Yes**　　**No**	My definition: _____ _____ _____ _____ _____
6 inspire (in-**spīr**) *verb* **Rating:** 1 2 3	Before a game or competition a coach tries to **inspire** the players. **Yes**　　**No**	My definition: _____ _____ _____ _____ _____
7 overcome (ō-vur-**kum**) *verb* **Rating:** 1 2 3	You can **overcome** a problem by working hard to solve it. **Yes**　　**No**	My definition: _____ _____ _____ _____ _____
8 unforgettable (un-fur-**ge**-tu-bul) *adjective* **Rating:** 1 2 3	An **unforgettable** experience is something you do not remember. **Yes**　　**No**	My definition: _____ _____ _____ _____ _____

B. Use one of the Key Vocabulary words to describe how you want to be remembered.

_____

_____

Before Reading To Helen Keller

LITERARY ANALYSIS: Analyze Style

A writer's **style** is the particular way he or she writes. Word choice and sentence structure help create a writer's style.

A. Read the passage below. Complete the chart with the effects that the writer's word choice and sentence structure have.

> ### Look Into the Text
>
> She,
> In the dark,
> Found light
> Brighter than many ever see.

Word Choice	Sentence Type

B. Complete the sentence about the writer's style. Use an example of the poet's words to explain your answer.

The writer's style is _____

_____

_____ .

FOCUS STRATEGY: Identify Emotional Responses

How to IDENTIFY EMOTIONAL RESPONSES

1. **Make a Journal** Jot words and phrases that create a picture in your mind.

2. **Visualize** Focus on the mental images. How do they make you feel?

3. **Respond** Describe your emotional responses.

A. Read the passage. Use the strategies above to identify emotional responses as you read. Then answer the questions.

Look Into the Text

> June 28, 1965
>
> Dear Helen,
>
> In my mind I can still see you clearly, standing for hours talking to the students and answering their questions. The questions were not always the most intelligent ones. For instance: "How can you ride horseback when you can't see where the horse is going?" But you gave a wonderful answer. "I just hold onto the horse and let him run wherever he wishes!" And you and the children had a good laugh over this description. Or when you said that after you had learned to speak, you became a real blabbermouth!

1. What words and phrases from the passage helped you create a picture in your mind?

   _____

   _____

   _____

2. Describe your emotional responses as you read the passage.

   _____

   _____

   _____

Selection Review To Helen Keller

 What Do You Do to Make an Impression?
Meet people who are or who want to be unforgettable.

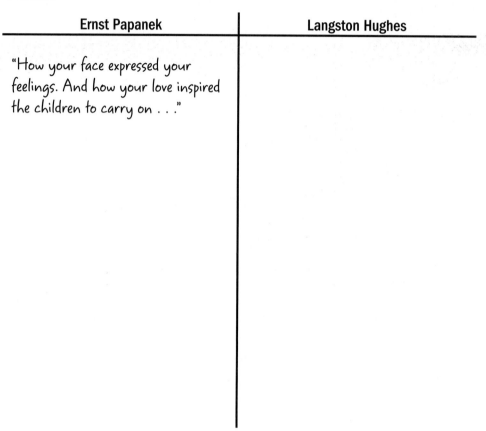

A. In "To Helen Keller," you read two writers' impressions of her. Complete
the T Chart with the writers' descriptions of her.

T Chart

Ernst Papanek	Langston Hughes
"How your face expressed your feelings. And how your love inspired the children to carry on . . ."	

B. Use the information in the chart to answer the questions.

1. Compare the writers' descriptions of Keller. How are their writing
   styles similar? How are they different?

   _____

   _____

   _____

2. How did Helen Keller inspire both writers? Use **inspire** in your answer.

   _____

   _____

3. Why do you think Keller is so unforgettable to so many people?

   _____

   _____

Connect Across Texts

Helen Keller made a strong impression on those around her. Read how these two poets feel about making a mark in the world.

Marked

by Carmen Tafolla

Never write with pencil,
m'ija.
It is for those
who would
5   erase.
Make your mark proud
        and open,
Brave,
        beauty folded into
10   its imperfection,
Like a piece of turquoise
        marked.

Never write
with pencil,
15   m'ija.
Write with ink
        or mud,
or berries grown in
gardens never owned,
20   or, sometimes,
        if necessary,
        blood.

Clearing the bark from sticks and arranging it in swirling patterns, 2003, Strijdom van der Merwe. Land art/photo documentation, Kamiyama, Tokushima, Japan.

Key Vocabulary
imperfection *n.*, defect, problem

Interact with the Text

1. Emotional Responses
Underline the command the speaker gives her daughter. What do you picture? How does it make you feel?

_____

_____

_____

_____

_____

2. Figurative Language
Circle the simile. What two things does it compare?

_____

_____

_____

_____

_____

About the Writer

Carmen Tafolla (1951–) grew up in San Antonio, Texas, and started writing poetry when she was a teen. She still lives in San Antonio, in a century-old house with her husband and mother. Tafolla writes fiction as well as poetry. She is also a professor and a public speaker.

3. Figurative Language
In your own words, explain what the simile in line 5 means.

_____

_____

_____

_____

_____

_____

_____

4. Emotional Responses
How does the poet want the reader to feel about her mother?

_____

_____

_____

_____

_____

_____

_____

_____

_____

_____

_____

Dusting

by Julia Alvarez

Each morning I wrote my name
on the dusty cabinet, then crossed
the dining table in script, scrawled
in capitals on the backs of chairs,
5   practicing signatures like scales
while Mother followed, squirting
linseed from a burping can
into a crumpled-up flannel.

In Other Words
scrawled wrote
scales music notes played for practice
linseed furniture polish
flannel cloth

5. Emotional Responses
Think about the images
the poet creates. What is
your emotional response to
these images?

She erased my fingerprints

10 from the bookshelf and rocker,

polished mirrors on the desk

scribbled with my alphabets.

My name was swallowed in the towel

with which she jeweled the table tops.

15 The grain surfaced in the oak

and the pine grew luminous.

But I refused with every mark

to be like her, anonymous. ❖

6. Interpret
What does the poet say
she does not want to
be like? What can you
conclude about the poet?

Key Vocabulary
anonymous *adj.*, unknown,
unnamed

About the Writer

Julia Alvarez (1950–   ) is the author of many
novels and books of poetry. Her family moved
from the Dominican Republic to New York when
she was ten. Alvarez believes that learning
English helped her become a writer. "I had to
pay close attention to each word," she says.

Selection Review Marked/Dusting

A. Complete the chart with examples of figurative language from the poems.

Types of Figurative Language	Examples from the Texts
Simile	"Like a piece of turquoise marked"
Personification	
Symbol	

B. Answer the questions.

1. Choose one example of figurative language from the chart in Activity A. Describe what image the words create in your mind. What responses do you have to the speaker's words and ideas?

   _____

   _____

   _____

   _____

   _____

   _____

2. How would each poet describe the other's idea of making an impression?

   _____

   _____

   _____

   _____

   _____

Reflect and Assess

WRITING: Write About Literature

A. Plan your writing. List details and ideas from each selection that show how someone can "make a mark."

To Helen Keller	Marked/Dusting
Helen Keller made a mark by being patient, even when people asked questions that were unintelligent or rude.	You can make a mark by being proud of who you are and what you believe.

B. Write a short poem to express your feelings and thoughts about how people can "make a mark." Use details and ideas from each selection to write your poem.

_____

_____

_____

_____

_____

_____

_____

_____

_____

_____

_____

Integrate the Language Arts

▶ To Helen Keller
▶ Marked/Dusting

LITERARY ANALYSIS: Analyze Alliteration and Consonance

Alliteration is the repetition of consonant sounds at the beginnings of words. **Consonance** is the repetition of consonant sounds within a line or verse of a poem.

Example of alliteration: **s**ignatures like **s**cales
Example of consonance: scri**bb**led with my alpha**b**ets

A. Find examples of alliteration from either "Marked" or from "Dusting." List the examples below. Then underline the repeated sound.

1. _____
2. _____
3. _____
4. _____
5. _____

B. Write a line of alliteration for each sound listed below.

1. *th* _I think three things constantly._____
2. *ch* _____
3. *dr* _____
4. *fr* _____
5. *scr* _____

C. Write a short poem using either alliteration or consonance. Use the lines you wrote in Activity B, if necessary.

_____
_____
_____
_____
_____
_____
_____
_____
_____
_____
_____
_____

VOCABULARY STUDY: Connotation and Denotation

Denotation is the literal, or precise, meaning of a word. **Connotation** is the feeling or idea that a word suggests.

A. Circle the word in each pair that has a more positive connotation.

Word Pairs	
1. scribble / write	**5.** encourage / insist
2. walk / stalk	**6.** exaggerate / embellish
3. stingy / frugal	**7.** wander / drift
4. noisy / loud	**8.** steal / take

B. Read the words in the chart below and list the connotation and denotation for each word.

Word	Denotation	Connotation
embellish		
exaggerate		
frugal		
stingy		

C. Use each of the words below in a sentence. Ask a partner to tell you if you have used the word with a positive or negative connotation.

1. stingy _____

_____

2. frugal _____

_____

3. exaggerate _____

_____

4. embellish _____

_____

Read for Understanding

1. Genre What kind of text is this? How do you know?

_____

_____

_____

_____

2. Topic Write a topic sentence to tell what the poems are mostly about.

_____

_____

_____

Reread and Summarize

3. Key Ideas Circle three words or phrases that best express the key ideas in each poem. Note next to each word why you chose it.

· Section 1: first poem
· Section 2: second poem

4. Summary Use your topic sentence and notes from item 3 to write a summary of the poems.

_____

_____

_____

_____

_____

_____

_____

I Believe in All That Has Never Yet Been Spoken

by Rainer Maria Rilke

translated by Anita Barrows
and Joanna Macy

I believe in all that has never yet been spoken.
I want to free what waits within me
so that what no one has dared to wish for

may for once spring clear
5   without my contriving.

If this is arrogant, God, forgive me,
but this is what I need to say.
May what I do flow from me like a river,
no forcing and no holding back,
10   the way it is with children.

Then in these swelling and ebbing currents,
these deepening tides moving out, returning,
I will sing you as no one ever has,

streaming through widening channels
15   into the open sea.

In Other Words

contriving planning
arrogant too proud and self-important
swelling and ebbing growing and retreating

A woman lying on her back playing the ukulele by the sea, Carla Golembe.

Make Music with Your Life

by Bob O'Meally

Make music with your life
a
        jagged
silver tune
5 cuts every deepday madness
Into jewels   that you wear

Carry 16 bars of old blues
wit/you
everywhere you go
10 walk thru azure sadness
howlin
Like a guitar player

Cultural Background

Blues music was created by African Americans in the early 1900s. It follows a specific progression of sounds divided into groups called bars. Blues has had a powerful influence on other musical styles, including ragtime, jazz, rock and roll, hip-hop, country, and pop.

Reread and Analyze

5. Compare Representations
Reread Rilke's poem. Underline the references to water. Then highlight the words telling what the speaker wants to set free. Notice how details about water and freedom are visually represented in the painting. What ideas and feelings do these details suggest?

_____

_____

_____

_____

_____

6. Compare Representations
Now reread O'Meally's poem. Underline details in the poem that are echoed in the painting. Highlight the key idea. How are O'Meally's and Golembe's ideas and feelings the same?

_____

_____

_____

_____

_____

_____

_____

_____

Discuss

7. **Synthesize** With the class, list some of the details that the poets and painter use to express their ideas. Discuss why they chose them.

Words and Phrases in the Poems	Details in the Painting That Convey the Same Ideas and Feelings
Detail:	Detail:
Detail:	Detail:
Detail:	Detail:
Detail:	Detail:

Then, with the class, discuss how poets and painters deliberately choose images to express ideas and create a mood. Make notes.

_____

_____

_____

8. **Write** Use your notes from question 7 to write about how poets and visual artists use written and visual details to express ideas and create a mood. How are their techniques alike and different?

- · What details do poets use?

- · What details do painters include?

- · Do the details help express an idea or a mood?

- · How do the details work together to create the overall message and mood of the piece?

_____

_____

_____

_____

_____

_____

_____

Connect with the EQ What Do You Do to Make an Impression?
Consider the role of self expression in your life.

9. **Viewpoint** Reread lines 6–15 of "I Believe in All That Has Never Yet Been Spoken" and all of "Make Music with Your Life." Would Rainer Maria Rilke say that is important to make a good impression on others? What about Bob O'Meally? Which is more important: making a good impression or expressing yourself?

_____

_____

_____

_____

_____

_____

_____

_____

10. **Theme** What is the message of the poets about self expression?

_____

_____

_____

_____

_____

_____

_____

_____

Key Vocabulary Review

A. Use the words to complete the paragraph.

anonymous	desire	personality	romantic
compliment	nervous	reveal	unforgettable

One day Rebecca found an _____ letter in her locker. The boy who wrote it must have been
(1)

too _____, or shy, to _____ his identity. He was very _____, and
(2)   (3)   (4)

he expressed his _____ to go out on a date with her. He gave her a _____ and
(5)   (6)

said he thought she had a nice _____. Rebecca said the letter was _____ and
(7)   (8)

that she would always keep it.

B. Use your own words to write what each Key Vocabulary word means.
Then write a synonym for each word.

Key Word	My Definition	Synonym
1. conceal		
2. conquer		
3. contribute		
4. elegance		
5. horizon		
6. overcome		
7. privacy		
8. recover		

Unit 7 Key Vocabulary

anonymous	conquer	elegance	imperfection	overprotective	• reluctant
ashamed	conscious	encouragement	inspire	personality	• reveal
compliment	• contribute	flirt	nervous	privacy	romantic
conceal	desire	horizon	overcome	recover	unforgettable

• **Academic Vocabulary**

C. Answer the questions using complete sentences.

1. In what ways can you reveal that you are **conscious** of a problem?

   _____

   _____

2. How can parents be **overprotective** of their children?

   _____

   _____

3. What is one **imperfection** you wish you could change?

   _____

   _____

4. What is one thing you would be **reluctant** to try?

   _____

   _____

5. How can you give someone **encouragement**?

   _____

   _____

6. In what ways do you **inspire** others?

   _____

   _____

7. Explain a time in your life you felt **ashamed**.

   _____

   _____

8. Who do you know that likes to **flirt**?

   _____

   _____

Acknowledgments

Laila Ali: "Showdown with Big Eva" excerpted from "Separating Right from Wrong" from *Reach* by Laila Ali, with David Ritz. Copyright © 2002 by Laila Ali. Reprinted by permission of the author.

Susan Bergholz Literary Services: "Dusting" by Julia Alvarez from *Homecoming*. Copyright © 1984, 1996 by Julia Alvarez. Published by Plume, an imprint of The Penguin Group (USA), and originally published by Grove Press. All rights reserved.

"Only Daughter" by Sandra Cisneros. Copyright © 1990 by Sandra Cisneros. First published in *Glamour*, November 1990. All rights reserved. All Reprinted by permission of Susan Bergholz Literary Services, New York.

BOA Editions: "miss rosie" by Lucille Clifton from *Good Woman: Poems and a Memoir 1969-1980*. Copyright © 1987 by Lucille Clifton. Reprinted with the permission of BOA Editions, Ltd.

BookStop Literary Agency: "Scene Seven" from *Novio Boy* by Gary Soto. Copyright © 1997 by Gary Soto, Reprinted by permission of BookStop Literary Agency. This material may not be reprinted in any form or by any means without the prior written permission of the publisher. CAUTION: Professionals and amateurs are hereby warned that this play is subject to a royalty. For more information regarding performance rights, contact BookStop Literary Agency, 67 Meadow View Road, Orinda, California 94563, (925) 254-2668.

Chronicle Books: "Oranges" by Gary Soto from *New and Selected Poems*. Copyright © 1995 by Gary Soto. Used with permission of Chronicle Books, LLC, San Francisco. Visit ChronicleBooks.com.

Dorling Kindersley: "Genes: All in the Family" by Robert Winston from *What Makes Me Me?* by Robert Winston. Foreword copyright © 2004 Robert Winston, text © 2004 by Dorling Kindersley Limited. Reprinted by permission of Dorling Kindersley Ltd.

Sheldon Fogelman Agency: "I Go Along" by Richard Peck, first published in *Connections*, edited by Donald R. Gallo, Delacorte Books. Copyright © 1989 by Richard Peck. All rights reserved. Used with permission of Sheldon Fogelman Agency, Inc.

HarperCollins Publishers: "Karate" from *The Land I Lost* by Huynh Quang Nhuong. Copyright © 1982 by Huynh Quang Nhuong. Used by permission of HarperCollins Publishers.

Excepts from "Household Words" from *Small Wonder: Essays* by Barbara Kingsolver. Copyright © 2002 by Barbara Kingsolver. Used by permission of HarperCollins Publishers.

Henry Holt: "In Giving I Connect with Others" by Isabel Allende from *This I Believe*, edited by Jay Allison and Dan Gediman. Copyright © 2006 by This I Believe, Inc. Reprinted by arrangement with Henry Holt and Company, LLC.

Houghton Mifflin Harcourt: "Ambush" from *The Things They Carried* by Tim O'Brien. Copyright © 1990 by Tim O'Brien. Reprinted by permission of Houghton Mifflin Company Harcourt Publishing Company. All rights reserved.

Lippincott Williams & Wilkins: Excerpt from "Do Family Meals Matter?" by Mary Story and Dianne Newmark-Sztainer from *Nutrition Today*, November/December 2005. Reprinted by permission of Lippincott Williams & Wilkins, WoltersKluwer Health.

Los Angeles Times: "Calling a Foul" by Stan Simpson from the *Hartford Courant*, February 19, 2005. Copyright © 2005 by the Los Angeles Times. Reprinted by permission.

Norman Mineta: "Why We Must Never Forget" by Norman Mineta. Copyright © 1992 by Norman Mineta. Used by permission of the author.

National Geographic Society: "Superstitions: The Truth Uncovered" by Jamie Kiffel from *National Geographic Kids*, October 2005. Reprinted by permission of National Geographic Society. All rights reserved.

National Youth Rights Association: "16: The Right Voting Age" from *Why the Voting Age should be Lowered to 16* by the National Youth Rights Association. Reprinted by permission of National Youth Rights Association.

NEA Today/National Education Association: "Should Communities Set Teen Curfews?" by Barbara Bea from *NEA Today*, December 1994. Reprinted by permission of NEA Today/National Education Association.

Robert G. O'Meally: "Make Music with Your Life" by Robert G. O'Meally. Copyright © by Robert G. O'Meally. Reprinted by permission of the author.

Oregon ACLU: "Curfews: A National Debate" adapted from material published on the ACLU of Oregon Web site. Reprinted by permission.

Penguin Group (USA) Inc.: "The Bicycle" from *The Color of Water* by James McBride, Copyright © 1996 by James McBride. Used by permission of Riverhead Books, an imprint of Penguin Group (USA) Inc.

"Ich glaube an Alles.../I believe in all that has never yet been spoken" by Rainer Maria Rilke from *Rilke's Book of Hours: Love Poems to God*, translated by Anita Barrows and Joanna Macy. Translation copyright © 1996 by Anita Barrows and Joanna Macy. Used by permission of Riverhead Books, an imprint of Penguin Group (USA) Inc.

Andrea Davis Pinkney: "Building Bridges" by Andrea Davis Pinkney. Copyright © by Andrea Davis Pinkney. Reprinted by permission of the author.

Aaron M. Priest Literary Agency: Excerpt from *Brother Ray: Ray Charles' Own Story* by Ray Charles and David Ritz. Copyright © 1978 by Ray Charles and David Ritz. Reprinted by permission of Aaron M. Priest Literary Agency, Inc.

Random House: "Caged Bird" by Maya Angelou from *Shaker, Why Don't You Sing?* Copyright © 1983 by Maya Angelou. Used by permission of Random House, Inc.

"Helen Keller" and "Theme for English B" by Langston Hughes from *The Collected Poems of Langston Hughes*. Copyright © 1994 by the Estate of Langston Hughes. Used by permission of Alfred A. Knopf, a division of Random House, Inc. and Harold Ober Associates.

Rebel Productions: Excerpt from *The Right Words at the Right Time* by John Leguizamo. Copyright © 2002 by The Right Words, LLC. Reprinted by permission of John Leguizamo.

René Saldaña, Jr.: "Jump Away" by René Saldaña, Jr. from *Every Man for Himself*. Copyright © by René Saldaña, Jr. Reprinted by permission of the author.

Scholastic: "Abuela Invents the Zero" by Judith Ortiz Cofer from *An Island Like You*. Copyright © 1995 by Judith Ortiz Cofer. Reprinted by permission of Scholastic Inc.

"Behind the Bulk" by Cate Baily from *Scholastic News*, July 6, 2006. Copyright © 2006 by Scholastic Inc. Reprinted by permission of Scholastic Inc.

"The Experiment" by Martin Raim from *Literary Cavalcade*, October 1960. Copyright © 1960, 1988 by Scholastic Inc. Reprinted by permission of Scholastic Inc.

"The Pale Mare" by Marian Flandrick Bray from *Stay True: Short Stories from Strong Girld*, compiled by Marilyn Singer. Copyright © 1998 by Marian Flandrick Bray. Reprinted by permission of Scholastic Inc.

"Violence Hits Home" by Denise Rinaldo from *Choices*, CHOICES, February/March 2005. Copyright © 2005 by Scholastic Inc. By permission of Scholastic Inc.

Scripps Howard News Service: "New research shows stark differences in teen brains" by Lee Bowman. Copyright © by Scripps Howard News Service. Reprinted by permission.

Simon & Schuster Adult Publishing Group: "He Was No Bum" by Bob Greene from *American Bean*. Copyright © 1983 by John Deadline Enterprises, Inc. Reprinted and edited with the permission of Scribner, an imprint of Simon & Schuster Adult Publishing Group, All rights reserved. Electronic rights by permission of Sterling Lord Literistic.

SLL/Sterling Lord Literistic: "Fear" by Terry Trueman from *Every Man For Himself*. Copyright by Terry Trueman. Reprinted by permission of SSL/Sterling Lord Literistic, Inc.

Sussex Publishers, LLC: "Trashing Teens" by Hara Estroff Marano from *Psychology Today*. Copyright © 2007 by Sussex Publishers, LLC. Used by permission of Psychology Today.

Carmen Tafolla: "Marked" by Carmen Tafolla from *Sonnets to Human Beings and Other Selected Works*, published by Lalo Press, Santa Monica, California, Copyright © 1992 by Carmen Tafolla. Reprinted by permission of the author.

Amy Tan and the Sandra Dijkstra Literary Agency: "Fish Cheeks" by Amy Tan. Copyright © 1987 by Amy Tan. First appeared in *Seventeen*. Reprinted by permission of the author and the Sandra Dijkstra Literary Agency.

Louise Bohmer Turnbull: Excerpt with adaptations from "Advice for an Unhappy Teen" by Louise Bohmer Turnbull as appeared in the *Denver* Post, July 13, 2005. Copyright © 2005. Reprinted by permission of the author.

The University of Utah: "How to See DNA" from learn.genetics.utah.edu. Reprinted by permission of the University of Utah, Technology Commercialization Office.

Christopher de Vinck: "Power of the Powerless: A Brother's Lesson" by Christopher de Vinck from the *Wall Street Journal*, April 10, 1985. Copyright © Dow Jones & Company. All rights reserved. Reprinted by permission of the author.

Weekly Reader: "Enabling or Disabling?" from *Current Health*, 2 January 1992. Reprinted by special permission granted by Weekly Reader, published and copyrighted by the Weekly Reader Corporation. All rights reserved.

David Yoo: "Heartbeat" by David Yoo. Copyright © 2005 by David Yoo. Reprinted with permission of the author.